Sharell Cook was born and brought up in country Victoria. After gaining a Bachelor of Business she moved to Melbourne, where she worked for ten years in the accounting and finance sector of the Victorian government. Then, India called. Sharell now writes about India travel for a *New York Times* company. In addition, she maintains a popular blog on her life in India called 'Diary of a White Indian Housewife'. Sharell lives in Mumbai, India, with her husband.

# Henna for the Broken-Hearted

## SHARELL COOK

MACMILLAN
Pan Macmillan Australia

*Some of the people in this book have had their names changed to protect their identities.*

First published 2011 in Macmillan by Pan Macmillan Australia Pty Limited
1 Market Street, Sydney

National Library of Australia
Cataloguing-in-Publication data:

Cook, Sharell.

Henna for the broken-hearted / Sharell Cook.

9781742610405 (pbk.)

Cook, Sharell—Journeys—India.
India—Description and travel.
India—Social life and customs.

915.4

Text design by Deborah Parry Graphics
Typeset in 13/17 pt Griffo Classico by Post Pre-press Group, Brisbane
Printed and bound in India by Replika Press Pvt. Ltd.

*To my parents for instilling their goodness into me and always being there*

*To my husband for creating this story with me*

*And to anyone who is comforted or inspired by it*

# Contents

# Preface

FROM a hand to a hand, an instrument to a canvas, the henna flows in a deep red thread out of the small pliable cone. The canvas of the hand is blank, ready to be transformed. The woman looks at it, anxious and expectant, as she waits for the design to take shape. At first, it is unrecognisable. Dark, formless and fragrant swirls that will stain her skin. It is hard to understand the significance of them. Yet, the artist has a vision of the end result. This vision guides him as he applies the henna, slowly and gently, like a balm. He's bent over his work in deep concentration.

Gradually, and with precision and patience, the design unfolds. From the challenge of shaping it, it blooms into something magnificent, intricate and exquisite. As the woman continues to observe her hand, she gains clarity. Her uncertainty melts away. She now sees what the design resembles, what it's supposed to be. The design, uniquely conceived by the artist, is the perfect expression for her. Each swirl and bend that he's crafted makes sense to her. She can see how necessary each one has been. How they've contributed to the creation of the bigger picture.

The healing and rejuvenating properties of the henna plant cleanse, condition and cool the woman's skin. Its pungent, earthy smell speaks to her of a mysterious land, eclectic history and rich spirituality. She breathes it in deeply. The henna soothes and inspires her.

A talisman on her skin, the henna bestows blessings, good fortune and protection. A catalyst for change, it colours her skin but reaches her spirit.

# PART ONE

# LOST

# The Crisis

'**I**'M sleeping with Kimberly.'

These aren't the words a wife wants to hear from her husband. It was three days after Christmas, early in the morning. I was almost 31 and we had been married for five years. My husband had again been out all night, his phone switched off. I had spent yet another sleepless night, wondering where he was, if he was all right, and why he had chosen not to be with me. It was a relief to find out the truth.

I first met Michael the summer before I turned eighteen. He was the friend of a friend. Three years older than me, he was studying for a degree in applied science at the local university. I didn't see him again until summer was over and I started my business degree at the same university. He found me crying in the library one day, heartbroken and confused. I'd been involved with his friend and it hadn't worked out. I really needed a shoulder to cry on, and Michael offered his. We spent hours together, talking until late in the night. Full of infatuation and possibility, I was drawn to his emotional nature. Here was someone who understood me in a way no one ever had. Inevitably, we fell in love.

Soon, it became apparent that Michael had his demons. They were significant enough to ensure that our relationship was never an unwavering one. A dysfunctional childhood, moving from place to place, and his parents' subsequent divorce had left its mark; his mind was a constant battlefield, pulled one way by his fear of commitment and the other by his fear of abandonment.

Our relationship wasn't exactly what you would call healthy: Michael would smother me with attention, then distance himself. Feeling rejected, I'd withdraw. He'd then feel scared of being alone and come back. It was traumatic, especially as Michael offered no explanation for his cyclical detachment. Some nights I would cry myself to sleep. Cosseted in the stability of my steady upbringing, I didn't appreciate the depth of his mental anguish. The constant ups and downs fed my insecurities.

Despite what some would call an idyllic childhood in the country, full of climbing trees, flying kites, chasing butterflies and catching tadpoles, I grew into a shy, closed and introverted teenager. I was a sensitive only child, used to spending time by myself among nature and absorbed in books. As a result, I didn't find it easy to relate to people. I found being at a large school uncomfortable. I was scared of what to say, so I chose not to say anything at all. The usual teenage growing pains of crooked teeth, braces and bad hair didn't help. Later, at university and during my twenties, I was determined to reject that unpopular person, and outwardly became the opposite. On the inside, I remained scared that people would still see the old me. I cared too much about what they thought, and feared their judgement and rejection, not believing they would find me attractive or amiable. I'd always been a conscientious student who did very well. My parents had devoted a great deal of time to helping me learn when I was young, and had been generous with my education. They sent me to a private school and encouraged me to get a degree – the first person in my family to do so. I started to develop control-freak tendencies towards the end of secondary school, when it felt like my whole future rested upon my grades. I had very high expectations of myself, and thought that I had to complete everything to perfection. I felt as though I had to do everything myself for it to be good enough, and was terrified of failure or anything going wrong. The sheer magnitude of life ahead overwhelmed me, and made me to want to control all aspects of it. It didn't work out, of course.

After we graduated from university in 1995, Michael and I moved to Melbourne together. I wanted to spread my wings and experience the freedom of the city. He agreed. We started work on our respective careers, mine as a financial auditor. It was the first job that I was interviewed for, and I got it. Never mind that auditing had been one of my least favourite subjects at university; I was gainfully employed.

Like many women, all I wanted was a big wedding and to look like a princess in a billowing white dress, long flowing veil, a huge bunch of long-stemmed red roses to match my red lipstick and a sparkling tiara. I desperately wanted to belong to someone, to have the security and the status of being a 'Mrs'.

Michael didn't want to get married at all. To him it was a constraint, and could go wrong like his parents' marriage had. He became restless and wanted to travel the world. I found the idea daunting and at first dismissed it. Then one morning, tired of the daily work routine, I agreed. We left for a six-month overseas trip. Tears trickled down my face at the airport as I waved goodbye to my parents. It felt like I would be away for an eternity.

Michael and I spent a month in America, three months working in London, and the remainder of the time travelling around Scotland, Ireland and western Europe. On the way home, we stopped over in Bangkok. We both enjoyed visiting new places and sharing new experiences, but it was overshadowed by my unsettling feelings about wanting to get married. I wasn't satisfied with our relationship. I wanted more commitment and didn't see much point in staying together if I wasn't going to get it. Even during the trip, I complained bitterly about not being married, while my friends from school and university all experienced that joy. In the end my persistence and Michael's fear of abandonment won. He proposed to me in Munich, despite his concern about the impact marriage would have on his life.

'It doesn't have to change anything,' I reassured him. 'We can still keep having fun and going out.'

Secretly, I hoped it would bring more stability into our lives.

Seven years after we met, with me at 25 and Michael 28, I had the wedding I wanted, in the same church my parents were married almost 30 years earlier. I was elated.

If I thought marriage would solve all of Michael's problems, I was wrong. An injurious cloud of nightclubs, parties, drugs and alcohol constantly intruded on our life. My initial curious participation gradually gave away to resentment, and I struggled to keep my emotions and life in order. There was no place for such a lifestyle in the accounting office I worked in. Neither could I share it with my conservative friends and family. I felt torn. Who was the real me? Where did I fit in?

Surprisingly, Michael and I continued to do well at work.

Another of his fears was not having enough money, which drove him to great lengths to succeed. He was constantly stressed about work, and pushed himself very hard. We had a classic double-income-no-kids lifestyle to match: outwardly, we were successful and on track to achieving the conventional Australian dream. We travelled and dined out frequently. We moved into a brand-new townhouse in Melbourne, and accumulated two investment properties in sought-after coastal towns in Queensland. We talked about moving into the property near Noosa and living a simple life. I dreamed of our two kids and carefree, sun-drenched weekends spent at the beach.

It was hardly reality, though. A couple of years after we were married, major cracks began to appear. I spent Friday nights at home alone while Michael partied with his single friends. He went straight from work and didn't come home until late on Saturday morning. Then he spent the rest of the weekend recovering.

'Why do you keep doing this?' I begged him.

'I just don't know,' was his usual reply.

After six months, I decided I had no choice but to join him if I was to share his life. I made new friends and spent nights and days with them, mostly in clubs. I also discovered shopping. Until then, I'd had little interest in fashion or expensive clothes, the legacy of growing up in rural Australia. I soon discovered that new clothes and expensive haircuts did wonders for my self-esteem. I could mould myself into someone else. Without these material thrills, my life seemed bland and stale. I was paying the price for pressuring my husband to marry me, but I loved him and dreamed of a better future together.

My job suited the control freak in me but totally quashed the creative person I'd been when I was younger. Unfulfilled and unmotivated by it, I nevertheless put up with it because it paid well and I didn't have the courage to try anything different. Change made me uneasy. Besides, my job had other benefits. I was home in time to prepare dinner, and was never stressed. I dreaded people asking me how work was, because I never had anything positive to say. I was hardly doing my life's passion.

On the weekends, our partying reached a peak. The more wretched I felt inside, the more compensation I required outside. I constantly sought attention from others, hoping they'd see me as different and worthy of approval. This me was bold, daring and pushed boundaries. I hardly recognised myself anymore, and I didn't like this new person I'd become very much.

I first met Kimberly (not her real name) at drinks with Michael's colleagues. Michael used to work with her and they became friends. She started to party with us, and even came to our house. Like Michael, she'd had a dysfunctional childhood, and this drew them to each other.

'I think I'm developing feelings for Kimberly,' Michael confessed one night.

I felt besieged and yet powerless to do anything about it.

'Those feelings don't have to progress,' I naïvely replied. 'You obviously understand each other, but it doesn't mean you're meant to have a relationship with each other.' I'd also sought emotional support and closeness from other people, so had some idea of how he was feeling.

We had divested ourselves of the responsibilities of marriage, and were living separate lives, yet I never really thought it would end. When he finally told me about their affair a couple of months later my stomach felt heavy and hollow, my heart pounded and my head spun. It was a strange feeling of knowing that my life had irrevocably been altered in that one moment. While I'd been searching for reasons for Michael's distance from me, I hadn't been particularly suspicious of an affair due to the ever-present state of flux of our relationship. Now that I had tangible evidence of what was wrong, I wasn't sure what to do with it. Neither was Michael. Our pain over the situation strangely united us. We wanted to cling to the remnants of our marriage, but at the same time we couldn't. Underlying issues prevented it.

'I just don't know who I am,' Michael said. 'I need to discover who I am.'

Having been with me since he was 21, he'd never had the freedom or independence to make that discovery. Despite our problems, we'd spent most of our adult lives with each other.

'I don't know what to do,' Michael continued. 'I think I need to move out for a while, but I don't know if I can do it.'

So many different emotions flew through my mind. Anger. Disbelief. Despair. Shock. I cried. I raged. Yet, I never told him not to leave. Deep down, I understood his need to find himself and grow. I didn't want our marriage to end, but neither could I cope with it the way it was. We both needed space to sort ourselves out.

'You must stop seeing Kimberly – you can't focus on yourself while she's in your life.'

He agreed. I believed him.

We decided to live apart for six months. I helped him look for an apartment. The weekend that he moved out, I fled to a friend's house in the country.

He called me in tears. 'This is so difficult. I really don't know what I'm doing. This is all so much harder than I thought.'

I consoled him, even though my heart was in tatters.

Michael continued to call me often, usually in an overwrought state. 'I've lied to you so much and I'm still lying to you, but I can't stop it.'

Our friends knew we were having problems, but we kept up appearances for a while. We went to a stage show together and even a wedding. Once I picked Michael up from his apartment. There were two dirty wine glasses next to the sink in his kitchen. Seeing that confirmed my fears.

I felt raw and tender. I couldn't sleep, and nothing made sense anymore. My life as I knew it was disintegrating, and I was powerless to do anything about it. I became obsessive, trawling the Internet for information on midlife crisis, which I was sure was Michael's problem. My husband was only in his early thirties but he wasn't behaving normally. Only people in pain do such painful things. I had to try and understand what was happening.

While Michael relied on antidepressants, a prescription of sleeping pills and Valium was my only comfort. Some nights, alone in our bed, I was so disturbed that even the strongest of sleeping pills didn't work. I had no appetite. I'd always been slim, but my weight started dropping alarmingly. My clothes began to hang on me, and I had to buy jeans two sizes smaller. Surely, I wasn't *that* thin? Concerned friends insisted that I eat dinner with them every night.

Michael tried a ten-day Vipassana silent meditation course but had to leave halfway through because it was too intense. A friend recommended a psychotherapist, and we went together to see if there was any hope for our marriage.

It wasn't pleasant. Michael, obviously anguished, had a long list of grievances against me. I was too controlling. I only saw things in black and white. I wasn't passionate. I wasn't spontaneous. I didn't understand him. I didn't share his interests. I was bad tempered. He didn't want to work through our problems together. He didn't think it was possible for me to change anyway. He couldn't even have coffee with me in the morning because I didn't drink it!

There was an upside. While some people turn to drugs and alcohol to drown their sorrows, I'd already been there. I stopped partying. I also stopped shopping. I wanted to do away with everything that reminded me of my past. I became very reflective and introspective. My agony slapped me in the face and forced me to look in the mirror, introducing me to my real self. I immersed myself in spiritual and self-development books. I wrote down all the issues Michael had with me and evaluated them. Which were legitimate and which was he using to justify his behaviour?

No doubt, I was controlling at times and very rarely spontaneous. Our life ran to a strict schedule, with every social event planned weeks in advance. While partying gave me confidence to be someone else, it came at the expense of who I really was – someone genuine, emotional, trustworthy and who needed solitude to regroup. The outrageous party person I'd been had destroyed my soul. With the ground ripped out from underneath me, I realised that I no longer wanted to impress people or prove anything to them. All I wanted was to stop doubting myself and finally accept me for who I was. To be more independent and confident. To make myself a better person.

What is a crisis but an opportunity for change? If I embraced the pain, maybe it would lead me to a new path in life that I could paint a new canvas with.

At work, I became very withdrawn. I didn't want to see or talk to anyone. It was a struggle just to be in the office. I couldn't pretend to be cheery. Neither could I explain what was going on in my personal life. My problem came to light under shameful circumstances one day. The boss was away. It was a colleague's birthday and we all went out to lunch. We were a festive group, and there was the usual generous consumption of alcohol, including tequila. I had earned myself a reputation in the past as a force to be reckoned with when it came to drinking tequila. That wasn't the case this time.

Back in the office, I started feeling sick, really sick. I crawled under my desk to try and sleep it off. Around 45 minutes later I woke up in a daze. I couldn't move but the tequila insisted on coming up. I vomited all over the floor under my desk. Not knowing what else to do, I called Michael on my mobile to come and rescue me. He came and carried me away. The saga didn't end there. In the lobby, hysteria welled up inside me and boiled over. I was panic stricken and incoherent. An ambulance was called and I was taken to hospital. They were concerned about my mental health and didn't want me to do anything harmful.

My recollections of the hours spent in the hospital are hazy. I remember bright lights and chattering voices. One of those voices told me to pull down my dress, which was crumpled and immodestly heading towards my waist as I lay on the stretcher. At the time, it struck me as an absurd thing to say. Wasn't nudity an everyday occurrence in hospitals? Besides, unlike other patients, I was wearing underpants and opaque tights.

As midnight approached, I remembered I was supposed to be a bridesmaid at my best friend's wedding the next day. I needed to get out of hospital as soon as possible. The doctor who attended me shared my same offbeat sense of humour, so I encouraged him to regale me with hospital emergency-room stories. Seeing that I was laughing, he pronounced me sane enough to go home.

Michael was extremely concerned about my wellbeing, and his remorse prompted him to suggest that we move to Queensland together. I felt a flicker of relief and hope. He did still love me and wanted to be with me after all.

A day later he called and said he couldn't do it.

The months passed. Michael couldn't let go of either me or Kimberly. He alternated between blaming me and himself. On the days he felt vulnerable he was tearful, said he missed me, saw many positive changes in me and wanted to work things out. On the days his barrier was up he was tense, said that in his heart he had moved on, didn't have what it would take to fix things between us and was driven a lot by guilt over what he did to me. His oscillations were tearing me apart emotionally, but I was powerless to turn him away when he phoned. I had little experience in dealing with rela-tionship break-ups, and my life seemed incomplete without him. I wanted to beg him to sort himself out and make everything better but I didn't. It would only pressure him, and he seemed incapable of change anyway.

My task was to remain detached and to keep the focus on improv-ing myself. Then he'd see the difference and want to come back of his own accord. I craved for the opportunity to confront Kimberly and to get closure so I could move on. Miraculously, the universe conspired to grant me my wish.

I met a couple of good friends for dinner after work one evening. They had missed their train home to Geelong, so we headed to the pub opposite Flinders Street station to pass the time until the next train came. I noticed her soon after we walked in. She was in a cor-ner surrounded by colleagues and had no way of escaping.

Like a puppet, I walked over to her. 'Hello Kimberly, what a surprise to see you after so long. How are you?'

She squirmed.

As I turned to leave, I addressed her colleagues, 'By the way, did you know she's having an affair with my husband?'

That was enough for me, but not for my feisty friend. While I stood there trembling, she ran out of the pub and across Swanston Street yelling abuse at Kimberly as she fled. It felt like an outlandish scene from a movie, not my life.

I was living an unending nightmare. I had no idea of the direc-tion my life was going in. I felt like I was treading water, but barely at that.

Michael talked about divorce. 'I want to know what it feels like to be truly free.'

He wanted to sell both of the houses we had bought in Queens-land. 'I never wanted to live in the Noosa house anyway,' he claimed.

That said, I didn't oppose him. I was thoroughly confused by his confusion, how he sometimes wanted to be with me and not at other times. Along with the houses went my dream for the future. Nothing that was left in my life inspired me. I felt uncertain, hollow and directionless.

At work, I arranged to take long-service leave. My boss was very understanding, but I felt that I couldn't continue to be there. I needed time away to regain my health and to heal. I needed to rediscover myself. After ten years, I was entitled to three months' leave at full pay or six months at half-pay. I took the six months.

I stayed home the first month. Time flew by, but none of the days was easy. I was mentally exhausted and struggled to keep it together. I wanted to sit down and cry and yell and run to someone – anyone – and ask them to take away the pain.

Then an old friend from university needed somewhere to live and moved into the downstairs bedroom. It felt incredibly good to have someone in the house. We cooked together, listened to music, danced, drank red wine late into the night and went on road trips.

My spirits lifted. I grew stronger. Gradually, with the distraction, my anxiety started receding, as did my need for the pills. My friend's presence was exactly what I needed, not just for the company, but because his personality forced me to confront a lot of the issues I had about myself. He was very independent, decisive, accepting of himself and stubborn. He had little patience with my wallowing, and often got annoyed with me for constantly comparing myself with him and others, and for thinking I was inferior. He just wanted me to give myself a break. He also wanted me to develop my own strength, and had the knack of disappearing every time I started becoming too reliant on him. I knew he was right, but it was tough all the same.

Michael resurfaced again, and so began another cycle of blame and recrimination. And as quickly as he reappeared, he disappeared again. Tired of being buffeted by these emotional waves, I decided I needed a complete change of environment. To move forward, I needed to throw myself totally out of my comfort zone and open myself up to new possibilities. It couldn't happen here, with constant reminders of the life I had once led. Besides, another Christmas was approaching, and I couldn't face the harrowing memories of the previous year.

I'd never been anywhere by myself before. A trip alone would help me grow, help me discover the blessings and purpose that seemed hidden in my life. I chose India for its unrivalled ability to challenge me, but looking back I think it was India that chose me. I'd been there twice before with Michael. We visited both the north and the south. I found it infectious. The contrasting crumble of Old Delhi and the orderly New Delhi, the regal splendour of Rajasthan, sacred Varanasi with its mystical rituals revealed openly along the Ganges riverside, the luminous Taj Mahal, extreme Mumbai, the spiritual merging of three seas at Kanyakumari and the hedonistic beaches of Goa. Everywhere, India teemed with life and paradoxes.

Like everything else I did, I had been meticulous when planning our trips. Daily itineraries were prepared, hotels and train tickets booked in advance. It was quite a contrast to how most backpackers saw India, but I didn't want to leave anything to chance.

Of course, India made sure that despite my extensive arrangements, things still went awry. Taxi drivers took us to the wrong hotels, trains were late and people gave us incorrect directions. We were lied to, cheated and sometimes even found ourselves stranded. Yet, it was during some of these moments that I discovered a wonderful sense of liberation.

Unable to get a taxi from the Ellora Caves to Aurangabad one day, the only option had been to pile into a local jeep. Our backpacks were thrown onto the roof. Inside, twice as many people than seats were crammed together, the smell of sweat masked by sticks of burning incense jammed into a little holder on the dashboard that sat next to a Ganesh idol. Hindi music blared from the speakers. The driver dodged other vehicles, people and cows.

I was mesmerised. India pushed me to let go and adapt, while the country's cultural clichés sucked me in and enveloped me. Ancient scriptures. Reincarnation. Snake charmers. Gods with multiple heads and arms. Curry. Chaos. Smiling people with few possessions. And all those holy cows.

To me, India felt like an old but unpredictable friend; one whose behaviour I could never be sure of, but liked anyway. Its allure was nebulous, but had a lot to do with the sense of possibility the country offered. While I felt that life was too immense and I needed to control it, in India it was the opposite. In a country addicted to religion, people put themselves in God's hands. They had faith in a higher power and believed that it could turn their fortunes at any time. I didn't – but that would change. As a result they spent a great deal of time engaging in rituals to please the gods. They even believed that man could become god, self-realised, through the practice of yoga and meditation.

For this trip, I decided to spend five weeks in Kolkata – chosen because I was yet to visit that city – doing volunteer work and giving something back. It would take my mind off my woes and it wouldn't hurt for me to be truly humbled by those less fortunate than me.

Michael didn't react well to my plans.

'I've made a mistake, please let's try again,' he begged. He even phoned my parents.

'We'll talk when I get back,' I told him.

I left my friend in charge of the house, packed my bag and boarded a flight into the unknown.

# Alone but not Lonely

A COMBINATION of fear, apprehension and excitement gripped me as the plane began its descent into Delhi. I wished someone special was sitting beside me to share the forthcoming adventure with. Yet, at the same time I was aware it was something I had to do for myself, on my own, to grow. And, just perhaps, to grow up.

India announced itself as soon as I stepped off the plane and made my way to the domestic terminal for my flight to Kolkata. The most recognisable reminder was the pungent, heavy air. It was winter, a season notorious for pollution and smog trapped between the upper and lower layers of the atmosphere. My nostrils welcomed it.

To a girl from Australia, the place fulfilled the definition of exotic, and left no doubt as to exactly where I was. Always absorbing, often confounding, but never boring. Love it, hate it, it's impossible to remain ambivalent about India. The sights, sounds and smells are so intrusive they cannot be ignored. Jostling crowds, blaring horns, the grate of rapid-fire Hindi, clanging of temple bells, cries of street vendors, brightly coloured saris, flashes of gold and the sweet smell of jasmine.

The shuttle bus to the domestic terminal was waiting near a carpark curiously designated for VVIPs (Very, Very Important Persons). Were there so many VIPs in India that another, more exclusive, category was needed? I wondered. Only later did I learn it was India's often corrupt politicians who received such special treatment. The bus finally lurched into life, taking us transiting passengers, both foreigners and Indians, over a dusty field away from the international terminal. Ignoring the looming signs that implored him to go 'Dead Slow', the bus driver proceeded to swerve violently around each corner. We passed dusty hangars sheltering aircraft in various states of repair, some with their seats ripped out and sitting dejectedly on the ground. To the side of the airport, airport employees slept on stretchers in makeshift huts, guarded by armed security. On the main road in front of the airport, roaming cows and monkeys greeted travellers. In the middle of the round-about, a group of men wearing suits and ties lay sprawled on the grass in the late afternoon light, smoking *bedis* (hand-rolled ciga-rettes) and playing cards.

Chaos reigned at the domestic terminal. It was December 2005, and Delhi airport was yet to be woken by change. Its terminals were unrenovated, JetLite was still known as Air Sahara, and the local airline, Kingfisher, had only been operating a week. The cramped and outdated domestic terminal was hopelessly inadequate for the volume of traffic that mercilessly converged on it every day. I strug-gled to negotiate check-in and finally settled myself in the departure lounge. The cricket dominated every television in the terminal, and almost every passenger was glued to it. Disinterested as I was, I was glad when boarding for my flight to Kolkata was called an hour before the scheduled departure time.

This didn't mean that the flight actually left on time. We were herded onto another shuttle bus and taken to our plane, which was stationed in front of one of the ramshackle maintenance hangars near the international terminal. It was well into the night by the time I arrived in Kolkata.

I was met at Kolkata airport by the volunteer coordinator. The volunteer program was administered by an organisation in the UK, and for a participation fee, I was to be provided with a place to stay, meals and a coordinator to look after me. Her name was Sucharita. She emerged from the depths of the human wall that had formed against the barricades outside the arrivals terminal. It would be hard to miss her. Her considerable height and short wavy hair, unusual for a middle-aged Bengali woman, made her stand out.

Waiting in the car was Tara, another newly arrived volunteer. She was born in India but had been adopted by a family in the USA. On vacation from college, she'd come back to rediscover her Indian roots.

Sucharita announced we'd be having dinner at a restaurant with a visiting representative from the volunteer program office in the UK. We drove through the streets of Kolkata to the venue. The air was softer here than in Delhi, and the architecture distinctly colonial. Slowly crumbling walls and flaking paint unceremoniously revealed tired, grey cement. Unwilling to preserve the legacy of the British empire, Kolkata's communist government left it to decay. A mammoth resoration drive, the first of its kind in India, was gaining momentum in the city but it would evidently take a while for it to rescue the facades of all the buildings.

Among the dilapidation, the restaurant was located atop a swanky new shopping mall. This wasn't the Kolkata I was expecting. I was soon to discover that in contrast to its impoverished past and ailing infrastructure, Kolkata had been developing at a swift rate since the economic reforms of the mid-1990s and the information technology boom that revitalised its economy. No longer identified with just slums, destitution and the heartening work of Mother Teresa, the city was reclaiming its title of the cultural capital of India, particularly known for its writers, poets, musicians and artists.

Our dinner companion from the UK couldn't wait to have a beer. 'Care to join me?' he asked.

Feeling the tension of travelling for almost 24 hours, I indeed longed to join him. However, I was fully aware of how disreputable it would look. Virtuous middle-class women rarely drank alcohol in India. My hesitation to say no must have been evident because a beer soon materialised in front of me. The waiter proceeded to take a particular interest in this apparently loose western woman who was drinking beer. Sucharita didn't seem impressed either.

'My name is Martin, like as in Ricky Martin. I sing like him also,' he announced with a grin. 'And what is your good name, madam?'

I'd forgotten how excitable Indian men could be. And there was that peculiarity of asking to know one's 'good name', as if I had a bad name. (In fact, the correct alternative is a pet name.) Fortunately, his curiosity didn't end with me. He soon turned to Sucharita.

'And who might you be, madam? You are with these people for what reason?'

Not keen to indulge his fantasies, she told him that we were from a hospital far, far away.

'Oh, I was thinking that you might be a nun,' he replied animatedly.

'He must be helping himself to the liquor while serving drinks,' Sucharita declared in disgust after he'd departed.

After dinner, Sucharita delivered Tara and me to our accommodation. Again, I was surprised. We would be staying at Hiland Park; by Indian standards, a luxurious new high-rise residential complex on the outskirts of town. It was the first high-rise development in Kolkata, and its gleaming white towers rose starkly from the vacant grassy surroundings. The complex contained nine towers in total, ranging in height from 17 to 28 floors. Within it were an astonishing 941 apartments. We were on the fifth floor of one of the shortest towers.

It soon became obvious that my accommodation wasn't ready. The apartment that my room was located in was unoccupied and mostly unfurnished. This was in contrast to the other volunteers, who were sharing a comfortably lived-in apartment down the hall. While my apartment had a couple of beds, couches still in their plastic wrapper, a coffee table and a fridge, there were no kitchen cupboards, no curtains, no wardrobe, no mosquito nets, no washing machine, no microwave, no cooking utensils and no hot water.

'You'll have to adapt,' Sucharita told me, adding that I'd be getting a flatmate and more furniture soon. I learned pretty quickly that though congenial on the surface, she was prone to emotional outbursts when volunteers failed to adapt as required. It also became apparent that 'adapt' was the most favoured word in her vocabulary.

In that empty apartment in an unfamiliar city that night, I was assailed by packs of massive and unrelenting mosquitoes as I tried to sleep. My loneliness was oddly offset by my gratitude at the opportunity to be alone for a while.

The next morning I drifted around the apartment, examining its whitewashed walls and marble floors and benches. On the floor in a corner of the other bedroom I found a small bronze statue of Lord Ganesh, a box of incense, incense holder and matches. I gently carried them to the coffee table in the living room and lit the incense. Its soothing, ancient smell instantly calmed and cheered me. Although it had only been a night since I'd arrived in Kolkata, I thought that I might actually be okay there.

It wasn't long before Sucharita arrived at the apartment. I had only the one day to settle in before starting work at the centre for underprivileged women that I'd been assigned to. She was keen to start the orientation process. Behind her was a small dark man.

'This is Kali,' she introduced him. 'Kali will be providing your food and cleaning the apartment.'

It was a curious name, one better known as the fearsome Hindu mother of death and Kolkata's presiding deity. With blood-drenched tongue jutting out of her black face, hands bearing bladed weapons, and ears and neck decorated with dismembered body parts, the true Kali is a terrifying sight. The name also means 'black one'.

It was obvious that Kali, the servant, was uneducated and couldn't speak much English. Communication would be interesting. He went about his work while Sucharita took me to the other apartment to meet the rest of the volunteers. They were all in their late teens and early twenties.

'You can't be!' they exclaimed, when I told them I was 31. 'You only look like you're 25.' Unconfident and unsure of myself, I certainly felt that young.

The youngest two girls, Georgie and Nicole, were also from Australia, on their first trip overseas. They were suffering from severe culture shock and couldn't engage with India's confronting personality and were keen to leave. Bubbly, blonde Claudine from England appeared to have settled in well. Cliona, who was from Ireland, was out, but I was told she had been there the longest and had apparently become almost Indian. She could speak Hindi, often wore Indian clothes and had made plenty of local friends.

It emerged that the girls were all volunteering together, teaching in schools and slums; I would be the only one working at the women's centre. Not only did I have to live by myself, I had to work by myself too.

I felt even more anxious when Sucharita told me I would have to take the bus to work. The journey would take an hour each way, and I'd have to change buses. I was in an unfamiliar city and I didn't speak the language. How would I ever cope?

'We will take a practice run,' Sucharita said. 'And on the way, we'll go to a shopping centre so you can buy some Indian clothes. You must wear Indian clothes to work to blend in with the women there as much as possible. They are poor and will feel more comfortable if you dress like them.'

This was getting harder by the minute. Sure, they might feel comfortable, but what about me? I'd wanted to be a bit less concerned about my appearance in India but I could see that it wouldn't be possible if I had to dress in a certain, and completely untried, way. I would be more unsure of myself than ever.

The bus stop was located on the main road, a five-minute walk from my apartment. Heaving, rusty, mechanical monsters that belched out pollution ground to a halt there at irregular intervals. Hordes of people scrambled to get on and off before the conductor bashed the side of the bus with his hand and shouted something incoherent to let the driver know he should proceed.

'We will take the number 1B to Dhakuria, okay?' Sucharita instructed. 'I want you to tell the conductor where we're going. It's important that you pronounce the name right and be understood.'

Our destination, which required a series of tongue acrobatics completely foreign to an English speaker, did nothing to put me at ease. The 'dha' is known as an aspirated, retroflex consonant. There's no equivalent to its pronunciation in the English language. The speaker has to touch her tongue to the roof of her mouth and flip it down, while breathing out and trying not to choke. The word 'Dhakuria' also requires a slightly trilled rolling of the 'r'. I was being thrown in at the deep end.

Inside the bus, I squeezed myself onto a cramped wooden bench seat and awaited my fate. Most of the passengers were men, neatly dressed in the customary pants and shirts. The few woman sat segregated, with their saris wrapped immaculately around themselves and the *pallu* (loose end of the sari) often draped over their heads. Their long dark hair was scraped back into tightly woven buns and their faces were devoid of make-up. The warm shades of their skin blended together but contrasted against mine. Combined with my western dress, I stood out like a beacon. Despite the teeming humanity, I was isolated because of my difference.

It wasn't long before the conductor stopped in front of me. No matter how much I tried, my tongue refused to position itself as needed. As all heads turned in my direction, the source of the shambling sound, I wished I was anywhere else but there. What had I gotten myself into? Whatever was I thinking coming to India by myself? I wasn't brave enough for this!

After my third hopeless attempt, Sucharita realised I wasn't going to make myself understandable and intervened. I resisted the urge to leap off the bus and run to the safety of my apartment. In this unfamiliar city that contained the population of Australia, I felt very much an outsider. I had no one to share my trials and tribulations with, empathise over the challenges or laugh over the misfortunes. I was going to have to rely on myself. I badly wanted someone to hold my hand.

As the bus crunched and groaned along, I distracted myself by looking out the window while the people of India played their lives out on the streets. So used to the quiet streets of Melbourne, it seemed like the whole of Kolkata was gathered by the roadside.

Vegetable vendors sat hunkered down, their bright array of produce laid out on the ground in front of them for finicky Indian house-wives to pick over. I'd never seen such varieties of gourds before. Men gathered around makeshift *chai* (tea) stalls, fashioned out of chunky bits of bamboo tied together. The richer shopkeepers were holed up in their small tin shacks, draped in assorted potato-chip packets and other consumable items. Cycle rickshaw *walas* rested, leaning up against their rickshaws, waiting for the next fare. People coughed and spat. Vehicles honked.

Around forty minutes later we reached Dhakuria. I took note that we disembarked next to a petrol station, and hoped I'd recog-nise it the next day.

'From here, we'll take bus number 45 to Park Circus,' Sucharita told me. It wasn't long before the required bus lumbered up to us and we were on our way again. I found some comfort in the fact that Park Circus, a name reminiscent of the British Raj, didn't present with any pronunciation challenges.

Park Circus, I soon discovered, was aptly named. A huge round-about with roads running off it in all directions, it had cars, buses, auto rickshaws, bicycles and a man carrying a heavy hessian bag on his head jostling for their place. Sucharita took me along Park Street, then down a side street to the women's centre where I'd be working. The centre was located on the top floor of a decaying, whitewashed residential building. The doorway was so low I had to bend down to enter. Inside, I met the people who ran the centre – Aarti, Meera and Nalini.

'So, what do you do?' they asked me.

'I'm an accountant,' I reluctantly replied.

'Ah, perfect, you can work in the showroom,' they decided. 'A stocktake is needed.'

Inwardly, I groaned. A stocktake! I'd come all the way to India to get away from accounting, and I was going to have to do a stocktake. The universe has a sense of humour sometimes.

My hours were to be 9 a.m. to 5 p.m., Monday to Friday, just like an office job. I knew the other volunteers were only working around five hours a day at their projects. It seemed unfair. However, the position would only be for five weeks, and I still hoped that I'd get to meet and work with the women who the centre supported.

While stopping to change buses at Dhakuria on the way back, Sucharita took me to the Dakshinapan Shopping Centre for my Indian wardrobe. This open-air shopping complex houses a number of handicraft emporiums, as well as row upon row of cheap, nondescript clothing shops. The task was to find a *salwaar kameez* or two that suited me. Every shopkeeper vied for my attention as soon as they saw me.

'Madam, madam. Come look my shop. Yes, madam, can I help you?'

After being shown dozens of outfits, I finally found a red-and-brown patterned *salwaar kameez* for 150 rupees ($5), and another in blue for 250 rupees ($8). The *salwaar kameez*, a loose-fitting pants and tunic combination with *dupatta* (scarf), hung like a tent on my thin body. But it would suffice.

Back at the apartment, I knew I was going to have to do something about the mosquito menace. Although Hiland Park was located in the middle of nowhere, on a road known as the EM Bypass, it wasn't completely isolated. There was a shopping mall right in front of it. And, in that shopping mall was the closest thing I was to find to a western department store, the Big Bazaar.

To the uninitiated, the Big Bazaar is India's version of a discount department store. It's a two-storey mecca that stocks everything from food to fridges, to cookware to clothes. With a slogan of '*Is se sasta aur accha kahin nahi!* (nowhere cheaper or better than this!)', it's been expanding through India and fuelling frenzies among shoppers at an alarming rate. No doubt, a sign of an emerging middle class with a disposable income.

That night marked the beginning of my strong love/hate relationship with the Big Bazaar. Blissfully ignorant, I was unaware that the colossal crowd milling around outside was also an indication of what was within. As I passed through a security check to be admitted indoors, the first thing that struck me was the complete disarray. Merchandise was clustered together in islands, piled onto tables and overflowing from large bins. Whole families hunted for bargains in huge groups, eagerly pushing past me in their hurry to unearth the next good deal. Trolleys acted as obstacles in already jammed thoroughfares.

All of this, I was later to learn, was no design flaw but purposely laid out that way. A neat and empty shop, which may appeal to foreigners like me, will never attract the masses in India. For Indians, shopping is entertainment. They like to be able to bump into people, chat, gossip and eat while shopping. The Big Bazaar, with its organised chaos, purposely facilitates this.

It certainly didn't make easy my mission of acquiring a mosquito net. My confusion only increased as I left the store. At the checkout, the mosquito net was placed into a plastic carry bag, which was then heat-sealed shut. At the exit, a security officer demanded to see my receipt, which was then hole-punched and returned to me. Neither process made sense, especially as it wasn't possible to check the contents of my sealed shopping bag against the items listed on the receipt. It would be a long time before I futilely stopped looking for logic in India!

The next morning, I managed to make my way to work and arrived on time. I was proud of the fact that I'd done it without any hiccups, or having to ask for help. I nervously stepped inside the building and, deciphering a handwritten sign instructing 'Please Open Your Shoes Down', removed my sandals.

Every day the women's centre opened with meditation and yoga, followed by music, singing and prayer.

'*Saab ka mangal, saab ka mangal, saab ka mangal, hoi re* (Let good happen to everyone).' It was touching and inspiring. Most importantly, for all the women from diverse backgrounds who attended the centre, it fostered hope and oneness. It was impossible to know, just by looking at the women, that they had suffered intense hardship and oppression, living in unhygienic conditions with the burden of having to meet the domestic and financial needs of their families. They were so composed and attractively dressed, although they looked at me with wary eyes.

Introductions were made over steaming hot cups of spicy *chai*. I felt as shy as the women, and didn't know what to say to them to bridge the divide between us. The women at the centre were taught skills that would empower them to earn a decent income and live a more dignified life. They learned how to read and write, make handicrafts, pickles and jam, market the goods and manage a small business. The showroom was a retail outlet for what they produced. It was stacked from floor to ceiling with eye-catching batik wall hangings, bedding, clothes, bags, aprons, greeting cards, leather purses and notebook covers. All of a sudden, the thought of immersing myself in their work and having to do a stocktake didn't seem so bad.

At lunchtime, Nalini and Meera invited me to join them in their office.

'Come, sit,' they directed me as they unfurled mats on the floor. I contorted myself into a cross-legged pose and positioned my lunch in front of me. It was a simple meal of rice and potatoes, cooked by some of the women at the centre. It suited me, as I'd always liked

Indian food and had never had a problem eating it. Fortunately, I was given a spoon, and so was saved from having to make a clumsy attempt to eat with my fingers. But I would learn and become familiar with eating with my fingers by the time I left the centre. The trick is to use the fingers to work the food into a ball. Then with four fingers acting like a spoon, gather it up onto the fingertips with the thumb, place the thumb behind it, and lever it into the mouth.

'So, tell us about yourself,' they asked. Used to living communally, Indians like to know as much as possible about each other. There is little concept of privacy, so prized in the west. 'How old are you and do you have a husband?'

Just the questions I didn't want to answer! I knew if I told them my true age but said I was single, they would think it strange since anyone over the ripe old age of 29 is looked on as being past marriageable age in India. I decided to be truthful but to say as little as possible.

'Um, I'm 31 and yes, I do.'

'How long have you been married? What is his work? He didn't mind you coming here?'

The questions kept coming. I answered them briefly, and then deflected their interest by asking some of my own.

'And what about both of you? Any husbands?' This prompted one of the most enlightening discussions I've ever had in India.

'Oh no, we don't want to get married,' they chorused. 'Once we get married, we'll have to give up working and look after our husband's family.'

'Really?' I said in surprise.

'Yes, in India, traditionally when a girl gets married she goes to live with her husband and his parents. Everyone lives together in the same house. A wife must take care of her husband's family while the husband earns the money to support them. We're not ready to spend our lives cooking and cleaning for other people all day. We like our work here.'

I was amazed. Coming from a country with a culture that cultivates independence, the idea of not only having to live with the in-laws but also to look after them was completely incomprehensible to me. Travelling around India as a tourist, I hadn't had the opportunity to find out much about daily life in India, and was keen to know more.

'So, how old are you both, and where do you live? And do you have any boyfriends?'

'We're 24 and 26,' they replied. 'And we live with our parents.'

It was no surprise to learn that they were still living at home, but all the same it was a little perplexing. Like most young people in Australia, I'd been so anxious to move into my own place as soon as I'd finished university and started work. I couldn't wait to taste freedom. But that kind of freedom, while not only a rarity, was also quite unacceptable in traditional Indian society.

'Boyfriends? No!' they giggled, embarrassed. 'Our parents will arrange our marriage for us.'

And how would they find prospective grooms?

'Our parents will talk to people or advertise,' the women explained. 'Then they will come to the house and we'll meet them. Of course, we can say if we don't like them but it's not the case for everyone. The most important thing is that both families agree. In India, it's not just the couple who becomes joined, it's the families too.

'See, for us Indians, love and affection grow after marriage. Husbands and wives learn to love and respect each other. It's not like in the west, where people initially try so hard to impress each other, have so many expectations, then fall out of love and get divorced. In India, marriage is about partnership and compatibility. A lot of effort is put into finding a compatible match with a good family of similar background and financial status. This helps ensure that the couple stays together.'

Given my situation, I could definitely see the merit in arranged marriages, difficult as the idea is for westerners to fathom. In India, marriage is more about duty, whereas in the west it's about finding 'The One'. Many westerners view the idea of having to marry someone who they hardly know, or aren't even attracted to, as almost barbaric. In India, the arranged marriage produces the best and most stable outcome because other factors, apart from emotions, are taken into consideration.

The conversation left me filled with wonder at the world and how two completely different, and in fact opposite, cultures existed on the same planet. It was a feeling that would remain with me as I continued to discover extreme differences between the cultures.

Western facilities were conspicuously absent at the women's centre. That afternoon I had my first encounter with the infamous Indian squat toilet. There it was, beckoning me, a porcelain basin in the floor, with a hole and space for my feet on either side. I soon discovered there are two challenges involved in using the squat toilet – aim, and the cleaning of body parts afterwards. Making a stream of urine go down a porcelain hole without splashing or spraying the sides and getting wet feet is no easy matter. And even if it is achieved, the task of cleaning the nether regions still remains.

Foolishly, I didn't carry any toilet paper. Cleaning would have to involve my left hand, the small mug nearby, and water. But with my bottom pointing downwards, and loose *salwaar kameez* pants bunched around my ankles, how would it be possible to pour the water onto myself without getting everything wet? I managed to splash the water around in a totally unsatisfactory manner, and had the displeasure of it dripping down my legs and on to my clothes as I stood up. A large bucketful of water was waiting by the side of the door, so I quickly tipped it down the toilet to flush it and beat a hasty retreat.

By the end of the day, I was exhausted and couldn't wait to go home. I dragged my weary body onto the packed bus and wedged myself in between the other commuters who were standing.

The one redeeming feature of the buses is their ladies only seating. While it really highlights the distinction between men and women in India, and how they interact, it also helps prevent any unto-ward incidents between the sexes. Unfortunately, during peak hour there's barely any room to move, let alone sit, on the bus. A portly Indian male's potbelly pressed into my back. No sooner had I man-aged to disengage myself from it than I felt a hand on my bottom. Its owner whispered something unintelligible to me as he squeezed past. I promptly rewarded him with a swift and strong elbow for his effort. The most disconcerting thing was that he looked so respect-able, like a decent family man.

It was a relief to wash the day's sweat and grime from my body. Somehow, I managed to summon my last remaining bit of energy to go to the apartment next door to reheat the curry and rice dinner that Kali had kept in the fridge for me. Then I promptly crawled into bed and fell into a deep sleep under my bright purple mosquito net.

As the week progressed, people at work seemed to become more open to my presence, and warmed to me more. I warmed to them too and was keen to befriend them. On the plus side, I always had company in the showroom. It was Nalini's job to oversee it. A very attractive Bengali woman, she was slight in build with sharp fea-tures, sparkly eyes and an engaging smile. We were often joined by the women who attended the centre. They would sit in the corner and stitch their handicrafts.

'Do you know any Hindi? *Bangla* (Bengali)?' they eagerly inquired.

'*Aap kaise hain*? (How are you?)' I offered. It was one of only a few things I knew how to say in Hindi. But it was enough to please them. They were even more amused when I pulled out my Hindi and Bengali phrasebook and attempted to read from it.

'*Aa-mi Bang-la bohl-te paa-ri-nai* (I can't speak Bengali),' I stumbled and they laughed. It soon became apparent that my phrasebook would be the thing that united us.

'Read, we will help,' they encouraged me.

I quickly grew very fond of two women in particular – an irrepressible girl named Lakhi, and a gentle older Muslim woman called Mastari Begum.

Lakhi taught me how to reprimand people in Bengali. *Baloh naa.* (Not good.) *Aap ni karap.* (You are bad.) *Aap ni dushtu.* (You are naughty.) Mastari, who didn't know much English, would just sit next to me and smile. When English was spoken, it was mostly broken Indian English, as the women hadn't been formally educated in the language.

It wasn't long before I got to see firsthand the impact the women's centre had on people's lives. Two volunteers from another organisation brought a mother and her young daughter to the centre one afternoon. They were extremely poor, distraught and dejected-looking. The daughter was still at school, but had already developed some skills in making handicrafts. The mother begged for advice and assistance for her daughter. After sitting down and talking to Meera in the office, the mother left, crying tears of happiness, knowing there could be a positive future for her daughter after she finished school.

'*Phir milenge* (We'll meet again),' I tried to reassure the mother as she left, in the only other Hindi phrase I knew. She reached out, grabbed my hand and kissed it. I felt like crying myself, it was so emotional. However, that I was almost moved to tears by her plight indicated that I wasn't really suited to a career in social work. I had actually given serious thought to it when pondering my future. Yet, the reality was that I didn't have the tough mind needed to deal with confronting situations and other people's suffering. I was sensitive and easily saddened. I wished I could wave a magic wand over her and take away all her problems. But life isn't like that.

Just seeing the depth of the mother's despair reminded me of how many positives I still had, and took for granted, in my existence. It left me feeling disturbed for the rest of the afternoon. My sombre mood didn't go unnoticed.

'Come, sit, drink tea,' the other women tried to make me feel better. Little did they know that I had had enough of sitting on the floor all day, and had had enough tea (try explaining to Indians that you don't want tea, and they'll look at you incredulously).

I was thankful it was already dark when I took the bus home that night. The dim glow of the lights took away some of the harshness of reality and gave the streets a magical feel. I leaned my face towards the open window and breathed in the sights and smells – the dust, the smog, the spices, the incense. Street vendors lined the pavements. Everywhere, people. The foreignness of my surroundings made me feel like I was a very small part of a huge, unfathomable picture. It was strangely reassuring.

Before long, it was Christmas Eve. Kolkata has a nostalgic relationship with Christmas, as a result of its colonial history. Tara, Claudine and I decided to go shopping in the heart of Kolkata. The taxi dropped us at the iconic stretch of Park Street near Chowringhee Road, at the opposite end to where the street connects with Park Circus. The city's most prestigious thoroughfare, it was named after a deer park that existed there in the late eighteenth century, during the glory days when Calcutta was the capital of British India. With those days long gone, and with Calcutta metamorphosing into Kolkata, the street has now been renamed Mother Teresa Sarani after the Albanian nun who dedicated herself to helping the poor.

It's clearly still a prestigious part of town, even if it doesn't glitter like it used to. There was a time when Park Street was the focal point of the whole city, if not the country. The street's grand old mansions housed the finest of shops and restaurants on their ground floors, and the richest of the rich in airy apartments on the upper floors. India's first independent nightclub opened there, with soulful voices and swinging six-piece bands, along with India's first department store.

Today, the main symbol of Park Street's pre-eminence is The Park Hotel. Restaurants are still filled to capacity but the class of diners has changed, and dinner jackets are no longer compulsory. DJs have replaced the live jazz and cabaret, and shops selling pirated books and fake perfume have encroached where once they wouldn't have dared.

Around the corner Chowringhee Road has been renamed Jawaharlal Nehru Road. It's now dominated by packs of pavement vendors selling cheap jewellery, western and Indian clothes and handbags. We tried to browse as we walked, but the clamour and commotion didn't make it a peaceful activity.

A bangle seller latched onto me.

'Madam, just looking. I show you. See, pretty bangles. Very cheap,' he assured me.

I made the mistake of smiling at him and pausing to take a peek. They didn't interest me, and I attempted to move away.

'No madam, I give you good price. How much you want to pay?' he persisted.

'Really, I don't want them,' I replied.

'But madam, best deal,' he beseeched.

I turned away and began to push through the crowd to catch up with the other girls, who were already well ahead.

He followed me. 'Madam! Madam! Wait!'

Some people find it easy to be abrupt and dismissive of these kinds of annoyances. I don't. I never want to seem rude and always find the attention hard to ignore, no matter how irritating. All of a sudden, I remembered why India can be so tiring.

The bangle seller was still pestering me by the time I reached the girls.

'Looks like you've got yourself a fan,' they laughed.

'I can't get rid of him,' I sighed.

At that point, I was feeling really hungry and dragged the girls into a nearby restaurant to eat.

'I'd have to be paid to eat here,' Claudine complained as I ordered my *aloo gobi* (potato and cauliflower curry). It was a dingy dining establishment, where functionality took priority over aesthetics and tasteful decorations were conspicuously absent. Yet, when the *aloo gobi* arrived, it was undeniably good. And it cost only 15 rupees (45 cents). Claudine helped herself.

'You really don't look like you're 31,' she said again as I got my bag to leave. 'But I can see that you act like a grown-up and have nice things like one.'

I was amused and alarmed. How were 31-year-olds expected to act? Did 31 really seem that old? And when had it stopped seeming old to me? I'd been happy to turn 30. I still felt and looked young, but was glad for the wisdom that I'd acquired during my twenties.

'You know,' she continued, 'I think the reason why you get hassled so much here is that you're smiling all the time. Every time I see you, you're smiling.'

No doubt she was right. Smiling came naturally to me. But it also disarmed people, and encouraged them to be persistent. Claudine, on the other hand, had her own way of dealing with unwanted attention. She waved, said 'See you later', and walked away without looking back. It was a non-offensive but effective technique that even amused many Indian onlookers. I'd seen them start laughing at their counterparts after witnessing it.

For the next few hours, we immersed ourselves in Kolkata's historic bargain shoppers' paradise of New Market. Another remnant of the British Raj, it sprawls over a series of buildings and the surrounding area on Lindsay Street. It had been established solely as a white man's market, providing exclusive goods to the affluent English populace. These days, locals claim there's nothing its 2500 stalls don't sell. We wandered through the warren of corridors, trying on Indian clothes in infinite shades and designs until we were exhausted. Afterwards, we headed to Peter Cat restaurant to replenish ourselves.

Opened in the swinging 1960s, Peter Cat had managed to survive the passage of time and remained as popular as it was back in its heyday. The dimly lit interior spoke of history. The waiters were resplendent in crisp Rajasthani white and red costumes, which matched the colours of the restaurant's interior but curiously contrasted with its name – a name that didn't give away much at all. However, a bit of research revealed that it's the namesake of a famous cat who lived in Lord's cricket ground in London from 1952 to 1964 (and Kolkata is a city obsessed with cricket).

I ordered a Tom Collins. Priced at only 74 rupees ($2), it was the cheapest cocktail I'd ever had, and was likely to ever get in India. Already drained by the day's activities, I struggled to stay awake after drinking it.

The Christmas lights twinkled warmly on Park Street as we climbed into a taxi to go home. Nevertheless, by the time we arrived back at the apartment building, melancholia had descended over me like the mist that falls over Kolkata night after night in winter. Kolkata's winter lacks the bitter coldness, cloudy skies and rain of the Melbourne winter. However, it's extremely dusty and the chill of the night air adds impenetrable thick mist and fog. Not only does it make it very difficult to breathe, it often grounds flights as well. My head pounded from the noxious blend.

Since childhood, Christmas Eve has been a magical occasion filled with anticipation for the day to follow. This Christmas just wasn't going to be the same. Music from a Christmas Eve party being hosted for residents in the apartment courtyard drifted through my apartment windows. But I couldn't summon enough interest to investigate.

Christmas day dawned bright and sunny, but with the usual layer of Kolkata smog. It was Christmas morning in India but it was already Christmas afternoon in Australia, where celebrations would be in full swing, eating and drinking at a relative's house. It seemed so far away, a detached and distant land. For me, Christmas morning had involved the same ritual since childhood – sitting on the floor and unwrapping presents with my parents. I had never spent a Christmas away from my family until now.

Just last Christmas, Michael was still in my life. We had the presents ritual as usual but he had later spent a lot of time out of sight on the phone, when we were at his father and stepmother's house for Christmas lunch. Looking back now, it was a sign. But although I noticed it at the time, in my ignorance I didn't really think anything of it. My, how so much can change in a year! If anyone had suggested to me that I would be spending Christmas in India, on the brink of divorce this year, I would have thought it totally obscene. Yet, here I was.

Claudine, Tara, Georgie, Nicole and I decided to go to the Christmas-lunch buffet at the luxurious ITC Sheraton hotel in our

Indian clothes. We wanted to give our appearance an Indian touch, but looked forward to eating something other than curry. I'm blessed with a very strong stomach and hadn't experienced any digestive problems at all, but some of the other girls weren't so fortunate.

At 1200 rupees ($30) per head, the buffet was affordable only to well-off Indians. The cost, which we regarded as quite a bargain for a sumptuous all-you-can-eat lunch with alcohol, was more than a week's wages for much of India's population. What we were entitled to as the middle class in our developed nations and were casual about was reserved for the privileged in India. I couldn't help noticing the distinction between us and the other portly Indian guests. Us, dressed in the cheap outfits we'd thrown together, and them resplendent in the finest of saris. Us, acting exuberant and unfussy; them, reserved but demanding. Us, with our bodies kept deliberately slim; them, displaying the desired roundness that comes from having more than enough to eat.

The disparity between rich and poor in India stretched deeper than that. The richest ten per cent of India's population owns over half the country's wealth, while the poorest ten per cent owns a mere 0.2% of it. Most of India's poor struggle each day just to make ends meet. Only yesterday, we had been alongside those people. Today, we were alongside the rich, playing the role of privileged tourists. The extremes seemed hard to justify.

Champagne flowed, a live band sang Christmas songs and a roving Santa stopped by our table to give us gifts and wish us Merry Christmas. His starkly white beard stood out against the deep coffee colour of his skin. It was Christmas, Indian style!

At the buffet, we had to search for roast meat among the dominating curries. I ate a plateful of curry because it looked so appealing. The roast turkey delivered to us by the chef next was delicious. And the desserts, laden with chocolate, were among the best I'd ever had.

After spending almost four hours in the dining room, we retired to an outdoor pavilion in the hotel's grounds. We reclined on the couches and admired the large marble bowls filled with colourful floating flowers, as fountains cascaded around us.

Outside the sanctuary of the hotel, the illusion was shattered and we were quickly reminded of exactly where we were. A short distance down the road, our taxi driver pulled over as a random Indian guy came running up alongside us. It seemed that he was a friend of the taxi driver and desperately wanted a lift. Despite the decrepit taxi barely accommodating the five of us, as well as the driver, he insisted on getting in the front with Claudine.

It was one of those mad Indian moments that we were completely unaccustomed to, and had no idea how to react. Vehicles are commonly burdened beyond their capacity: motorbikes carry whole families on them, with children gripping the handlebars in front of their father and sitting on their mother's lap. Any available space is used. The taxi lurched forward, with all of us aboard and the two Indian occupants clearly amused by the unexpected situation they'd found themselves in. It was probably the first time they'd been crammed in a car with a bunch of hyperactive white girls. The brakes were slammed on multiple times by the distracted driver, who had a few near misses as we shrieked in unison.

The day spent with the girls did wonders for my mood. They were young, innocent and carefree, and they made me feel that way too. Bonding with them gave me a huge boost.

'You always seem so positive and happy,' the girls said during the day.

This was a welcome revelation. I was relieved to know that, apart from the fact that I was noticeably underweight, the difficult year hadn't had an obvious impact on me. And, perhaps, I was more likeable than I thought.

Two days later, on what I thought was going to be an uneventful day, I arrived back at the apartment after work to find that my flatmate had moved in. My clothes and belongings had been picked up off the other bed in my room, which was acting as my wardrobe in the continued absence of any furniture, and unceremoniously dumped onto mine. Not long after, the door opened and a mature-looking Indian lady entered.

'Hi, I'm Panna,' she introduced herself in a British accent. She must have noticed the less than enthusiastic look on my face because she quickly added, 'I didn't do that, by the way. It was Kali.'

'No one told me you were coming today,' I replied. 'Otherwise I would've moved my things.'

It transpired that she had also been shifted without notice, and was equally unimpressed about it. What's more, she'd apparently been comfortably ensconced in a properly furnished apartment on one of the upper levels of the building. In her late thirties, she didn't appreciate having to live in this barren and inhospitable environment or sharing a room with me.

The feeling was mutual. I was even more underwhelmed by the prospect when Panna told me her routine: 'I only have to work for a couple of hours a day, so I go out every night and don't usually come back until late.'

She was enjoying living the life she didn't have back in England. This was a massive difference from my eight-hour work days and two-hour commute, which meant an early bedtime and waking to a 7.30 a.m. alarm five days a week.

Despite the fact that the apartment was generously sized and had three bedrooms, Sucharita had insisted to Panna that we share one bedroom because it was the rules.

'She said that since we were volunteers, we must learn to adapt,' Panna relayed.

Ah! Adapt. That word again.

What was even more illogical was that Sucharita had conceded to let us keep our clothes in one of the spare bedrooms until a wardrobe arrived, whenever that would be. So we could use the vacant room for storage, but not for sleeping?

'There's no point discussing it with her anymore,' Panna advised. 'I've tried, but it got me nowhere. Indians have their own ways of doing things.' Although assertive, Panna had failed to resolve anything in our favour with the unreasonable Sucharita. Our only option was to adapt, and try and make the best of it.

Having spent a considerable amount of time in India, and being of Indian descent herself, Panna was right. Indians can be extremely adjustable or extremely stubborn, depending on the perception of power. Rules are created or bent at will to suit situations. Definitions of right or wrong are never absolute, and instead depend on the context and the desired outcome.

In any case, I was quite thankful for the company; I was beginning to feel lonely in the apartment.

# New Beginnings

THERE'S something invigorating and exciting about the impending start to a new year. I'm always one of the excited ones, keen to clean the slate of a year, refocus, and fill the next one with new goals. I was particularly keen to put the past year behind me. It had been life-changing for me and I wanted to know what the future had in store.

Georgie and Nicole were leaving for Darjeeling on New Year's Eve, so we went out the night before to have a farewell party for them. Little did I know, that night would set my life towards a whole new direction.

It had started simply enough, with a delicious dinner at Kewpies Kitchen restaurant. Located in the owner's home, the Bengali restaurant is intimate and unique, and one of the most sought after

45

in Kolkata. This comes as no surprise, given that the owner's wife wrote two cookbooks on Bengali cuisine.

It wasn't until we ended up at Roxy, the stylish 1960s-inspired cocktail bar at The Park Hotel, that things took an unexpected turn. World-class bars and clubs are not something that people readily associate India with. And many tourists who visit India for purposes more spiritual never bother to seek them out. However, in modern-day India, they do exist in abundance. India's young and rich are cosmopolitan and well travelled. They like to live western lifestyles, and expect the finest facilities.

I felt comfortable in Roxy's sleek and contemporary interior. Cocktails were sipped, and conversation was light. Then Utsav, a close friend of Panna's, suggested a mystery cocktail. Named 'God Knows Fucking What' by the barman who created it for him, it contained a lethal concoction of unidentified ingredients. I was the only one game enough to try it. The mood turned upbeat and energetic as the alcohol coursed through our bodies. We hit the dance floor and grooved to retro, electro and everything in between.

'Can I dance with you?' a mature Indian gentleman approached me.

Although he must have been around 60, he had the stamina of someone half my age. I couldn't keep up with him.

'Please, you've worn me out. I need a break,' I begged him, as I fled back to the bar.

Before we knew it, it was 4 a.m. Unlike the rest of India, where bars and clubs had to close by 1.30 a.m. or even 11.30 p.m. in some places, Kolkata didn't have a curfew.

Then it happened.

Just as we were about to leave Roxy, I saw an Indian guy enter the room. He stood near the entrance with a friend. I looked at him, noticing his full lips and beautiful eyes. To my surprise he came over. He was to later admit that he surprised himself by talking to me; he thought I looked quite intimidating. I would later admit that I was surprised that I wanted to talk to him. With everything that had gone on in my life over the past year, I wasn't interested in meeting anyone, especially Indian guys who were keen to try and get somewhere with a white girl.

'Are you really this tall or are you wearing heels?' he asked.

It was an understandable question. I must have been around 10 centimetres taller than him. My 175-centimetre frame was tall by western standards, but in India I was more like a giant.

'Yes, I really am this tall,' I said, amused.

His name was Aryan, and he was a resident DJ at The Park Hotel's nightclub, Tantra. Chatting with him felt effortless and comfortable. He smiled and laughed readily. There was no tension or pretension, just a tangible and uplifting lightness of being. We went upstairs to chill out on the sofas where it was less noisy.

I was surprised to find out that Aryan and I were the same age. What's more, astrologically, we were supposedly very compatible. He was an emotional water sign like me. From the way he spoke and acted, he certainly did have a gentle calming manner about him.

'Come to Tantra tomorrow night. New Year's Eve will be big,' he said as we parted.

Although I'd enjoyed spending time with him, I had no intention of going. Back at the apartment the next day, Panna couldn't understand my reluctance. She was enjoying knowing people in Kolkata, and going to bars where she was known and recognised. It was new and exciting for her.

'I've had enough of the party scene back home,' I tried to explain. 'It doesn't hold the same attraction for me.'

More than anything, I didn't want to be distracted from the real reason I came to Kolkata – to learn more about myself in a different environment. Hanging out in bars and clubs was hardly a different environment for me, and I wanted to avoid it.

So for New Year's Eve, I found myself at a rooftop party hosted by Linda, an American friend of Panna's. She spent six months of the year in India, and even had an Indian boyfriend. I was quite in awe of her extraordinary life. I wondered what it would be like to be so much a part of another culture like that. And how did she manage it? I tossed the idea around in my mind, but it seemed unfathomable. I doubted I could ever create a life like that for myself. I wouldn't even know where to begin.

The party was attended by an interesting mix of people. Two of the guests had graduated in accounting like me, but had gone on to pursue completely different paths. One was now a filmmaker, the other a musician. The filmmaker had recently won an award for a documentary about his parents' experience of the 1947 partition of India by the British into Muslim-controlled Pakistan and Hindu-dominated India.

I envied the two guys for where they had ended up; filmmaking and music were pursuits so opposite to accounting. The creativity of my younger years had been replaced by structure, logic and analysis. It was a long time since I'd painted, sewn or written poetry or stories. All those things were a significant and enjoyable part of my life when I was growing up. Sadly, that wasn't the case anymore. But perhaps there was hope yet for me: if those two guys could make the transition to a creative field and pursue their passion, maybe I could too?

Claudine, Tara and I stayed at the party until after 3 a.m. We were among the last to leave. Meanwhile, Panna and Cliona had gone on to their usual hangout, Roxy.

'Aryan was there last night. He was looking for you and asked us numerous times if you were out,' Panna informed me in the morning. Clearly, even if I avoided The Park Hotel, I couldn't avoid

the situation. And, despite being flattered that Aryan was so interested in me, I still had no intention of pursuing anything with him.
Instead, I put him out of my mind.

That afternoon, Panna, Claudine, Tara and I joined the rest of
the city and spent the day at the horse races at the Royal Calcutta
Turf Club. It was a New Year's Day tradition, and a popular one at
that, despite the revelry of the previous night. The Turf Club, built
by the British in 1820, had managed to retain its colonial name. Its
buildings were grand and imposing, at its centre a lofty clock tower.
Looking around, it wasn't difficult to imagine the refined manner in
which the British lived during the rule of the Raj. Nowadays, the
Indian elite were making bold fashion statements in bejewelled saris
and suits, short dresses and ridiculously ostentatious hats. Clearly,
like everywhere else, it wasn't just about the horses. Those with new
money and generous allowances were the most obtrusive, while the
old money put on a more refined display. There were ordinary folk
there as well, like us, casually dressed.

As we strolled along soaking up the atmosphere, the anticipation
was obvious. We followed Panna to the members' area where she
was to meet yet another friend. Occupying the top third floor, the
privileged space provided an unbeatable view of the racecourse and
the Victoria Memorial in the distance.

Much money changed hands that day; fortunes were made and
squandered.

'I lost 27,000 rupees ($700) today,' one unlucky fellow unbur-
dened himself to Claudine. 'But you look nice and sexy,' he continued.

Tara and I sniggered in amusement over her latest admirer. Being
the only blonde among us, the Indian men were most generous with
their attention.

Even Kolkata's formidable policemen were reduced to unusual
behaviour in Claudine's presence. She had us howling with laughter

one day as she entertained us with the tale of her five-hour visit to the Kolkata police station to report the theft of her wallet.

'The Chief Superintendent himself personally attended to me. I received a number of offers of marriage, and even caught one policeman sneakily taking my photo,' she said. 'And then, another policeman took me all the way back to the apartment on his motorbike. He offered to pick me up and take me to work every day.'

By the time we arrived back at the apartment that evening, we were completely worn out. The crowd leaving the races had merged with that coming from the nearby zoo to create a seething mass of people, young and old, and overburdened buses and taxis on the roads. At the traffic lights, engines were turned off to save fuel. Crossing the road was almost eerie as the silent lanes of banked-up traffic waited, ready to start up and come charging.

A week later, Claudine dragged Tara and me out to spend time with her new friend Raj, the springy-haired son of the Police High Commissioner. It seemed that her liaisons with the Kolkata police weren't over after all. We met him on Park Street, just outside the Oxford Bookstore. He looked at the personal development book, *The Monk Who Sold His Ferrari*, which I had just bought and was carrying.

'One has to get a Ferrari first,' he commented disdainfully.

Raj took us to visit his palatial family home in central Kolkata, where we were fed snacks and harassed by the family's feisty gaggle of pet geese. Regrettably, our visit had coincided perfectly with their walk and swim. The house was a rambling two-level, burgundy-coloured mansion, complete with guards and an extensive collection of Ganesh statues. It was an imposing sight. Raj obviously lived a life of luxury, wanting for nothing.

That evening, Raj and his driver collected Claudine, Tara and me for dinner at the Tollygunge Club, where we were joined by his friends, a lawyer and a pipe-smoking businessman.

The Tollygunge Club, another vestige of the British occupation, prides itself on being among the top twenty country clubs in the world. It offers all sorts of sports, from horseriding to golf, on its sizeable 100-acre grounds. I was amazed at how India had preserved aspects of traditional British culture better than the British themselves, and how much India's elite clamoured to be a part of these exclusive English-style clubs. By restricting its membership to a select 3500, the Tollygunge Club has ensured that the list of wannabes waiting to sign up is always long and the queue slow to move.

Over dinner, Raj's interest in me grew, buoyed by the red wine that was flowing. When we decided to move on to The Park Hotel, he ordered me into the car with him and the pipe-smoking business-man. Tara and Claudine went with the lawyer in his car.

'Don't worry, he's a nice guy and different from the others,' Claudine reassured me.

I was unconvinced. By that stage, Raj had already tried to put his arm around me. We were to soon discover that the lawyer was actually the least offensive of the trio.

Panna, Cliona and Utsav were at Roxy as usual, but seemed reluctant to talk to us. It didn't bode well. Raj seemed unhappy that we knew people, and quickly whisked us out of there and into Tantra. All I could think about was one thing: I would see Aryan again.

He noticed me as soon as I entered and climbed the stairs to the Bodhi Bar on the second floor of the club. The DJ cabin was located on the same level, on the opposite side of the room. We smiled and waved at each other across the distance. Then Raj called me to have a tequila-and-lime shooter. His arm was again on my waist. I slid away. Claudine and Tara had escaped to the dance floor and were chatting to some Norwegians by the time I found them. Again, Raj and his friends seemed keen for us to leave. None of us was interested in going.

I returned to the Bodhi Bar, where I could see Aryan, with Raj in hot pursuit. He ordered another shooter, and another. Before long, he was drunk and hoping that I was as well. Then he lunged and tried to kiss me. I turned my head quickly so it landed on my cheek. Unimpressed, I fled to the bathroom.

'I've had enough of this. He won't leave me alone!' I shouted over the music to Claudine. She was about to accompany Tara, who'd also had enough, back to the apartment. 'I'll stay until Tantra closes, then go home with Panna, Cliona and Utsav,' I told her. I wanted to at least try and get some enjoyment from the night.

'I bet I know whom you're going to see,' she teased.

Aryan came out of the DJ cabin to greet me as soon as I knocked. He looked every bit as attractive as I remembered.

'I've been asking your friends where you were.'

'I know. But I didn't feel like partying. Tonight Claudine convinced me to come out to dinner with her and some other people. That guy you saw me with earlier was one of them. He tried to get me drunk and kiss me. I had to run away! It was awful!' I explained.

Aryan laughed. 'It's good you're here now then. Come and sit inside.'

There was a beanbag on the floor. I relaxed into it while Aryan and another DJ played music. It wasn't long before the club closed, and we had to leave. Aryan wanted me to join him and his friends.

'No, I have to go home with the others,' I declined. I didn't want to take any chances, especially after my encounter with Raj.

I met my friends at the front of the club. Raj was still on my mind as we got in a taxi.

'I'm so annoyed he kept forcing himself on me. I expected him to be better behaved, considering who he was,' I kept complaining.

'I agree. He's not a nice person. I went to school with him and his friends,' Utsav replied. 'But Indian guys are no different to guys anywhere else. Actually, they can be worse.'

We stopped for *chai* at a roadside *dhaba* (restaurant) on the way home, and crawled into bed as the sun was rising.

Claudine woke us all up mid-morning with a knock at the door. 'I was just checking to see that you'd gotten home safely.'

Still feeling sleepy and a bit hung-over, I went over to her apartment and curled up on her bed for a chat.

'Tara and I are keen to see the Norwegians again,' she confided.

I laughed. 'Well, anything would be a better alternative than revolting Raj. Fancy telling me he was a nice guy! And anyway, how come I got stuck with him? I'm not coming out with you on anymore of your dinner dates,' I grumbled.

'So, tell me, how was Aryan? Any flirtations?' she changed the subject.

'He was really sweet. But no, I didn't get to spend much time with him because he was busy working and then Tantra closed,' I told her. 'Besides, I'm really not up for it.'

She knew what my situation was like, and didn't press me.

# Fork in the Road

IT turned out that three new volunteers had arrived during the night. They were all from England, and aged in their late teens and early twenties. Daisy would be staying in my apartment, while Tess and Miriam were in the other apartment with Cliona, Claudine and Tara.

Unlike Panna and me, Daisy was yet to get curtains in her bedroom. Kali had decided that the solution was to fully cover the windows with newspaper to keep out the light, which he busied himself doing. It was impossible to determine from his response whether or not curtains would be hung, but it certainly didn't look promising. At least Daisy, who had been allocated the master bedroom to herself, had an ensuite bathroom and a wardrobe in her room.

Panna and I suspected we wouldn't be getting a wardrobe after all. Kali had suspended rows of string from one side of our room to the other for us to hang our clothes on. We had, however, been granted a water heater in our bathroom.

'Welcome to India,' we joked to Daisy.

It was a relief the water heater had finally been installed. It's the little things such as hot water, easily taken for granted, that mean a lot when you're in a foreign place devoid of the usual conveniences and comforts of home. In India, it was hard to get the most straightforward tasks done, amid systems that were confusing to learn. Even having a standalone hot water heater in the bathroom wasn't something I was used to.

The weather had become more uncomfortable; the nights cold, and the mist and dust thicker than ever. I struggled to breathe properly as I made my way to work in the mornings. I'd added a maroon shawl with a paisley pattern to my Indian ensemble.

'This weather will last for around two weeks, before it starts warming up again,' the women at work informed me. 'There are six seasons in Kolkata: summer, rainy, autumn, cool, winter and spring.'

Unused to the climate as we were, it wasn't long before both apartments were infected with colds. Tara was first to get sick, followed by Daisy. The virus progressively claimed more victims. Then the water heater in Panna's and my bathroom blew up. I had turned it on to warm the water for my shower but its light kept flickering strangely. Naturally, Panna was out. I called Daisy to look at it with me. We were both standing there staring at the heater, wondering what it would do, when sparks flew and it emitted a loud bang.

A call to Sucharita failed to garner any sympathy. 'I can't help you. The apartment complex electrician will have to come and fix it.'

By now, the apartment was becoming a challenging place to live

in. A huge pane of glass was missing
allowing mosquitoes free entry into the
to fix the handbasin in Daisy's bathroo
all. The broken water heater meant co
cian arrived. Without a functional kit
water on the stove.

The electrician who arrived spoke only Hindi. No Eng
Bengali. The water heater kept tripping the circuit breaker every
time he tried to turn it on. He left it unplugged and hanging from
the wall. Unable to communicate with each other effectively, the
only confirmation that we could elicit was that it was indeed *accha
nahi hai* (not good). As it turned out, our hot water heater wouldn't
be fixed for quite some time. Sucharita had a kettle delivered to our
apartment so we could heat water for bathing.

Repetitive banging from construction in a nearby apartment
complex and neighbours playing loud devotional music meant that
there was precious little chance for a Sunday sleep-in. We got up
and lazed around, reading and drinking coffee. In contrast to the
cold nights, warm air blew gently through an open window in the
living room, while the sun streamed in. Our choice of relaxing music
blocked out the external disturbance. For once, the apartment felt
quite homely. Panna and I both commented that it was almost like
a Sunday 'back home'.

That afternoon, Daisy, Tess, Miriam and I planned a trip into
New Market. I would act as tour guide. I'd recently taken Tess and
Miriam on a brief tour around Kolkata, but Daisy had been too
tired to come along. We'd caught the 206 bus to the Esplanade,
and went on an exhaustive walk through the grassy expanse of the
Maidan and over the Howrah Bridge. Part of the Maidan had been
overtaken by hundreds of thousands of pilgrims who'd come for the
Ganga Saga Mela, a three-day festival held in the middle of January

Sagar Island not far from Kolkata, where the holy Gan-
meets the Bay of Bengal. It's believed that those who bathe
Ganges River at an auspicious time during the festival will
absolved of their sins. The countless number of pilgrims were
all camped out in the open in makeshift facilities. Their living conditions were the picture of austerity; I was struck by the lengths
people were prepared to go to for their faith.

The walk showed us the different sides of Kolkata's indomitable
spirit. Miriam was mobbed by an aggressive group of beggar children,
who surrounded and latched onto her. So determined were they not
to leave her alone that I had to forcibly remove some of them.

Not long after, we saw a group of men pulling an overburdened
cart. It was buried underneath its cargo of colossal packages, all
stitched with a cover of white cloth and stacked at least six high.
The men were shouting words of encouragement to each other, as
they tried to get the heavy cart to move. It was a backbreaking job,
and yet their faces beamed widely when we took their photo. The
beauty of India is that there's always a positive to the negative, if you
take the time to notice it.

As we approached the Howrah Bridge, our attention was drawn
to the stark yellow and orange hues of the piles of marigolds, strung
together in garlands being sold at the wholesale flower market on
the ground below. The garlands would eventually be offered to the
gods during temple visits and daily *pujas* (prayers) in homes.

Walking over the Howrah Bridge left us in no doubt why the
bridge was said to be the busiest in the world. The sheer volume of
traffic – including cars, buses, bicycles, bullock carts and innumer-
able people bearing heavy loads on their heads – makes arresting
viewing. Incredibly, the bridge crosses the river in a single span,
without any pylons connecting it to the riverbed.

That Sunday, when we left the apartment to embark on our latest adventure, Panna warned us, 'Be careful. Some taxi drivers have been making their meters increase faster than they should.'

With her caution ringing in our ears, halfway through our journey we noticed with alarm that the meter was ticking over rapidly. It was already double what it should be.

'Daisy, check the meter,' I whispered. She leaned over the seat and saw the driver sneakily yanking on a piece of wire down beside the steering wheel. Instead of saying anything, we decided to wait and see what he'd do at the end of the trip. I reassured the others that I would handle it somehow.

The taxi came to a halt near the Oberoi Hotel on Chowringhee Road. Despite the widespread renaming of streets, people commonly continued to use what they were familiar with. The driver quickly reached for the fare conversion chart, which converts the number shown on the meter into the price to be paid, without being prompted. This was a surprise. Normally, repetitive requests had to be made while the driver pretended not to understand, and kept quoting an inflated fixed price.

'236 rupees,' he demanded.

From my forays around Park Street and Chowringhee Road, I knew that the fare was only supposed to be about 130 rupees.

Remembering Lakhi's series of Bengali rebukes, I put them to good use. '*Aap ni karap* (You are bad),' I shouted at him. '*Baloh naa* (Not good),' I continued, pointing to the meter.

The shock on the driver's face was visible. Outside the taxi, a curious crowd had started to gather, attracted by the commotion.

'He's trying to cheat us,' we exclaimed. 'The fare is only supposed to be 130 rupees.'

Other people also began shouting at him. Realising that he wasn't going to get away with his deception, he dropped his asking price to 160 rupees.

'Take 130 rupees and no more,' I growled at him, and shoved the money into his hand as we walked away.

One month in India had certainly improved my assertive skills; once, I couldn't even fend off the bangle seller. My unwavering smile had now been replaced by forceful frowns where needed.

The matter didn't end there. The next day, Daisy encountered the same taxi driver on her way to work.

'He apologised profusely for trying to overcharge us and even gave me a discounted fare. All the other taxi drivers at the taxi rank were telling him off too. His excuse was that the meter was broken and he was trying to fix it.'

We didn't believe him. It was another common Indian trait to always find an excuse and never admit liability.

All too soon, Tara's four weeks were up. I only had a week left myself.

We chose Oh! Calcutta, a fine dining Bengali restaurant, for our farewell dinner. We all struggled to find the energy to get to the dinner though, as our colds were making us weary. Once there, we decided that a bit of fun would lift our spirits. We ordered some tequila.

After watching us intently from the sidelines, one of the more daring waiters came our way. Focusing his attention on me, he began his inquiries.

'Which country are you from, madam? I am from Delhi. We are opening a branch of Oh! Calcutta in Delhi. Will you be coming there for tequila as well?'

How could I say no and disappoint him?

'I'll definitely come if you'll serve me the tequila,' I assured him with a grin.

Literally bouncing up and down on the soles of his feet, he responded grandly. 'Madam, I will even serve you champagne.'

'You heartbreaker,' Claudine said after he'd gone. We all left smiling, including the waiters who'd also had an entertaining night.

As we walked into the mirror-lined lobby of the apartment building, we saw a typed, official-looking notice adhered to the wall. Curious to know what it was about, we went over to have a look. The security guard stationed in the lobby observed us with interest. Most apartment buildings in India have watchmen who monitor who comes and goes.

'It is to inform you that there will be a consecutive fogging operation which will take place on and from tomorrow evening to control the massive mosquito problem . . . the area will be covered with a smoke discharged from fogging machine, so residents are hereby requested not to worry about the smoke,' Daisy read out.

A fogging operation. None of us had ever heard of a fogging operation before. This popular, but often ineffective, method of mosquito control in India involves spraying chemical insecticides around in a thick, noxious diesel- or kerosene-fuelled fog. It sounded ominous, particularly because of the missing windowpane in our kitchen. What was going to happen? Would the apartment be filled with smoke every day?

As it turned out, we needn't have worried.

'I saw some smoke around five this evening,' Panna commented.

It seemed to have had little impact on the mosquitoes though, which were just as plentiful and as eager to bite as usual. I was relieved that I wouldn't have to put up with them for much longer.

I was in two minds about the fact that my time in Kolkata was almost up. While I was definitely looking forward to being back in my comfortable surroundings at home, I also felt I needed some time out by myself. I hadn't been able to relax and contemplate anywhere near as much as I'd wanted. Claudine, my closest friend, would be leaving the week after me; I knew that even if I were to stay, it wouldn't be the same without her around.

And I was disappointed I wouldn't be remaining at the women's centre for longer. Work had recently become interesting. Everyone was excited about an upcoming handicrafts exhibition the centre was going to hold, and I wished I could be a part of it.

Nalini also seemed sad that I would soon be leaving. We'd enjoyed each other's company and had had some meaningful conversations. I'd even felt comfortable enough to tell her a little about my situation.

'I'm really uncertain about going back to my life in Australia. My husband is having some kind of crisis and doesn't know if he wants to be with me,' I confessed to her.

'Be patient and understanding, and one day he will decide that he wants the relationship. There's already too much divorce in the west,' she counselled.

She was only young, but I admired her wisdom. And she was right about divorce. I guess if I was looking for a sign about what to do with my future, then that was it. Patience and understanding were two of my strong qualities: I should put them to good use.

I thought I'd come to Kolkata and gain a sense of satisfaction and self-worth from helping people. I thought it would be good to feel needed. Instead, more than anything, I felt overwhelmed that I couldn't do enough for them. In reality, *I* was getting the greatest boost to my self-confidence from the friendships I had made.

Daisy thought I was open, honest and well balanced. Claudine liked how we were so upfront with each other, and could come out and say whatever we thought. From Panna, I learned the importance of good communication to prevent misunderstandings. We'd initially clashed as we came to terms with our forced living arrangement, but had ended up friends. She also encouraged me to be more assertive, and helped me realise that I wasn't always to blame for people's reactions.

On my last Friday night in Kolkata, Panna unexpectedly invited me to Roxy and Tantra with her. All the girls insisted that I go. They wanted me to see Aryan.

'You're always asking about our romances, go and have one of your own,' they implored.

Aryan was delighted to see me. His smile lit up his whole face. As usual, we talked and laughed so easily.

'C'mon, let's get out of here and go back to my place,' he suggested.

'But what about your work?' I was unconvinced.

'It's okay, there are other DJs here,' he replied.

I was still unsure. I really didn't feel relaxed about going home with him alone, and I certainly didn't want him to get the wrong impression.

'You have to promise to look after me though. And, I'm only coming as a friend. Don't expect anything else from me,' I warned him up front.

As the taxi turned off Park Street, I realised we were heading towards the women's centre where I worked. When it pulled up right in front of the centre, I was stunned. Out of all the districts in Kolkata, we had ended up there. Was this meaningful coincidence? Synchronicity? Were Aryan and I so destined to meet that, if I didn't talk to him in The Park Hotel, this was the back-up plan?

'This is where I've been volunteering,' I pointed.

Aryan took my hand and led me into the neighbouring build-ing where he lived. His studio apartment was simply furnished and overlooked a garden. I noticed a chair near the doorway.

'I often sit here and look out, and think about things,' he told me.

I was pleasantly surprised. Although Aryan seemed like a sen-sitive guy, I didn't expect that, given his work, he'd be so quietly contemplative.

As I stepped inside the apartment, I wondered whether I should take off my shoes. I didn't know how to behave in an Indian home. I felt stiff and formal, and was worried about making a mistake.

'It doesn't matter to me,' Aryan replied. From his lack of concern, it appeared he wasn't very traditional.

The first thing I noticed about the room was the large hand-painted backdrop that dominated one wall. It was of a woman's face in the ocean. She looked incredibly attractive under normal light. Under ultraviolet light, she became ethereal and almost eerie.

Aryan lit some incense, pushed the sticks through the crack in the door, and put on some world music with an Indian flavour. The mood was set perfectly. We sat together, and talked and laughed some more. Then he turned to me.

'So, tell me, what are you really like?' he asked. 'I want to see the real you.'

I was slightly thrown by the question. It wasn't something that I'd anticipated.

'People don't take the time to show me who they really are, and they don't care about who I really am either. There's so much pretending,' he elaborated. A typical, extroverted alpha-male DJ, he certainly was not.

Having spent plenty of time in the clubbing scene, I knew what he meant.

'Seriously, this is the real me. What you see is what you get. I hate pretending too. Honestly,' I assured him.

'So you're always this well mannered?'

I was to later discover that normal western manners appeared extreme in India, where 'please' and 'thank you' were rarely used or expected. At the time though, I was more bemused than anything.

'Can I kiss you?' he asked me.

It was such a simple request, I couldn't say no. And I didn't really want to. The kiss was soft and tender, but felt profound and end-less. I was totally unprepared for the prospect of anything more, and wanted to leave. This wasn't how I expected the night to turn out. I was no longer in control.

'Don't go. Stay here,' he implored. He tried to kiss me again. I felt panicky and pushed him away.

'No, really, I must go,' I insisted.

Although Aryan was obviously disappointed, he was kind enough to find a taxi for me and offered to come with me to make sure I got home safely.

'It's okay. I'll be fine. Plus, I live a long way from here.'

I couldn't wait to flee to the safety of my own apartment and bed.

The next day, the girls were very excited by the fact there had been romance. They insisted that we go out again that night – my last night in Kolkata – despite my protests. After dinner at Peter Cat, we went straight to Tantra where we ended up meeting some very sociable Icelanders from an airline company. They had a couple of bottles of vodka permanently on the bar. Rarely were we without a drink in our hands. I managed to sneak away from them for a short time to see Aryan.

'You came! I didn't think you would after last night,' he said in amazement.

I was quite amazed as well. I thought his overt advances would have made me run, like I did from Raj, but I was attracted to his gentle nature and calmness. He was very non-threatening.

'I brought you something. Put out your hand,' I told him. In it, I placed the small bronze incense holder I'd found in my apartment.

'Take this. I noticed you didn't have one in your room.'

He smiled his wonderful disarming smile. 'Wow, that's so thoughtful of you.'

Tantra closed at around 5 a.m., but none of us was in the mood to go home.

'Music, we want a party with music!'

Aryan obliged and took us to a friend's elegantly furnished and sprawling apartment not far from Park Street, where there was indeed a party with music. We drank and danced and indulged until way after the sun came up.

One of the people I got talking to at the party was an older guy named Rajiv.

'I can tell you're a genuine person because of the smile lines on your face. You must always be smiling,' he complimented me. 'I can also see that you and Aryan obviously have a lot of affection for each other.'

He'd seen us hugging each other. I'd slipped into showing Aryan affection much more easily than I expected. It felt natural. In a way, I almost felt protective of him. But I was still determined not to get too intimate.

After the party, I went back to Aryan's apartment again, sure that nothing physical would happen between us. I just wanted to spend some time with him before I left. We lay down on his bed, held each other tightly and talked about life.

His family lived in Mumbai. He had two older sisters and two younger brothers. He'd moved to Kolkata to take up a DJ residency at a club in a luxury hotel when he was in his early twenties, and had been happy to have his freedom. It sounded like he'd put his freedom to good use, too. By Indian standards, he was worldly, to say the least. But it was a lifestyle I could easily relate to.

'What about your parents? You're the eldest son. Won't you have to look after them?'

I was curious to know how the information I'd gathered from my Indian workmates applied to real life.

'My youngest brother lives at home with them, but I guess I'll have to move back there eventually,' he said.

He seemed lost as he spoke about it; more responsibilities than I could fathom awaited him. I didn't envy him.

'I really miss being a child sometimes,' he said.

What I also loved about Aryan, apart from his tenderness and sensitivity, were his sense of humour and fun-loving nature. He was uncomplicated and joyful. We were adults, but we'd behaved like children in Tantra, throwing ourselves onto the beanbags that were scattered all over the floor upstairs. He even surprised me by doing a backflip into one (he'd been an excellent gymnast at school). It had felt so good to play and laugh in an uninhibited fashion.

As we talked, I looked into the dark pools of his eyes, past the surface of his party-scene existence and saw so much depth there. It wasn't like I'd only just met him. I felt like I'd known him for a very long time.

'I'm going to have to leave soon,' I told him.

'Here, take this CD of mine. It's of the music we were listening to last night,' he handed it to me. 'Now, let's sleep for a while,' he grabbed my arm.

Very quickly, he fell into a deep slumber that I couldn't wake him from. I had too much going on in my mind to sleep. I found it hard to believe that I had only hours left in Kolkata.

Dreamlike, I wrote Aryan a goodbye note on a piece of paper, opened the door and walked out into the street. I was thankful I had a *dupatta* (scarf) with me to wrap myself in. Not only did it protect me from prying eyes in the light of the day, it also served as a barrier against the vulnerability I felt.

I sat in the departure lounge of the airport with a very heavy heart. The moment that had seemed so far away had arrived. I was leaving many people I cared about, people who had shared my life in different ways over the last five weeks.

Claudine and I wept on each other's shoulders. She gave me a framed photo of the both of us with the far from ravishing Raj, who'd been captured leering close to me. Daisy, Miriam and Tess had written me letters saying how much they appreciated me welcoming them and the fun I'd shown them. The women at the centre where I'd worked had given me a silk scarf and signed a card that they'd made. Such simple but touching gestures spoke so much.

During transit in Hong Kong, I looked out the airport window at the plane that was going to take me home. The sun was setting in the background, a fiery ball of red and orange. I didn't know what would await me when I got home but I knew that I had options and time on my hands. And thanks to Kolkata, I had discovered in myself some new skills, too, for dealing with life.

I arrived home to a blistering 38-degree summer's day in late January. My bedroom on the second floor of my townhouse was stifling. The streets were full of cars but curiously devoid of people. My surroundings appeared orderly and sterile. The silence was almost deafening. I tried to remind myself Kolkata was a temporary diversion. I had a life in Australia, one I couldn't keep running away from. Instead of daydreaming about an imaginary life, I needed to appreciate the enjoyable time I had in Kolkata but keep my mind on the present.

Being in India had enabled me to put my real life on hold. Now that I was back, I needed to face it and resolve things. Michael had written to me while I was in Kolkata. Initially, his messages had been frequent and heartfelt about wanting to be with me. Over the course of the five weeks, they had become sporadic and unemotional.

My beloved Nanna passed away the week I arrived back in Melbourne, and it was a day later when Michael called.

'I'm so sorry, I've been deceptive again,' he said. 'I want to be completely honest with you now. I was lonely while you were away and I've been seeing Kimberly.'

It was deja vu.

I was shattered.

Although Michael had told me that he didn't respect her and had decided not to see her again, the same disturbing pattern had resumed. Michael couldn't offer any consolation over my grandmother's death, nor did he show any interest in coming to the funeral. At that point, I realised that I'd rather be on my own than have to deal with the uncertainty and instability that Michael brought into my life. I was done.

We signed our divorce papers a couple of weeks later. I surprised myself by applying for the divorce jointly; I'd always resisted doing so when Michael had brought it up in the past. Maybe it now meant that I was ready to properly move on. Since we didn't have any children, and had agreed to split our assets equally, we didn't need the intervention of a lawyer or even a court appearance. We'd been separated for more than twelve months. All we had to do was complete a form, get it signed by a Justice of the Peace, and deliver it to the court. It almost seemed too easy.

The day was an extremely emotional one for us. In what seemed like a fitting death to our marriage, the Justice of the Peace who we selected was a funeral director and the meeting took place at her funeral parlour. We both cried.

'I really do love you,' Michael said as we were about to go our separate ways. 'I just lost my way. Thank you for everything that you did for me during our time together.'

His acknowledgement somehow took a little of the pain away. It felt like my role in his life had been to offer him support and stability while he needed it.

'I honestly hadn't wanted to be in a relationship for a number of years,' he went on. 'Kimberly was my way out.'

Michael handed me a book as a parting gesture. I'd given him a gift on our wedding day and now, he was giving me one on the day of our divorce. It was a book titled *Embracing Uncertainty*. It showed me how far he had progressed.

'I've been meditating and coming across these books on my own now,' he said.

Really, that's all I ever wanted. He was at last finding his own way, and it was time for us to move on to the next stage of our lives.

For him, that meant relocating to Queensland. For me, that meant going back to Kolkata on a one-way ticket. I would stay for a few months, until I had to return to my job after my long-service leave was over, and see what happened. Apart from my family and friends, everything I'd held dear in my life was now gone. With all that I'd learned, surely there had to be something amazing for me out there in the future.

Whatever it was, I had no idea.

PART TWO

# SEARCHING

# Desperately Seeking Sharell

IT remains the most daring and out-of-character thing I've ever done: throwing caution to the wind and returning to Kolkata on a one-way ticket.

A little more than a month after I first left, I was back, with no plans apart from seeing what would happen. I felt I needed to be there, that there was unfinished business I had to sort out. I flew out of Australia the day I turned 32, chosen deliberately as a sign of a fresh start and new possibilities. The plane was less than half full, and the Qantas flight attendants were generous with the drinks. When I mentioned to one it was my birthday, he disappeared into first class and came back with a huge glass of champagne for me. It was a fitting beginning to a new adventure.

Daisy, Tess, Panna and Cliona had decided to stay on in Kolkata, so I'd still be able to spend time with them. But since I was no longer volunteering, I couldn't go back to my old apartment. Rajiv arranged for me to stay by myself at The Saturday Club for a few weeks.

The Saturday Club turned out to be another century-old, colonial-style country club. It had maintained its refined English atmosphere, but was now patronised by prominent Kolkata businessmen and the city's younger elite. Like the Tollygunge Club, only those of appropriate financial and social standing were granted membership. The Saturday Club was a remarkable place to find myself in, and I longed to blend in and observe the interactions. However, I soon attracted attention of the staff – initially due to the colour of my skin, and later because of my late nights, which often resulted in my getting locked out of the building.

My first priority was to see Aryan and the girls again. Panna and Cliona were away travelling in India but would be coming back. Daisy, Tess and I had our reunion at Some Place Else pub in The Park Hotel. Only a month had passed, but the transformation in them was astonishing. I'd left them still unsure of their surroundings, and trying to make sense of the city. Now, The Park Hotel had become their second home and they had new Indian male friends of their own.

Daisy wasted no time in dragging me to Tantra to meet Aryan. I was reluctant and nervous; so many questions ran through my mind. What if he wasn't so keen to see me again? What if his feelings had changed? What if it wasn't the same between us?

I needn't have worried. He came running down from the DJ cabin, grabbed my hand and pulled me away. It was hard to believe I was with him again. His hand felt so soft on mine, and he was so cute. But I'd forgotten how much taller than him I was! I found myself having to lean down to hear what he was saying over the music. I mentally dismissed the height difference as unimportant. After all, I was in India, and normal notions of what should or shouldn't be didn't matter.

We spent the night in a corner of Tantra, discussing what we liked and disliked, and what made us happy.

'Having someone to come home to at the end of the day is what would make me the happiest,' he said.

I agreed.

'So, when are you planning on getting married?' he innocently asked.

I swallowed. It wouldn't hurt to tell him the truth. After all, there was nothing at stake. I had no reason to hide it from him. It wasn't like I needed to be a 'suitable girl'. We had separate lives in separate countries, and there was a limit to the amount of time we'd be spending together.

'I've already been married and have no plans to get married again soon,' I admitted.

'Oh, really?' he was surprised but didn't appear to be bothered. No doubt it was because he didn't see his long-term future with me either.

It seemed I'd timed my return to Kolkata well. Aryan needed me as much as I needed him. His circumstances were also less than ideal and he felt alone. He was getting over the break-up of a relationship with a girlfriend he loved a lot. He had to find a new place to live. And his close friend Lloyd, another DJ, had returned to Mumbai to take up a residency at a new club called Poison.

'I've been really quiet and retreated back into my shell,' he said.

The next day, Aryan came to collect me from The Saturday Club. He took me to a friend's house to eat Kolkata mutton *biryani* (a fragrant rice dish) for lunch. The friend, Manny, came from a wealthy family and lived in an old colonial mansion. Its white walls looked pristine, fresh from a recent repainting. Kolkatans claim their *biryani* is the best in the country, due to the rich combination of spices (saffron, nutmeg, cumin, cloves and cardamom), soft meat and potato. My unaccustomed tastebuds certainly appreciated the fact that the spices weren't as heavy as many other styles of *biryani*. Yet, the majority of Indians will tell you that nothing can beat the original *biryani* from Hyderabad, prepared in the kitchens of the Mughal rulers, because of the more involved cooking methods and intricate layering of flavours. Afterwards, we walked back to Aryan's apartment. The afternoon air was balmy. I hardly noticed the chaos in the streets or the staring as Aryan boldly held my hand. The fears that I'd had about being back in Kolkata melted away.

My reintroduction into Kolkata's social circle was swift and surreal. This time, I didn't resist it. Although I had no real desire to go partying again, I wanted to meet new people. After all, it was the friends I'd met during my previous five weeks in Kolkata who had had the greatest impact on how I viewed myself. People who knew nothing of me or my past. Just people who saw who I was in the here and now.

For me, self-discovery in India wasn't about ashrams and meditation. I wasn't a stranger to meditation, and I'd already done enough introspection over the previous year. Instead of closeting myself away in a confined environment, I wanted to spread my wings, see where life would take me, to say yes to whatever came my way. And if I was to spend time with Aryan, I needed to do so in his nocturnal world.

Rajiv invited me to a whirlwind of parties. In Melbourne, I had partied destructively with a need to fill various voids. This time, the element of neediness no longer existed and was replaced by a curiosity to see how people would react to me if I was myself, rather than the over-the-top person who snorted tequila off the bottom of a shot glass. And curiosity to see how people from all levels of society lived in Kolkata. India's poverty was all too obvious, but what about the other extreme? What were their lives like?

I soon discovered that Kolkata had plenty of rich residents who partied every bit as hard, if not harder, as people back home. They lived a lavish lifestyle replete with expensive cars, body parts emblazoned with designer labels and the latest consumer gadgets. The parties started at someone's spacious home, progressed to two or three lounge bars and clubs, and ended at another abode well after the sun had come up, just like anywhere else in the west. Some people had personal issues, some people had too much time on their hands, some just wanted to enjoy themselves.

Psychedelic trance had just found its way to Kolkata and was the genre of choice for the hardcore party people. In the early hours of Sunday mornings, Aryan dominated the dance floor at Tantra with his psy-trance sets. People went there especially to hear them. I felt an incredible energy and danced tirelessly until the last track was played at 6 a.m. It was like I was sharing part of him through his music.

As we were leaving Tantra one night, Aryan grabbed some coloured powder and smeared it all over my face. Outside, remnants of bonfires littered the streets, bathed in full moonlight. Winter had turned to spring, and I was about to experience my first Indian festival. It was Holi, the festival of colours.

During Holi, India turns into a gigantic, over-enthusiastic playground. Those who venture outside can expect to be covered in coloured powder and drenched in water. Children become miniature snipers, armed with high-powered water guns and water bombs. No one is spared. *Bhang*, a substance that's derived from cannabis and is sacred in ancient Hindu scripture, is widely consumed as the traditional Holi drink. Nothing is off-limits, as restrictive social norms are gleefully discarded for a day. People throw Holi parties for their friends especially to indulge and have fun.

On this occasion, it's Lord Vishnu (the Hindu god of preservation) and his much-loved human incarnation Lord Krishna who are being worshipped. Legend has it that Lord Vishnu intervened to save the life of an ardent devotee by making it possible for the demoness Holika to be set on fire and destroyed. Bonfires are lit on Holi eve to mark this victory of good over evil, and to burn evil spirits. It also presents the opportunity to burn away bad feelings that may be lingering from past events, and to let bygones be bygones. For me, it was a time to forgive and forget, and put the previous year behind me.

The next day, everyone emulates the pranks of mischievous Lord Krishna, who liked to drench the village girls in water and colours. There can be no half-hearted participation. Those who don't want to get grimy hide in their homes for the day.

I couldn't wait to be a part of it. I rushed out and bought myself a cheap 150 rupee ($4) *salwaar kameez*, ready to be ruined.

The owner of a bar cleverly called B.E.D. (the acronym for Bars Entertainment Dining, which always produced a smile when someone invariably said, 'Let's go to B.E.D. tonight') threw a Holi party in a farmhouse on the outskirts of Kolkata. No expense was spared. A band and DJs provided entertainment. A substantial selection of alcohol flowed liberally. We drank shooters and *bhang lassis* all day, ran around drenching each other in colour, and danced until we dropped. It was a crazy day. When I got back to my room, I was shocked to see myself. Unrecognisably covered in bright red colour, I looked like I'd been bleeding profusely from a severe accident.

That night, I scrubbed my face until it was raw. The colour still refused to budge. It had stained my pale skin a vicious crimson. Even worse, a patch of flesh had come off the side of my nose where

I'd overdone the scrubbing. Everyone's aversion to the red colour suddenly made sense. As did their glee in putting it all over me. Naïvely, I hadn't applied hair oil to my face beforehand to prevent the dye from absorbing. Now, I'd have to stay inside for a few days.

Luckily, Aryan was going to be too busy moving into a friend's apartment to meet me. He had caught up with his ex-girlfriend at the Holi party and clearly wasn't over her. Startlingly, she reminded me of a younger version of myself, the one who ran around entertaining everyone, getting people drunk and doing zany things.

Even though it hurt a little to see him like that, I knew what he was going through. It was becoming obvious that the universe had brought us together for a reason. Some may, unflatteringly, refer to it as a rebound relationship. At that stage, neither of us expected to remain together forever. We would simply be there for each other, and bring fun and laughter back into each other's lives, before moving on to whatever the future held.

Utsav invited me to his apartment for dinner one night. I accepted. The conversation was interesting and insightful. An investment banker aged in his mid-twenties, he was mature beyond his years.

'A guy's mind revolves around three categories of women: friends, flings and relationships,' he explained to me. 'And the categories don't overlap. For a guy to want to have a relationship with a woman, he must see some special quality in her that makes her different. Otherwise, it will only be about sex, and he'll move on once he's had enough.'

I couldn't help wondering which category Aryan placed me in. No doubt, part of the reason why he was attracted to me was because I was a foreigner. But would he see beyond that?

Aryan's friend Lloyd was visiting from Mumbai. My face had barely recovered from the after-effects of Holi when he called me with a proposal.

'How would you like to be a model for an advertising photo shoot? They want a foreigner who can convincingly dress up in Indian clothes. Someone saw you at the Holi party and recommended you.'

It sounded appealing. 'Sure,' I agreed.

The work was for a money exchange company whose slogan was 'We change everything.'

Hours spent in hair and make-up transformed me. My long dark mane was pulled back in a bun and my eyes rimmed in thick black kohl. Heavy foundation made my skin flawless. Weighty earrings made my ear lobes droop. A *tikka* (forehead jewellery) was hung by a chain from the top of my head to the centre of my forehead. The sari was draped, and one end placed over my head. As the finishing touch, a huge round *bindi* (dot) crafted out of red *kumkum* (turmeric) powder was positioned between my eyebrows at the location of my third eye chakra. I could hardly recognise myself. The person who stared back at me in the mirror looked half-Indian.

'Sit on this stool,' the photographer instructed.

I ungainly shuffled over to it, trying not to trip on the sari or cause it to unravel. Lights flooded the room and dazzled me.

'Hold your hands this way, turn your head that way, put your chin down, smile a little more.'

The work wasn't easy. I'd been a reluctant model a couple of times previously, but I was no less wary in front of the camera.

It came as a relief when the photographer announced, 'That's it, finished.'

'Yes! *Aa mar shesh!* (I'm finished!),' I responded jubilantly. The first Bengali that I'd spoken since being back in Kolkata slipped out. I surprised myself by remembering it.

There was laughter all round. 'You do look really Indian and beautiful. How much Bengali do you know?' the curious young daughter of the woman from the advertising agency asked me.

'Actually, not much at all.'

It was one of the few phrases I'd learned at the women's centre. Apart from that and Lakhi's insults, my Bengali remained very limited.

That evening I hit Roxy and then Tantra with Daisy, Tess and Cliona. At Tantra, the moment I'd been dreading took place. I came face to face with Raj again. It was bound to happen, but was so much worse than I ever imagined. His hair had grown longer and was brushed into an outdated male bouffant. To my dismay, my rejection of his previous advances hadn't deterred him at all. This time, he actually winked while leering at me.

Daisy, who was standing next to me, tried not to laugh. I quickly turned and headed in the opposite direction.

'Did you see the expression on his face? It was exactly like in the photo Claudine gave you!'

Daisy had been attracting a few men of her own. She was juggling a couple of Muslim boys. Cliona, on the other hand, had developed an attraction to Sikhs. While I only had eyes for Aryan, the girls were revelling in the attention that being white foreigners had brought them.

'It's too competitive in London, but here there are so many men to choose from,' Daisy was delighted.

I didn't envy them; it looked like it was more trouble than it was worth.

'Oh no, both Hussain and Imran have turned up at the same time. And they're both calling me on my phone,' Daisy shouted in alarm, as she hid behind a pillar.

Tantra wasn't a safe place to be that night. A dancer from Mumbai was performing, bringing India's moustachioed middle-aged men out in full force. Having a moustache was considered to be a supreme sign of status, manliness and virility in India. It indicated traditional values and a conservative mindset, but in this case also highlighted the paradox of behaviour in India. These men had happily left their wives at home, probably not even informing them of their whereabouts, while they went out to feast their eyes on a skimpily dressed woman dancing like she was in a Bollywood movie. Armed with their phone cameras and knocking back drink after drink, they were overexcited by what was around them. As it turned out, it was Daisy who saw quite a bit of one of the men. She came running out of the female toilets to where I was waiting for her, screaming hysterically, 'There's a drunk man in there with his willy hanging out!'

Clearly upset, she grabbed me by the arm and dragged me inside with her. By the time I saw him, he'd put it away. His pants were unzipped, however, and he threateningly looked like getting it out again. I went to find the manager. He happened to look over just in time to see the guy stagger out of the toilets.

Far from being concerned, both the manager and the security staff erupted into laugher. The security staff escorted the guy out into the foyer and left him swaying there, clearly intoxicated, while Daisy continued to wail.

'Madam, cover yourself up,' the manager rebuked her, as he tried to place a *dupatta* (scarf) over her shoulders and impressive cleavage.

Fortunately, Aryan noticed the uproar and came running over to see what had happened. Only then was the guy duly evicted from the club.

'You're not taking this matter seriously!' Daisy shouted at the manager. He was too bemused to offer any further solution. It was clearly a case of power and status at play. The flasher was no doubt a high-spending member of the club. Daisy, on the other hand, was an immodestly dressed female tourist. Loyalties lay where the money was.

After Tantra, Aryan and I ended up at another party before heading back to The Saturday Club. As with most hotels in India, The Saturday Club banned guests in rooms after 11 p.m. However, the rules didn't stipulate when guests could start arriving in the morning. Sunrise seemed like a good time, so I invited Aryan in.

'What music shall I put on?' I asked him as I grabbed my iPod.

'How about retro?'

'As in 1970s and 1980s?'

I was surprised. Back home, my love of retro was often ridiculed. Songs by The Carpenters, Air Supply and Bruce Springstein were just some of my unfashionable favourites. But here I was in India, with a guy who actually wanted to hear such music. I could hardly believe it.

'You to Me Are Everything' by the Real Thing started playing. We sang to each other and absurdly danced around. The significance of the lyrics – about growing closer to someone – drew me in. I had to admit that any distance between Aryan and me was rapidly diminishing. I was filled with admiration for his diverse knowledge of music, coupled with his willingness to sing a mushy song with me at some ungodly hour of the morning.

We moved on to country classics: Kenny Rogers, Johnny Cash and John Denver. Then we kissed. A tender kiss that we got lost in. One that went on for longer than ten minutes and three tracks.

Aryan had Mondays and Tuesdays off work, and we spent those days and nights together. We'd go to the movies, eat out, laze around and drink beer in the evenings. Often, we'd just curl up together and not say anything. It was a pleasurable, easy silence. Words just weren't necessary.

'You two don't talk much, do you?' Mukesh, the friend that Aryan was now living with observed, amused. In India, people usually had too much to say.

It didn't take long for me to realise that true to his gentle personality, Aryan was indeed not a guy of many words. He conveyed his emotions through his smile, the expressions in his eyes, his child-like laugh and his singing. When he was carefree and happy, he sang Hindi songs and answered my questions with popular lines from English songs.

'I feel like my life is turning into an old Hindi movie. There's a song called *"Pardesiyon se na ankhiyan mila na"*. It means don't fall in love with a foreigner,' Aryan told me one day.

'Oh, why's that?'

'Because they always have to leave.'

It was true. The day would come when I'd have to return to work and my Australian life. I dreaded the thought of it. I felt like I'd come so far, it would be taking a step backwards.

I wondered if I was becoming too absorbed in my relationship with Aryan. I also worried about what he really felt about me. The insecure, control-freak part of me wanted to make a fuss and question him. Then I realised he had his own fears and insecurities too.

'I never believed you'd come back to Kolkata, especially not for me,' Aryan admitted. 'I'm just as unsure of your feelings for me as you are of mine for you.'

I was from a country that Aryan was unfamiliar with. And, as a foreigner in India, I unwittingly attracted a lot of attention.

'If you don't look up at me when you walk into the club, I feel anxious,' he elaborated.

Meanwhile, I often deliberately didn't look at him because I didn't want to appear too interested, like a girl who wanted to hang off a DJ. I genuinely liked him for the person he was. It was a fine balance.

'We have our own issues, but we'll get through them,' Aryan said.

When he did speak, Aryan was always reassuring and positive, and rarely said a bad word about anyone or anything. I wondered what a sweet and genuine guy like him was doing in the party scene. Obviously, music was his passion. But he lacked the superficiality and self-interest that often characterised the scene, and made me want to turn away from it. He had a rare humility and depth about him. He was good-looking, fashionable and obviously took care of his appearance. Yet, he was down to earth and kind-hearted. He didn't seem capable of hurting anyone. There was a certain vulnerability about him that made me want to look after him.

'I've noticed so many little things about you, from the way you tie bedsheets around yourself like a dress to how you stop doing your make-up if I come into the room. You never criticise me for my flaws like other girls. And all the while you're concerned with trying to look your best for me. I don't care anymore. I want to see you at your worst. I've stopped looking at your face and now I look at what's inside.' The more time we spent together, the more Aryan revealed himself to me and opened up to me about his thoughts.

Without a doubt, I was having fun in Kolkata but nevertheless, I guiltily felt that I wasn't being very constructive with what I was doing. Previously, I was dissatisfied with my volunteer work taking up all my time. Now it was the opposite. I was always with Aryan or doing the rounds of the party circuit. I consoled myself with the thought that my eyes were being opened to the world, and I was getting to see another side of India, one that very few visitors experienced.

Most foreigners get taken advantage of at some stage during their trip to India. On past occasions, as a tourist, so had I. My interactions with India's well-off upper class were different. Because everyone had money, no one tried to pull scams. Instead, the opposite was the case: people couldn't do enough. My offers to pay for anything were rebuffed, friends refused to let me take taxis and went out of their way to drive me home, and others called me to make sure I'd reached home safely. I felt so warmly enveloped and protected. It was a different India altogether. Not one that I aspired to remain in, as it didn't encourage me to grow as a person, but one that I appreciated all the same.

Staying at The Saturday Club was becoming expensive. Plus, the staff were bothering me.

'Madam, you like to party, isn't it?' the guy at reception asked me one day when I picked up my keys.

I was also receiving strange internal phone calls every Sunday morning. I'd answer the phone, but no one would speak. After a month at The Saturday Club, I decided to move.

Daisy and Tess were also keen to move out from under Sucharita's control at Hiland Park. Aryan was keen to move in with us too, so we decided to look for an apartment to all share together. There were plenty of affordable places advertised in the newspaper, so we didn't think it would be too difficult to find somewhere.

How naïve we were! There was no anonymity of dealing with real estate agents like I was used to in Melbourne. Instead, we had to meet the potential landlady and be scrutinised by her, while she laid down any number of archaic conditions.

'No alcohol, no staying out after 11 p.m. and no members of the opposite sex sharing the apartment.'

I couldn't believe what I was hearing. Had I travelled back in time? Surely it couldn't be 2006? And I couldn't be 32 years old? Everywhere we looked, we encountered the same response. Most property owners didn't even want to rent their apartments to foreigners. And a man could definitely not, under any circumstances apart from marriage, occupy it with us. Indian values were strict about that sort of thing.

In the end, we had to give up on the idea. Daisy and Tess managed to find an apartment for themselves at Hiland Park through a friend. They'd be sharing with another volunteer named Krista, who'd already been living with them. I went to stay with Aryan at his friend Mukesh's apartment.

It was an interesting set-up. Mukesh didn't actually live in the apartment. Like most Indian guys, he lived at home with his parents. In order to get some privacy, he'd rented the apartment as a place he could visit during his spare time. He worked in the family business, but was also into music. In the evenings, he'd come and drink a couple of glasses of whisky, practice his DJing skills, and sometimes invite his girlfriend over. On Sundays he rented out one of the rooms to his friends who were in relationships and wanted somewhere to be alone with their partners. It was a profitable idea. India's communal living style and conservative values ensured that opportunities for intimacy outside of marriage were hard to find.

It was there that I had my first encounter with an Indian-style bathroom. Up until then, aside from the squat toilet at the women's centre, I'd led a sheltered existence of modern bathrooms designed for foreign use. These had areas cordoned off for showers, usually with shower curtains, and a minimal collection of buckets. This bathroom was the opposite. In what I would eventually discover was standard practice, there were at least five buckets of varying shapes and sizes in the bathroom. There was also a shower head on the wall near the door but no drain below it for the water.

As I looked around, perplexed, I noticed only one hole in the floor, situated over the other side of the room, near the toilet. If I turned on the water and stood under the shower, the whole bathroom floor and toilet would get wet. I wasn't to know it was a wet bathroom – and a typical feature of most Indian homes.

Carefully, I filled a large bucket with water, stood in it and attempted to wash myself without getting any water on the floor or any other surface. But where to tip the dirty water? Was that hole in the floor really a drain? Or something else? I had no idea. So I left the bucket full of dirty water sitting there.

Since the infamous small mug replaced toilet paper in this bathroom too, I decided that I'd better figure out how to use it properly. I'd tried, unsuccessfully, to picture how it was done. I certainly couldn't imagine Aryan using it. He must, though – he was an Indian guy. Now was the time to be brave and ask. I'd noticed he was very comfortable with himself, and that, in turn, made me feel comfortable enough to approach him.

'Um, you know that mug in the bathroom, for washing up,' I tentatively started. 'The water. How do you use it?'

He looked at me curiously.

'It's just that, well, there's no toilet paper here. And I don't think I'm doing it properly,' I tried to clarify.

He laughed and unabashedly answered me. 'Well, you have to kind of lean back, pour the water with your right hand, and cup your left hand to direct it.

'So you do it from the front?' I asked, surprised.

'Yes,' he laughed again.

Ah. No wonder I'd found the process quite cumbersome and messy. I'd been trying to pour the water, unguided, onto my bum from behind.

While I learned to deal with the mug, I was less than impressed about the wet bathroom arrangement. The whole bathroom floor and toilet did indeed get wet after showering. In order to get to the toilet, it was necessary to walk across the wet floor. Footwear had to be worn when going in and removed when going out. Sitting on a wet toilet seat wasn't exactly pleasurable either.

To minimise the amount of water that went everywhere in the wet bathroom, many Indians prefer to take a bucket bath. This is done by filling one of the large buckets full of water, lathering the body with soap, then proceeding to use the small mug to pour the water from the bucket over oneself. As I was used to showering under a constant flow of warm water, taking a bucket bath didn't appeal to me at all. Sucharita's unsympathetic words rang in my head, 'You must adapt'.

While Aryan was at work, I studied Hindi from my textbooks. Instead of taking classes, I'd purchased a few textbooks and was determined to teach myself. A language very different from English, I found it challenging and absorbing. Instead of saying, 'Pleased to meet you', it was, '*Aap se mil kar badi kushi hui* (Having met you great happiness happened)'. To casually ask someone how they were wasn't 'How's it going?' but '*Kyaa haal hai*? (What's your condition?)'. Yet, the discovery that intrigued me the most was that the word '*accha*' could have at least five different meanings depending on the tone and placement in a sentence. Commonly said in a neutral tone, it means 'good'. However, it could also mean 'really?', 'I understand', 'okay', 'listen up' or 'oh!'. I imagined telling someone that I wasn't feeling well, and mistaking their reply of '*accha*' as good. Awkward social situations could easily eventuate if I didn't get it right.

'Say *accha* in all the different ways for me,' I pestered Aryan when he got home. He recited them and we both laughed.

'I love it when you're happy. It feels like I don't have a care in the world,' he told me.

It was true, Aryan's moods had started reflecting mine. When I was quiet, he seemed withdrawn. When I was laughing, he was too.

A couple of weeks later, I was again living at Hiland Park. Tess and Krista had gone to Goa and Daisy didn't want to be alone in the apartment. Aryan initially stayed with me there during his days off. Soon those few days stretched into weeks.

We shopped, cooked together and entertained friends. At night there was soothing music, candles and incense, so much hugging and kissing, passion and sleeping enmeshed in each other's arms. It was exquisite and divine, a bonding of two bodies and souls.

'I'm so thankful for you being here. I'd been feeling so sad until you came along. It's like you've been sent from another planet or something,' Aryan remarked.

Our relationship did seem surreal. I felt just as grateful to have him in my life. We were healing each other's wounds and filling the emptiness.

Yet, there were times when Aryan became lost in deep thought and was unresponsive. It troubled me. I wondered how I was going to detach myself when it was time for me to go home. I thought that I might be falling in love with him.

'Why do you think you can't have a future with Aryan, if he treats you well?' Utsav asked.

There were so many reasons. How would it ever be sustainable? I just didn't know. I didn't have a job in India and didn't know where to find one. I no longer wanted to live my life in the party scene. And there were so many cultural barriers that stood in the way of us being together.

Then we found ourselves inadvertently confined to the apartment for a week, which brought us even closer. Daisy had a severe throat infection, while Aryan and I both caught colds after getting drenched in a sudden downpour. We'd been waiting for our *masala dosas* (thin and crispy crepes made out of rice flour batter and filled with a spicy potato and onion mixture) at a nearby snack shop one evening, when the clouds broke open. The wind whipped up gritty dirt into our faces. The storm was unrelenting and frightening. We huddled in the shop with the roller doors slammed down, the lights flickering on and off, waiting for the worst of it to pass. It was almost May and the monsoon had started brewing.

Just as we were recovering, a government election was held. The whole of Kolkata shut down and it was unsafe for anyone to go outside while voting took place.

'It's common for people to be killed in elections here,' Aryan said, as the news flashed reports of rival political parties clashing across West Bengal. The state had a long history of political violence. Party supporters intimidated opponents into not casting their votes. Militant Communist groups, known as Maoists, were a particular threat and aggressively boycotted voting. Doctors and central paramilitary forces were stationed at polling booths in case things got out of hand. In Kolkata, streets were deserted but, unexpectedly, nothing untoward took place. The Left Front, led by the Communist Party of India (Marxist), returned to power with a landslide victory. As the world's longest-running democratically elected Communist government, it ruled West Bengal for three decades until recently when the government was knocked out in an election.

Uncertainty loomed darkly and heavily in our lives, like the monsoon clouds. Time had flown. Two months had already passed. The reality was that I had to leave India in a little over a month. My visa was about to expire and I was also due to return to work. This time, I didn't know if I would ever come back.

One night, I went to Park Street to meet Emily, a friend of a friend from Australia. She'd already spent a number of years in India, and was leasing and running a small guesthouse in the beach town of Varkala, in southern India's tropical state of Kerala. I'd emailed her, suggesting that I pay her a visit. Fate had placed us both in Kolkata at the same time. We drank cheap cocktails at a bar called Floriana, affectionately known as Sam's Pub, and talked into the night.

'What is it about India? It's so confronting, takes so long to get anything done, we can't wear the clothes that we normally would in this heat, we're constantly stared at, and many women are treated oppressively, but yet, we're still here!' We were incredulous.

Undoubtedly, India had a special knack of holding us under her spell.

I filled Emily in on what I'd been doing. 'I'm seeing one of the DJs from Tantra.'

'Oh, Tantra. A friend of mine got kicked out of there for jumping around too much on the dance floor.'

It sounded familiar. I also knew an Irish guy who'd been evicted from Tantra for engaging in some vigorous Irish dancing.

'Would you believe there was a drunken flasher in the female toilets there recently, but no one cared to kick him out? Who would have thought that dancing is worse than a guy exposing himself?' I exclaimed.

'I came to Kolkata to open a vegetarian café. But I got attacked a couple of months ago by a heroin addict who was showing me an apartment. See – the scars,' Emily unveiled them.

I was stunned. There were many. And they were deep.

'The police caught the guy, and now I have to wait for the court case.'

I'd had no idea, just from sitting and chatting with her, that she'd gone through something so horrific. And that she was such a brave person to recover from such an ordeal so well. We vowed to keep in touch.

My stay at Hiland Park neared its end. I'd found a furnished apartment of my own to live in for my remaining month in Kolkata. It belonged to an Indian friend of Panna's, who had quite a few apartments that he leased out to foreigners. Refreshingly, he was open-minded and didn't care if Aryan stayed with me. Located in south Kolkata's Deshapriya Park, the place was only fifteen minutes from Park Street.

Moving into the apartment was bittersweet. On our first evening there, Aryan and I bought small clay statues of a Hindu god and goddess from a pavement vendor. For me Saraswati, the goddess of learning and creativity, and Ganesha for him. Fresh from our showers the next morning, we carefully set them up on a silver tray.

'It's necessary to be clean in body and mind when doing this,' Aryan explained. He lit some incense and placed the sticks in the incense holder I'd given him on my last night in Kolkata. Then he performed a small *puja* (prayer) with his hands together to give thanks. The spiritualism of the ceremony, modest and humble as it was, was touching to see.

My time in Kolkata was running out. Emotional at the prospect of my departure, and enveloped in the warm glow of candlelight at night, Aryan said, his dark eyes intense with feeling, 'You're the best girl I've ever met. A sweetheart. Everything you do and the way you do it is wonderful. I could see myself marrying someone like you. Of all the things to love in this world, I love you.'

His words touched me deeply. He'd been my constant companion for the last two months. We'd shared so much together, emotionally and physically. I'd been worried he didn't feel as I did, but he must.

'You're so different too. I'm so comfortable around you, and I've shared things with you I've never shared with anyone,' I whispered.

We both had tears in our eyes. Neither of us had imagined this for ourselves. It was so far beyond our expectations.

'Shh, no more crying now. We can do that before you have to leave. Let's make the next month the happiest time possible,' he said.

Being happy was easier said than done. The challenges of living in India, away from hotel rooms and swanky residential complexes, soon interfered. It was well into summer. As the days became hotter, the apartment became more uncomfortable. It was located on the first floor, at the back of a whitewashed art deco-style building. Unlike the apartment at Hiland Park, this apartment didn't have air conditioning. I sat under the fan, waiting and hoping for a cool breeze to flow through the window. The temperature soared above 40 degrees Celsius, and the humidity ensured that I was constantly bathed in a layer of sweat. Coming from a dry climate, I was unused to such high humidity. The locals were less affected by it, having lived with it all their lives. They sweated less, but it still sapped their energy. Adopting Aryan's nocturnal habits, I went to sleep when the sun rose and woke up mid-afternoon. There was no point being awake during the day because it was too unbearable to move around.

Fortunately, I didn't have to do any housework. Aryan's maid from his apartment came for an hour every day to clean and wash our clothes. I found having a servant around awkward, and was ill at ease in her presence, especially if I was still in my pyjamas when she came. She must have thought I was so lazy! I was used to doing housework myself, using fancy equipment such as washing machines and dishwashers. In India, most households employed staff to do it by hand. Home help was cheap – Aryan's maid cost him less than $20 a month.

Doing the grocery shopping at the local market was another challenge. The Big Bazaar may have had its quirks and frustrations, but at least I could get what I wanted in a cool environment, no matter how much time it took. In the fresh food market, where fruit and vegetable sellers were clustered tightly together, their produce piled high on worn wooden trestle tables, dozens of eyes followed me wherever I went. It was impossible to browse for groceries because the stock was kept behind the counter of the ramshackle, hole-in-the-wall outlets. Everything had to be asked for by name. Vendors couldn't understand me.

'Sorry, madam. Not available,' they'd tell me when I asked for items that Aryan had previously purchased from them.

Vegetable vendors would try and charge me double the price. Shops that sold alcohol were usually located down dim, dirty alleyways, and considered disreputable places that only men could visit. On one occasion, not wanting to stand alone in the street, I waited in the vicinity of one for Aryan while he bought the wine.

'You shouldn't be anywhere near here. It's not good for women,' a man warned me in passing.

Aryan, ever perceptive, asked me after a few days at the new apartment if I was happy. I couldn't complain that I *wasn't* happy. After all, I was living the life that I'd chosen for myself. However, I was beginning to realise that I couldn't live with fewer liberties and under the peculiar brand of strictures that India imposed. Indian culture lacked not only privacy, but also equality. Sure, I could learn to negotiate it but at the time, I wasn't sure that I wanted to.

'What do you like most about living in India and what do you like the least?' I asked him.

'Hmm, people are too interfering here. But I like the freedom that being a guy offers. As a guy, I can do most things. It's not the same for women.'

Perhaps I didn't belong in India. I would always stand out as a foreigner, no matter what I did, trying to be a part of a culture that wasn't mine. While I felt relatively normal around the progressive upper-class Indians, with their western dress and lifestyle, at the end of the day, despite their cultural bilingualism, they were still Indian and India was their home. I was neither upper class nor Indian. I didn't belong. When I stepped outside their privileged bubble, my foreignness was often a bane. Life was gruelling. Society was conservative and restrictive. Western comforts were rare and expensive. I didn't have the means to support that kind of lifestyle. The common perception among Indians was that white skin equalled wealth, but it wasn't true. Constantly having to fend off people who asked me for money, or who lied and cheated to try and get it, was draining and irritating.

The upper class certainly didn't care for my attempts to try and be Indian. 'Why learn Hindi? We all speak English. Why dress in Indian clothes? We all dress in western clothes.' They appreciated my foreignness for what it was.

In the evenings, as the sun set, Aryan and I sat on the plant-filled rooftop where it was cooler. We gazed at the moon and stars, drank beer and told stories about ourselves and our past, the good and bad things in our lives.

'Of course, you're the best thing in mine. If it wasn't for you, I'd be wasting money trying to make myself happy. I'd also be spending a lot of time alone, not wanting to be around people.'

I understood all too well, having done these things myself.

'Most likely, I'll go back to Mumbai after you leave. I'm feeling frustrated at work. I don't get to play the music I like at the club. Most of the time, we have to play commercial stuff. The same tracks over and over again,' he sighed.

It was true. I could accurately predict which songs I would hear and when.

'I miss my old friends. I also need to sort out the situation with my parents. I feel sad that I haven't lived up to what they expected of me,' he continued.

'Oh no, what did they want you to do?' I was curious.

'My dad makes furniture and wanted me to be an interior designer. I always wanted to go to music school. My parents didn't allow it because they didn't think it was an honourable profession. I started studying interior design at college and hated it. So I left and joined my friends who were DJs. I'd met most of them at school. We all went to a Catholic school together.'

I knew that Aryan going back to Mumbai would be the end of us. How could it be any other way if he had to try and please his parents?

'My mother tried to arrange a marriage for me once. She insisted I go with her to meet a girl from the village. I wasn't interested at all and didn't want to be there.'

I was enthralled. 'Tell me more. What happened?'

'My mother introduced me to the girl's family and talked about me to them. I just sat there and didn't say a word. Afterwards, I told her there was no way that the wedding would take place.'

I couldn't picture Aryan in a village, meeting a prospective bride. He seemed so western to me, I sometimes forgot he was actually Indian. It even surprised me to hear him speaking Hindi. I had to remember he was completely Indian, from a hardworking family full of expectations of him. A family where his mother no doubt compared notes with the other mothers, and was disappointed by her son's choices in life.

'Wouldn't she be aghast if she knew you were with me?' I asked.

Aryan nodded. 'I don't think we could ever be together in Mumbai. My parents would never accept it. They're conservative because they come from a village in Orissa. My brother had a love marriage with a Maharastran girl. They didn't approve and it took over a year before they accepted her.'

I felt miserable, but I knew Aryan had to take responsibility for his life. I couldn't interfere. I just hoped the good times we'd shared would be enough to sustain us through the challenges we'd face in the future by ourselves.

Yet I couldn't help but marvel that, halfway around the world, I'd found the one person who was so like me, who even had a similar background to mine. Although Aryan was born in Mumbai, his family came from the country. Mine were still in the country. His dad was a talented carpenter who could make anything. Mine, an electrician who could fix anything. One from the east, one from the west. Would the twain meet?

A few nights later, Aryan came home early from work just as I was finishing one of my infrequent meditations. I was concerned he'd think I was strange and mock me. When I told him, he surprised me by asking me to show him.

'After you've gone, I'm going to spend six months alone reading as much as I can. You've taught me so much and left such a positive impression on me.'

I was taken aback.

'But I haven't even been trying to.'

'It's your energy. You have this amazing light around you,' he explained. 'And I keep hearing about it from so many people. Everyone comments on your good energy.'

I felt a rush of emotion. I didn't think I was the only one with such remarkable energy though. Aryan had the calmest, gentlest, most loving soul. When he slept, he sometimes wrapped himself around me, his lips touching my skin. With him, I'd experienced a love I never thought possible, a love that came from feeling safe. In turn, his lack of inhibition and unconditional acceptance of me meant I didn't have to hide anything from him. It freed me from my fear of judgement and rejection. The nagging insecurities that used to bother me had been replaced by an acknowledgement that people liked me for being me. The real me, not the attention-seeking me. Instead of feeling like I had to prove my worth, others naturally saw it for themselves.

People really do come into our lives when we're ready and when we need them. Apart from destiny, there was no way of explaining how we'd found each other. Aryan's unexpected presence, at a time when I was struggling, had proven to me that there was a greater power looking after me. His acceptance of me had healed me.

'You've been given the gift of making people feel good with your smile. I'm so glad to have met you,' one of the DJs at Tantra told me. It was a humbling thing to hear – no one had ever put it so eloquently.

I'd been much blessed in this soul-searching journey of mine; it's nice to know I'd also been a blessing to others. Just a few months ago I'd arrived in Kolkata, terrified and knowing not a soul. My white skin may have opened doors but people consistently looked past the superficiality of my skin colour to see me as a person. They'd welcomed me and touched my life in special ways, as I'd touched theirs.

As May progressed, the weather became more and more unsettled. It matched my moods. There was a thunderstorm every few days. It cooled everything down, then the humidity built, and another thunderstorm happened. The coolness was refreshing, but the humidity was dreadful. I felt dizzy, nauseated and dehydrated. Rivulets of sticky sweat ran down my face during the day; the back of my neck was always perspiring and clammy. A wet facecloth became my constant companion.

Sometimes I wanted to leave India. Other times, I wanted to stay. Some days, I felt so serene alone in the apartment, surrounded by incense and candles. Other days, I felt lonely and stifled. The indecision was unsettling.

As my departure date loomed closer, Aryan started to pull away. He would get lost in his music, then announce he was going out with the boys. Afterwards, he'd come home drunk. I felt rejected and sought the company of my friends. But I took comfort in the fact that we were all facing ambiguous circumstances, none of which offered us any stability or security.

Panna had returned to Kolkata. I went shopping at the street market in Gariahat, a suburb of Kolkata, with her. She was also feeling displaced and uncertain of what was to come. Cliona now had an Indian boyfriend who practically lived in their apartment, so she had less time to spend with Panna. She thought she might leave Kolkata and go travelling again.

Daisy, Tess and Krista also decided to leave India temporarily in the wake of their tumultuous liaisons. People were talking – things had come to a head after a frightening encounter with the bar staff at Venom whom they suspected had spiked their drinks. They were fleeing to Thailand to renew their visas and have some time away.

We said our heartfelt goodbyes at our usual Sunday recovery session at Flury's restaurant, on Park Street.

Tess's parting comment made it much less sad than it could have been. 'Krista finally tried washing her bum with water after going to the loo!'

Daisy was horrified. I giggled. Aryan was amused by the ordinary Indian things that amused us. Sucharita would have to be pleased with how much we'd adapted.

The previous night Aryan and I had been to an all-night party. We'd again ended up talking about our relationship.

'I think you know by now that I really love you. If it wasn't for what's inside you, I wouldn't still be with you. That's how I know that I love you. But I don't feel responsible enough for you. I still need to grow up. There are things in my life I need to sort out. We should concentrate on ourselves and our careers,' he declared boldly.

Even though what he was saying was right, it felt like my heart was being ripped out. But, really, what future could we have together?

I went out to the terrace to get some air. I stood there, looking over the Kolkata skyline and the *chai-wala* (tea vendor) who'd set up his stand on the roadside. It was the dawning of another day, one of my last in Kolkata. The pre-monsoonal air was so wet and heavy on my body, like my emotions. Aryan and I loved each other but we weren't supposed to be together. This chapter in my life had brought me so much, but it was time to move on. The good times, as we knew them, were coming to an end for all of us.

The unbearable weather also seemed to be coming to an end. Thunderstorms were becoming more frequent, accompanied by temperature drops, booming thunder and power outages. Streets flooded with water; rats could be seen swimming along in the current.

In the mid-afternoon, the light dropped so much that it felt like evening. In our apartment I lit candles and incense, and felt strangely relaxed as I sat by the window and watched the storm. The monsoon was due any day, but no one could predict with certainty when it would arrive, just like I couldn't predict with certainty how my life was going to turn out.

Two nights before I was due to leave Kolkata, fate again intervened. I was supposed to meet Panna at Roxy but, feeling listless and lethargic, struggled to find the energy to get ready. I was half an hour late by the time I arrived. The queue to get in was long, and who should be there but Emily. I'd thought she was in Kerala.

'I'm heading back to Australia in a couple of days,' I sadly told her.

'Really? Do you think you'll return to India?'

'I just don't know. I'd like to but I'd need a good reason,' I despaired.

'Well, I want to hire someone to look after the guesthouse in Varkala for the tourist season. My priorities have changed and I don't want to go back there. I need some time to make up my mind about whether I want to keep leasing the property. Would you be interested?'

I was completely astounded. I'd often fantasised about running a guesthouse. And I loved the beach. It was too perfect.

'Are you serious? Of course I'm interested!' I spoke excitedly.

Could I actually go through with it? It was a huge decision. I would have to resign from my job. We agreed to talk about it some more once I was back in Melbourne.

I told Aryan about the proposal.

'Take a chance and come with me to Varkala instead of going back to Mumbai. You could play your music in the beach shacks there.'

'I'll think about it. Let's see.'

The afternoon before I left, Aryan disappeared from the apartment and came back with a sari.

'Here, every girl should have one,' he handed it to me. Made out of deep maroon and gold silk, it was the most exquisite gift I'd ever received. It almost seemed too delicate to wear. I wondered how he managed to choose something so lovely.

'I gave a similar one to my mother a few years ago and she liked it. So, I thought you might too,' he admitted.

We went up to the rooftop to enjoy our last evening together.

'Please come back,' Aryan said simply.

Our brave plans to go our separate ways had faded now that there was a possible opportunity to stay together.

Leaving Kolkata wasn't as traumatic as I expected. Aryan and I decided to pretend it wasn't happening.

'I'll see you in a few months,' I assured him, even though we knew that there was a very real chance that we'd never see each other again.

'I want to keep your Saraswati and you can keep my Ganesh. We'll put them together again if we ever meet up,' he said by way of goodbye.

There was nothing more to say. We'd said it all.

# Beach Girl for a Season

THE numbness lasted for over two weeks. Gradually, it was displaced by feelings of loss and directionlessness. I couldn't make up my mind about what to do. Did I really want to quit my comfortable job and return to India? It would mean completely separating myself from my old life. There would be no going back. Was I capable of it? I wasn't sure. No matter how much I wanted to reinvent myself, the prospect was daunting.

I returned to work to try and make a go of it. Quickly, I realised that although I earned plenty of money and lived well, it just wasn't enough anymore. I didn't want to spend the rest of my life confined to a profession that didn't inspire me, accumulating possessions and being in an environment that didn't appreciate or understand my growing spirituality.

'Be careful,' my boss warned me, when I spoke to him about returning to India. I knew he didn't want me to leave. 'It could be risky, and you need to be able to continue to support yourself.' Cutting ties with the place where I'd worked for ten years would be a big change. Yet, I'd been away from the office for six months, effectively putting distance between myself and my job. I'd discovered a whole new world away from it. Plus, the office was going through changes of its own. A new head had been appointed. People were coming and going. It seemed that transformation was taking place everywhere.

I couldn't overlook the fact that I'd been presented with an opportunity that might bring me closer to discovering my life's purpose. I'd be a fool not to take it. My subconscious thought so too. It filled my dreams with scenes of a palm-lined beach. I didn't need to worry about money; I would have free accommodation in India and Emily would pay me a basic Indian wage. Friends would continue to live in my townhouse in Melbourne. All I really needed to do was resign, pack my bags and go.

I spoke to Aryan on the phone almost every day. The conversations were long. We laughed and cried as usual. He'd grown more frustrated at work and was keen to leave. It seemed both our circumstances were pushing us in the same direction.

'A friend of mine said it's necessary to take chances in life,' he said.

I decided to throw caution to the wind. This time, he joined me.

\*

'Ten bags, including three large ones,' Aryan counted and announced.

The essentials of our lives had been compressed into these bags, which now occupied the roof, trunk and most of the interior of the taxi. We were heading to Kolkata's Howrah railway station. There we would take a long-distance Indian Railways train to Varkala in Kerala, a two-night, two-day journey.

As the taxi pulled up at the station, a *coolie* (porter) swiftly unloaded the luggage from the car and effortlessly hoisted one of the large bags onto his head. Other coolies appeared and did the same, while I watched in amazement at their agility and strength. With a quick glance at our ticket, they adeptly located our carriage and compartment. Our luggage was duly deposited there.

We were travelling in a three-tiered, air-conditioned carriage, commonly known as 3A. These carriages are divided into open-plan compartments, with six beds in each. The beds are stacked vertically in three tiers on either side of the compartments. During the day, the middle beds must be folded down flat against the compartment walls to allow passengers to sit on the lower beds. 3A offered a significant step up in comfort from the raucous sleeper class, which accommodated most of India's thrifty middle class. Nevertheless, the layout was the same. There was absolutely no privacy, and no escape from becoming intimately acquainted with the daily routines of strangers.

Women reached for food they'd cooked and crammed into silver tiffin containers for the journey. Men reached for packs of playing cards. Shoes were taken off and bodies relaxed.

It wasn't long before our excessive pile of luggage and contrasting coloured skin attracted attention.

'You are coming from where? And are going to where? What will you do there? And for how long? And who is she?' the questions started.

'She's a family friend,' Aryan told the inquisitive interrogators.

I was dismayed. A family friend? His family didn't even know about my existence! Why did he hide the fact that we were together? Was he embarrassed?

When I asked him later, he assured me it was the easiest answer. I didn't know it then, but telling the truth would only prompt even more unwanted questions and perhaps disapproval. Up until then, my relationship with Aryan had felt normal to me, as it would have anywhere else. But the people we spent most of our time with in Kolkata were hardly representative of Indian society in general – most Indians were much more conservative. Indians didn't have relationships with foreigners. And, as I would later learn, according to acceptable social norms, unmarried couples didn't traipse around the country together like we did.

With nothing much to do, people started retiring early for the night. I climbed into my bunk bed on the upper row and prepared to sleep. A stout, moustachioed Indian man lay opposite me, less than a metre away. He punctured the air with a curt fart as he settled himself in for the night. The elderly Sikh gentleman below me carefully removed his daywear turban, and replaced it with a more comfortable night version before reclining. As the lights dimmed, the snoring started. First, it was a solitary sound. Before long, a cacophony of snorers from every compartment joined in. I resisted the urge to leap out of bed and beat them all with pillows.

The gentle rocking of the train did its best to lull me into a slumber. But it didn't seem long enough before the drone of the early morning *chai-wala* woke me.

'*Chai, chai, chaiya, chai,*' he chanted loudly as he made his way through the carriage, serving the sweet milky tea that Indians so adore.

The morning brought a rush for the handbasins as toothbrushes, soap and towels were retrieved from luggage. A few Indian men had decided to partially disrobe to perform their ablutions, swanning around topless in simple *lungis* (cloth worn like a sarong).

The train had both Indian squat toilets and western ones. The toilets in 3A were cleaned, although not frequently enough. The theory was, if the user aimed well, the waste would drop directly on the railway tracks through the visible hole. The reality was different though. It was one thing to see, from the window of the train, the smiling brown bottoms of guys openly relieving themselves alongside the railway line. But it was another to be confronted with human excrement in close proximity, all over the toilet bowl. Amusingly, one of my Indian friends likened the display of bare bottoms to the shameless shows put on by dancing male peacocks. *Mor nach raha hai* (the peacock is dancing), he called it. A lot of peacocks liked to dance early in the morning in India.

Aryan loved the train environment. He happily roamed through the carriages, bringing back all kinds of interesting snacks from the vendors. Fortunately for him, he could do it inconspicuously. I, on the other hand, stood out like the proverbial sore thumb and preferred to remain in the compartment. The changing scenery revealed a rural India untouched by progress. Women toiled in fields. Herds of buffaloes and sheep roamed freely. Dung, shaped and dried into perfectly round saucer shapes, was used as fuel and insulation. The appearance of the people on the train also changed as we moved south. The colour of their skin deepened, moustaches became thicker and hair bushier. Many men also donned the traditional Keralan dress, a white *mundu* worn in a similar manner to a *lungi*.

At one of the main stations, I got off the train with Aryan to have a look around. There was no hint of what its exterior looked like. Some railway stations in India had glorious colonial architecture, while others were unremarkable. Yet, all platforms looked the same; shabby, soiled and congested with vendors, passengers and porters. Passengers inundated the carriages and all tried to embark at once.

'*Jaldi, jaldi, aage, aage* (Fast, fast, forward, forward),' they yelled, as they carelessly pushed and shoved one another in a rough scramble. Steel trunks full of belongings and heavily laden jute sacks were used as weapons in the battle to board. Eventually, when people and luggage were all on the train, peace was restored. Heads wobbled in acknowledgement of fellow passengers, and everyone unwound for the rest of the journey.

I soon discovered that southern Indians are particularly enthusiastic head-wobblers. This curious gesture, which looks like a cross between a nod and shake, has a multitude of uses. The non-verbal equivalent of 'accha', it can mean anything from 'good' to 'I understand', depending on the speed of the wobble. But most importantly, it's a universal gesture that unites all Indians. Cultural and language barriers miraculously dissolve with a wobble. I'd never seen Aryan wobble his head before but all of a sudden he was doing it like he'd done it all his life. (Actually, it's very difficult not to return the gesture if someone wobbles their head at you.)

In the dark of the night, our train finally pulled into Varkala station. Frantically, we struggled to offload our ten bags in the two minutes that the train would remain there. In our favour, our stop was near the end of the line so there weren't many people to get in our way.

Then the train departed, leaving us standing in a daze on the platform.

We'd arrived.

Aryan and I had easily picked up our relationship where we'd left off. Seeing him for the first time in two months had been overwhelming. He met me at the airport, his heart beating fast. We looked at each other in wonder, incredulous at this crazy-brave adventure we were about to go on. Love gave us courage.

It was only on the windy road to our hotel in Varkala that Aryan and I sighed in relief.

'This place is just like Goa, but less developed,' he commented. Perhaps we weren't so crazy to come here after all. Perhaps it would all work out okay. We'd find out soon enough what living here for eight months would be like.

As we discovered in the light of day, Varkala was indeed a beach paradise. Its feature was a long winding stretch of cliff, with views that extended over the Arabian Sea. A paved footpath ran along the length of the cliff, bordered by coconut palms, touristy shops, beach shacks, hotels and guesthouses. Nestled at the bottom of the cliff was an elongated stretch of sparkling beach, reached by steps leading down from the clifftop.

Emily's guesthouse turned out to be three simple but bright and spaciously constructed bungalows on a large block of land set back from the beach. Coconut palms, leafy green plants and hibiscus flowers were in abundance around the property. The ravages of the recent southwest monsoon could be seen everywhere, and quite a bit of restoration work would be needed to make it habitable. The bungalows had to be re-thatched and the long grass cleared. Emily had been in the process of expanding the guesthouse, and there was also a semi-complete outdoor kitchen and eating area that needed to be finished off.

Aryan and I moved into one of the bungalows. Daisy had also decided to join us in Varkala, and would be taking one of the others. That left one bungalow for guests. Most of the time, it would be occupied by a couple from Italy who came and stayed for a few months every year. All I had to do was keep the property clean and manage the finances. It was September, and the tourist season wasn't due to start until December, so we had plenty of time to settle in. Shopkeepers had arrived but the rest of the folk were predominantly locals.

Tess stopped by on her way to Thailand. Cliona and her Indian boyfriend, who were travelling around India together, also visited. Goodbyes had become meaningless as we continued to reunite so many times.

Waking up to the sight and sound of nature every morning was a joy. I actually wanted to go outside, unlike in Kolkata. Aryan and I had leisurely breakfasts at the beach shacks, enjoying the salty sea air and ocean view. Some afternoons, we'd share a beer or two and stroll along the cliff, exploring the shops that sold everything from clothes to spices. In the evenings, candlelight flickered over dinner, as the powerful waves pounded the rocks below in the darkness.

Self-proclaimed 'God's Own Country', the state of Kerala is like a world where time and tradition have stood still. Its palm-fringed canals, verdant mountains and fertile farming land offer a tranquillity that's difficult to find anywhere else. Silence and solitude calm the soul. At the same time, the state remains relatively undeveloped and lacks the infrastructure of other parts of the country. Bicycles are a common form of transport. People still grow their own vegetables, catch their own fish, prepare oil from coconut and grind their own sun-dried spices. The people of Kerala also keenly distinguish themselves from the rest of India, particularly by speaking the state language, Malayalam, as opposed to Hindi. Many locals are involved in seafood, agriculture, and handicraft and coir production, while the more enterprising ones have jumped aboard the tourist industry, which has grown rapidly since the 1980s.

While Varkala Cliff was undeniably picturesque, Varkala Town was a different matter altogether. Located a ten-minute drive away from the Cliff, it was dusty, noisy and nondescript. The town had a few small supermarkets, strings of small specialty shops and numerous roadside fruit and vegetable vendors. Right in the centre of town was the only alcohol store. Depending on the time of day or night, a queue of eager men could stretch around the corner. Of course, no women were in sight.

The difficulty of finding what I wanted in the town meant that it didn't take me long to develop a dislike for it. Staff unnervingly followed me around in the supermarket and constantly interrupted my attempts to browse. Once I scoured the shelves looking for roll-on antiperspirant.

'Oh no, madam, you will have to go to a Fancy Store for that,' one hovering employee informed me. A fancy store? What was a fancy store? Tramping from store to store to look for supplies in the heat and crowd quickly made me wilt.

The lack of infrastructure was apparent back at the guesthouse too. There was no municipal water supply. Instead, water had to be pumped from a well. There was no hot-water heater, so we had to bathe under cold water. The electricity supply, while inadequate, was at least predictable. It would go off daily at around 9 a.m. and return at around 5 p.m. The term given to this government-imposed power cut, as a means of dealing with the shortage of electricity, was 'load-shedding'. Since the tourist season was yet to start, load-shedding was at its peak.

As was to be expected, washing machine facilities were non-existent. The local *dhobi-wala* (laundryman) came to everyone's homes on his bicycle to collect dirty laundry. A couple of days later he would return it washed, ironed and folded. I couldn't justify paying him to do all our washing, so I decided I'd wash our clothes by hand myself and only give him the bed linen. Without a laundry sink, it was time for me to get intimately acquainted with the many uses of the Indian bucket.

In Varkala Town, I bought my own bucket collection. Five large buckets. Besides soaking clothes in buckets, I'd need a few for washing dishes.

From Aryan, I learned the special way of washing clothes in India. Laundry detergent comes in the form of a soap bar. It's smeared onto the clothes, and rubbed in with a brush. The clothes are then picked up and repetitively bashed on the floor or any other hard surface, sometimes rocks, to dislodge the dirt. It was a tiring process that I undertook in our wet bathroom.

Two workers came to cut the grass around the bungalows and the kitchen. By hand, I might add. The kitchen was similar in structure to the shacks along the Cliff. Made mainly out of bamboo, it had a tin roof, painted concrete floor and no water supply. Inside was a fridge, TV, stove and bench. The stove, a portable silver cooktop with two burners fired by gas from a cylinder, and standard in most Indian kitchens, reminded me of a piece of camping equipment. I was to discover that it was necessary to learn how to predict when the gas would run out, or end up with a half-cooked meal.

On another trip to town, Aryan and I stocked the kitchen with utensils. Armed, I decided to celebrate by making us a fish curry for dinner. Living by the ocean meant that fish was plentiful. The daily catch was sold fresh at the local fish market every morning.

Aryan and I returned with three whole fish, complete with heads, tails and fins attached. Having only ever cooked scaled and filleted fish, I was at a loss at how to prepare it. I randomly chopped off body parts and attempted to extract organs. It was gory and disgusting; more of the fish ended up in the scrap pile than could be cooked. After watching me massacre the first fish, Aryan took over.

'Here, do it like this.' He started cutting the fish into pieces crosswise, the way he'd learned to do it from his mother.

The curry ended up tasting surprisingly good.

As well as feeling a little at sea domestically, I was also experiencing some difficulty dealing with the guesthouse owner. She, and a male relative who'd been deployed to take care of the day-to-day running of the property, seemed intent on extracting as much money from us as possible. Not only did they demand that we pay a premium for rethatching the bungalow roofs, they expected us to pay the property tax.

'Legally, it's not our responsibility,' I told the landlady.

'But Emily paid it in previous years,' she insisted.

'It doesn't matter. Emily was mistaken. It's your responsibility as the property owner.'

I refused to budge.

Then the water pump seized up.

The relative, who we called 'Uncle', as per Indian custom, was supposed to pump the water for us every day. When he was unable to come, we had to do it ourselves. Inevitably, we forgot to turn off the pump and the motor seized up.

'You have to pay for it to be repaired. You've maliciously damaged the pump and it's intolerable,' the landlady ranted at me down the phone.

I was offended.

'It's not fair to blame me for this. The pumphouse isn't on the lease and it's not our responsibility. If Uncle had come to pump the water like he was supposed to, it wouldn't have happened. I'm not paying you anything. Emily has already invested so much money in developing this property. Come and discuss it with me when we finalise the lease,' I argued.

Later, as Aryan and I lay in the hammock between the coconut trees at the guesthouse, I asked him what he thought my best and worst characteristics were. He contemplated a while.

'You believe in your views and think about the big picture. But you lack commonsense.'

The commonsense that Aryan referred to was Indian commonsense. He often found my inability to think in an 'Indian manner' exasperating. Only recently, I'd become upset over an announcement for a special Saraswati *puja* (prayer) at one of the beach shacks. I rushed there with high hopes, only to find nothing happening.

'You should have known it was just an advertising strategy,' Aryan chided me when I objected.

Used to western standards of conduct, I readily believed what people told me. I was always punctual and expected that others would be too, unfamiliar with the concept called India time. Five minutes often meant thirty. Ten minutes meant an hour. And an hour commonly had no fixed duration.

'I'll come at 9.30 a.m. to sign the rental agreement and discuss the money,' the landlady informed me. The appointed day and time passed. She didn't turn up or tell me that she wasn't coming. Aryan, on the other hand, was relaxed about such things. Nor was he surprised at all. It was clear that I had a lot to learn.

Aryan had had no problem getting work at the shacks on the Cliff. Two beach shacks, the Groovy Beach Café and Dolphin Bay, dominated the party scene.

'Make friendship in the night, like sea waves at Groovy. Get yourself free and enjoy yourself with your unknown humans', a party flyer from the Groovy Beach Café invited everyone.

I loved dancing under the stars until the early hours, with the surf only metres away at the bottom of the Cliff. It was such a world away from the craziness of Kolkata, and even Melbourne. Neither alcohol nor late-night parties were permitted on the Cliff, but the police were appropriately persuaded, usually with money and boxes of beer, by the shack owners. The shack owners seemed charming but were divisive under the surface. It soon became apparent there was a lot of competition for business and foreign women on the Cliff.

The afro-ed Kama, owner of the Groovy Beach Café, was the smoothest talker I'd ever come across. From humble beginnings as an auto-rickshaw driver, he'd built a small empire. Besides the Groovy Beach Café, he also provided travel services and lodging. He was friendly, exceedingly helpful and knew how to please customers as well as women. Most of the tourists who visited his beach shack left with the impression that he was a delightful, genuine guy. What he really excelled at, however, was bedding the foreign women who visited his shack. It didn't matter that he had a wife and two children secreted away somewhere, he could frequently be seen leading a gullible woman by the hand up to the second floor of his shack.

'I am the master of sex. I love wild animal sex,' he boasted to us one night. The thought of it left me reeling.

The local men wasted no time in getting acquainted with Daisy. Kama lured her in by giving her an opal ring, then pretended to be extremely hurt when she rebuffed him in favour of a waiter named Vincent from Dolphin Bay. Vincent, a tall and brawny Malayalee man, was one of the best-looking guys on the Cliff. It wasn't long before he was practically living with Daisy in her bungalow. It was a more appealing alternative than the benches that the staff used for beds at the back of the beach shacks.

Most of the guys who worked in the shacks quickly found out that I was with Aryan and kept a respectful deference. It didn't stop them from following in Kama's footsteps and doing their best to snare as many other western women as possible. I soon came to realise that they didn't have to try very hard. There were many single white females looking for a good time on Varkala Cliff.

'Have you heard about Kama and his beach weddings?' Vincent asked us one night.

We hadn't.

'Last year, he held four of them with different girls who he'd met.'

'What, real weddings?'

'No, mock ones but with a proper ceremony on the beach.' Maybe the wild animal sex was better than it sounded.

To make it easier to get around, Aryan and I purchased a second-hand moped. Riding home on the back of it, with the wind whipping my hair, I felt so vibrant and content. We took a trip to nearby Kappil Beach, located a short distance north of Varkala Beach where the backwaters met the ocean amid swaying palm trees and a rocky shore. Kappil wasn't as developed as Varkala.

After the break in the rain from the departing southwest monsoon, the northeast monsoon arrived with a vengeance, delivering unpredictable downpours. Unlike many regions of India, Kerala received two monsoons a year. The southwest monsoon travelled up the west coast of India from June until September. Then, the heavier northeast monsoon made its way down the east coast, covering Kerala from October to December.

The monsoon rain made me melancholy. Mould grew everywhere in the humidity. Intermittent heavy downpours flooded the guesthouse grounds and caused shops to close. The neighbours' children came running over to our place holding plastic bags over their heads for protection, and with sticks to clear drains for the water to escape.

Caught on the moped at another time during a downpour, Aryan and I were saturated in less than 30 seconds. The rain was so heavy I could open my mouth and drink the water. A local river burst its banks, and two of the streets near the Cliff turned into rivers, complete with fish. I got another dose of viral fever, the second in as many weeks. Again, I was bedridden for three days.

To help myself recuperate, I went to see a Reiki master on the Cliff for a healing session. Reiki, the Japanese word for universal life energy, is an alternative therapy developed by a Japanese Buddhist named Mikao Usui. It involves the channelling of universal energy through the hands to the body's energy centres, known as *chakras*, to unblock and rebalance them. Each chakra vibrates at a different speed, and has a different function in a person's wellbeing. When we react to negative experiences by blocking out our feelings, it also blocks the energy flow to the chakras. I'd been interested in Reiki for quite a while and wanted to study it. I was still waiting for the right opportunity and teacher to come along.

'The energy in your solar plexus chakra is very strong, indicating that you have great willpower,' the Reiki master proclaimed after the session was complete. 'However, the energy in your heart and root chakras is weak. This indicates that you don't feel connected with life and your environment, and haven't found what you want to do with yourself yet. You have the capacity to achieve whatever you want because of your willpower. But you need to learn how to control your emotions, so that you're less giving and won't be taken advantage of. Lastly, you need to focus your beliefs only in one religion. This will strengthen your aura. You should find a guru. One will appear when the time is right,' he concluded.

My religious beliefs had always been confused. Born to a Catholic father and Anglican mother, neither of whom much practised, I was left to make up my own mind about what I wanted to believe in. I grew up feeling that Christianity didn't really have all the answers.

I was always attracted to New Age spirituality – palmistry, tarot, crystals. In my twenties, I dabbled in Buddhism and meditation. It greatly changed my outlook on life, but I was no closer to figuring out its meaning and forming concrete beliefs. In India, I'd begun exploring Hinduism.

The Reiki master's assessment of my character was accurate. I readily went out of my way to please people, seeking approval and reassurance. A lot of the time, I felt like I didn't receive as much consideration as I gave. I also felt detached and disconnected from life. Despite the progress I'd made, I was still trying to accept how my life had turned out. And I had to find my way.

It appeared I was no closer to uncovering the right path. Until I felt grounded, I'd likely struggle with my self-image and be unable to move on from the past. If my self-doubt turned my desire for Aryan into a need to control him, it also had the potential to affect our relationship. I needed to find my destiny, preferably soon.

It wasn't easy to develop a sense of belonging on the Cliff. I met many travellers but struggled to relate to them.

'What? You live here?' they invariably expressed their shock. I had work responsibilities while they were simply out to have fun. I found their views about India, often discussed in a haze of hash, as a destitute but spiritual country limiting.

'I'm having a "real India" experience in this market,' an Israeli guy proudly informed me in Varkala Town.

But what was the real India? To me, it was all real. Dual, but real. India was as rich as it was poor. Some people consumed a plethora of desirable brand names, while others struggled to consume one proper meal a day. A luxury hotel was just as much a part of the 'real India' as a vendor selling vegetables from his wooden cart. My time in Kolkata had proven that.

The foreigners living long-term in Varkala were a motley bunch. Most infamous and intriguing was a middle-aged Englishman who was on the run with his wife and eight children. He believed he'd uncovered a secret government and religious conspiracy, and could usually be seen sitting in a beach shack warning some hapless traveller about it. He'd even documented his questionable evidence in a self-published book called *Little Book, Big Secret*.

Aryan and I connected best with another young foreigner–Indian couple, Faye and her boyfriend, Michael. He was a talented chef from Darjeeling in north India. They ran a restaurant on the roof of their nearby home. It was there that I finally got to experience the pleasure of eating a variety of *ghar ka khaana* (home-cooked Indian food). On days that wine was available at the shop in Varkala Town, we lay on cushions under the stars, and drank and ate until we could barely move. Those moments of bliss were what we'd hoped living in Varkala would be.

As more tourists trickled in for the season, however, a range of untoward incidents started taking place. It began with a power outage at the Groovy Beach Café while Aryan was at work one night, just as the party got under way and everyone was dancing.

'Sulfi from Dolphin Bay has cut the power line,' a murmur arose.

Next, we heard a fight had broken out in Dolphin Bay. A foreigner had his passport and money stolen in the fracas.

Just when it seemed like matters had settled down, the situation took a more sinister turn. Once, Aryan and I were woken by a phone call from Daisy at 3.30 in the morning.

'There is a group of guys outside. They were at my window and have opened up one of the shutters,' she whispered in alarm.

We rushed out of our bungalow to see what was going on.

'I think I saw them standing near the kitchen but they have disappeared now,' Aryan said. The darkness made it impossible to distinguish anything from the shadows of the trees.

When we returned to our bungalow, we discovered the guys hadn't gone far. My phone and handbag, which held my camera and purse, were missing. A wave of shock and dread hit me. I felt sick and dizzy. How could we have been so foolish?

In the morning, the neighbours saw us sitting outside, looking distressed.

'Check over the fence. A similar thing happened last year,' they informed us after we told them what had taken place. Aryan scaled the high concrete fence that bordered the adjacent vacant land and looked over it. Much to my surprise, my bag and purse were there, minus the valuables.

I hit a new low. Who could have done it? I didn't want to live among thieves.

'How do you feel about being here?' I asked Aryan uneasily. I was waiting for him to say that he wasn't happy so we could pack up and leave.

'It's been great until now, and I still want to stay. I don't want to let this bother us.'

Reassured by his attitude, I resolved to be strong and get over it.

A trio of moustachioed policemen came to investigate the theft but did nothing of use. One of them made himself at home in the hammock. The other returned to the car. The remaining one snooped around. He checked out our moped and asked irrelevant questions.

'So, what do you do back home? Do you work or study?' he asked me.

Then he proceeded to tell us off. 'You shouldn't have left your bungalow in the middle of the night. You should have called us instead.'

After learning of the policemen's movements for the rest of the night, however, I doubted that would have been useful either.

'The police came to Dolphin Bay and collected a couple of boxes of beer to drink. They found one of the waiters drunk on the premises and also took him with them,' Vincent told us. 'I had to go to the police station this morning and pay a bribe to get him out.'

Sulfi, the owner of Dolphin Bay, remained in trouble with the police. They sent him a court order that required him to go to jail for seven days for serving alcohol. It didn't matter that they'd taken two boxes of it for their own consumption. Sulfi's solution was to call a friend from Kochin, who was a Malayalee actor, to come and deal with the problem. In status-driven India, this friend had the power and the contacts to get things amicably resolved.

After the strain of the robbery, I started noticing small positive changes in Aryan's behaviour. He was drinking less and helping me out more.

On the other hand, Vincent was driving Daisy to distraction. A huge power struggle was going on between them. She packed his belongings for him to move out of the bungalow but he refused to go.

'My last boyfriend did everything possible for me and treated me like a queen. Vincent is controlling and picks on everything, but then sulks if I hurt his feelings. Now, I've discovered that he's been in contact with an ex-girlfriend, and has made up all these lies. I don't know what to do with him!'

As December progressed, and the northeast monsoon finally dispersed, the tourist season started to get busy. A friend of Aryan's visited us from Kolkata and the Italian couple moved into their bungalow. The German proprietor of the Skylark Art Garden organised a sunset parade, complete with elephant, along the Cliff to promote unity between businesses. She wrapped me in a red foil dress, painted my upper body and face in fluorescent colours, and plonked a huge hat adorned with doves on my head. I was a creature of her imagination.

The after-party was held at Coconut Grove, near the black sand beach. Aryan was the DJ. Almost everyone from the Cliff was there. But it wasn't enough to conquer the mounting tension between the locals and the outsiders. The buffet had different prices for foreigners and Indians. The bar staff refused to serve Aryan's friend vodka shots because he wasn't a local. And the festivities came to an abrupt halt with a fight on the dance floor.

A group of local guys had been drinking Michael's beer. When he refused to give them any more, one hit him. The fight continued near the parking lot, where they beat Michael up quite badly. Faye came to see us the next day in a state of distress.

'Please tell me what happened,' she begged as she tried to make sense of it.

Not long after the incident, Faye and Michael decided to leave for Goa. He didn't feel safe in Varkala anymore. It was such a shame, as we were just starting to get to know them.

Between the fights and the robberies, I didn't feel very good about staying in Varkala either. Fortunately for us, Aryan's profession made him popular with many of the locals. He had some disreputable but influential people on his side, and was never bothered.

The thief returned. Aryan and I had been to the opening party of the Skylark Art Garden. After coming home, we relaxed in the hammock for a while before going inside our bungalow. We'd had a few drinks and foolishly fell asleep with the light on and the door unlocked. I woke up around 45 minutes later, only to notice that the shutters on the window were slightly ajar and my handbag was again gone. In it was my iPod and money. The thief also took Aryan's phone and an umbrella. Once again, I found my empty bag outside the bungalow. I was in a state of disbelief. The feeling of knowing that someone had been watching us so closely and had so boldly invaded our privacy was awful.

All of my electronic items had now either been stolen or broken in India. The thought of it made me crazy. What more could go wrong?

This time we didn't even bother reporting the incident to the police. The last thing I wanted was another rebuke for being careless. Besides, we weren't the only ones suffering. Michael had found his expensive yellow motorbike pushed over and badly damaged one day. It was another sign of the simmering tensions on the Cliff.

The parties continued on the Cliff amid altercations between shack owners. Kama had a new lust interest, a sweet Belgian girl called Julie. When she wasn't hugging Kama in one of the hammocks, she joined me on the dance floor. We were trying our best to imitate a tall moustachioed Indian man, whose curious combination of dance moves was a cross between John Travolta and the Karate Kid. He executed them wearing the facial expression of David Hasselhoff, and at one point sang into a banana-leaf microphone.

He wasn't the only source of entertainment. A bespectacled officer from the Indian Navy, who had come to Varkala Beach to study the movement of the tides, had an impressive repertoire of Bollywood dance moves. Regrettably, he directed them all at me and in very close proximity.

'You're incredibly special. Are you sure you're not a Punjabi girl?' he kept asking, until Aryan called me away.

Soon, it would be Christmas – my second away from home. This year, being away didn't feel so monumental. The fancy stores in Varkala Town had started stocking decorations, and rows of huge brightly coloured paper stars adorned shopfronts, along with Santa masks and flashing lights. Aryan and I bought a small Christmas tree and decorations for the guesthouse. The neighbours built a nativity scene, and Aryan and I went around handing out Christmas cake. On Christmas Eve, ten of the local boys dressed up in masks and Santa suits, roaming from house to house, chanting loudly and singing Christmas carols. Even the dog ran for cover.

Daisy, who had been renewing her visa in Kathmandu, and Vincent arrived back on Christmas Day, and we treated ourselves to the buffet at the luxury Taj Garden Retreat Hotel on a grassy hill overlooking the Arabian Sea. Swathed in the sari that Aryan had bought me in Kolkata, it was another Christmas where east met west.

Tess returned to Varkala to spend New Year's Eve with us. Dolphin Bay promised a 'sleepless nite of thunder and lightning' from 5 p.m. until 5 a.m. The substantial crowd sprawled out onto the footpath, unable to be contained within the walls of the shack, as sweaty bodies danced together. A guy from Australia hoisted me up onto his shoulders, spinning me around as we jubilantly heralded in the new year.

Gallingly, the new year began with further visits from the thief. Soon after Daisy gave her dog to one of the shack owners on the Cliff, Aryan and I awoke to find the shutters on our bungalow open. That made it not once, but three mornings in a row.

Daisy, Tess and I resolved to uncover whoever it was. We came home early from a party and took up strategic positions. After waiting hidden in the shadows of the fence for over an hour, I grew tired and went inside to sleep. It was 4.30 a.m. and there was still no sign of the thief.

'He came to my window and peered in at around 5 a.m.,' Tess announced the next day. 'I was awake but couldn't see anything in the dark and was too scared to move.'

We sighed. Again, the person had managed to avoid getting caught.

The police raids continued on the Cliff, however.

'The owner of the supermarket next door complained about the music, so the police came and took away my CD player and ten of my kitchen staff so I couldn't serve any food. My business is ruined,' Kama said dramatically.

His lust life was also creating problems.

'Kama's wife turned up looking for him on New Year's Day. She was insane with anger,' Julie told me. 'I had a huge fight with him and ran off. He didn't even bother to come after me, and sent two of his kitchen staff instead. Now he's being so affectionate with me again, I just don't know what to do. I don't want to believe that he's a bad guy.'

It was almost time for her to return to Belgium. If she didn't realise what he was really like before then, I feared that another mock beach wedding might eventuate.

There was only a month left of the season. What would happen to us after Kerala remained unasked, and unanswered. My visa was about to run out. It seemed that the best option would be to get a new visa from Kathmandu, like Daisy did. Aryan agreed to come with me.

The four-day journey from Varkala to Nepal via Delhi and through India's poor heartland of Uttar Pradesh was arduous and tested us in every way possible. Poverty-stricken, overburdened and uncivilised, most of Uttar Pradesh isn't welcoming to visitors. The state is home to the Taj Mahal and Varanasi, two of the most popular tourist destinations in India. Yet, most of it consists of rural farming land that is unable to support the largest population, of almost 200 million inhabitants, in India. Crime, lack of education, unemployment and 'eve teasing' (sexual harassment of women) plagued the state. Colleges banned girls from wearing jeans to stop men from being aroused. It was seen as the only way to curb crime against women.

We arrived at Gorakhpur, a few hours from the Sonali border crossing, on a train from Delhi. It was 5 a.m. when we disembarked, only to discover that a *bandh* (closure) was in place due to political unrest. As dawn broke, we snuck out of town via the back roads in a solitary escape vehicle. It was one of the very few local bus services running. I had little understanding of the situation, including the violence that apparently would have ensued if we'd been caught.

The conductors on the bus were particularly lecherous and uncouth. I couldn't help noticing that one of them had a large hole in the crotch of his pants, which he freely used to access and scratch himself. The male passenger seated in front of us enthusiastically chewed *paan* and regularly opened the window to let out a stream of tainted red spit. Blasts of chilly air slapped my face each time.

The conductors decided to have some fun by asking Aryan about me and making lewd remarks.

'*Chup rao!* (Be quiet!)' I shouted at them in rage.

They looked at me in surprise.

'Shhh, don't say anything and don't acknowledge them,' Aryan ordered me.

Later he told me that they were discussing taking both of us away, beating him up and playing games with me. It made me feel sick.

Twelve hours later, after taking another bus from the border, we arrived in Kathmandu. I was exhausted but filled with aggression towards the crude Indian men who could get away with behaving so offensively.

The atmosphere was noticeably different in Nepal. Despite being a very poor country, a certain dignity was apparent. People greeted me with a 'Namaste'. Staring was minimal. And there were no rude comments even though Aryan was often mistaken as a Nepali. At worst, they thought he was my Nepali guide. We had encountered similar assumptions in India as well. It was frustrating and demeaning, but there was little we could do about it. People did not expect Indians, or Nepalis, and white people to have relationships with each other.

Foreigners in a foreign country together, the maze of narrow winding streets and Kathmandu's medieval architecture enchanted us. We wandered around aimlessly, getting ourselves lost and discovering something new at every turn. Afterwards, we hired a motorbike and explored the surrounding temples. More than 300 steps on a hill to the west of the city led us to Swayambhunath Stupa, the oldest holy shrine in the Kathmandu valley. Its piercing eyes looked out in all directions (north, east, south and west), symbolising the all-seeing nature of the Buddha. Its nose was the Nepali character for the number one, symbolising unity and the 'one' way to reach enlightenment – through the Buddha's teachings. In a rare display of his roots, Aryan was also overwhelmed to visit Pashupatinath Temple, the oldest Hindu temple in Kathmandu and one of the most significant Hindu temples of Lord Shiva in the world. 'My mum would really appreciate me doing this. She would love to come here,' he explained to me as I waited outside. Unfortunately, only Hindus were allowed to enter. It seemed so mysterious to me, and I wondered what went on inside. In the evenings, we drank wine and listened to live music in the bars of the pulsating tourist district known as Thamel. One day, I got an unexpected taste of home when we discovered an Australian exhibition, complete with didjeridu-playing Aboriginals. The fact that Aryan loved the barbecued meat confirmed to me that our blend of cultures seemed to merge relatively effortlessly. I'd never had a problem eating Indian food, and now he was enjoying the food from my home. I suspected that he'd fit in well in Australia.

On the return train from Delhi to Varkala we found an unusual man seated opposite us.

'I'm Lokesh,' he introduced himself. Aged in his mid-twenties, Lokesh was a recent but ardent devotee of Lord Krishna. He was also deeply into astrology and claimed he could predict the future.

'If you give me your birth details, I'll prepare your charts,' he offered, to pass the time during the journey.

The results were intriguing. He said some surprisingly accurate things as he addressed Aryan.

'Your family's financial situation was difficult in the early years but is okay now. Although you're emotional, you often keep your feelings to yourself. You didn't plan your career, it's just something you fell into. You're loyal in relationships, and it's always been the girls who have created doubt in the past.'

Turning to me, he warned, 'You need to be more forthright in giving Aryan guidance. But I believe you will both marry next year, around March,' he concluded.

It was a bold prediction but one that Aryan and I both found comforting. The future of our relationship had been on our minds a lot. Whether or not Lokesh's prediction eventuated, it gave us hope that we would remain together.

Our relationship was always going to attract a great deal of attention, and at times scorn, in India. How would it affect us? Could I cope with the challenges and disapproval? Living in Varkala without the facilities that I was used to had shown I was adaptable, but it had also revealed that there was no utopia.

Life slipped into a peaceful pattern in Varkala upon our return. Daisy had fled with Tess to Kolkata to escape from Vincent. The ongoing police raids had subdued the Cliff. There were no parties to tempt Aryan into staying out late and over-indulging. Days were long and slow, and ran on Indian time. The weather was warm and breezy. I sat around reading books and studying Hindi. Aryan devoted his time to learning new music production software. Without interference from anyone else, our relationship moved to a new level of contentedness.

Our reverie was unexpectedly interrupted by a phone call from Aryan's mother.

'She was again asking me if I'd met a girl. She really wants me to get married and is keen to arrange a wedding.

'Do you think it would be possible for us to be together forever? If I don't marry you, I'll probably give in and have an arranged marriage. It'll be easier that way. I don't want to love anyone like this again.'

So many thoughts flooded my mind.

'Do you really think you could be a good husband?' The prospect of being locked into another party lifestyle wasn't appealing.

'I can. I'm willing to learn,' he assured me.

When he looked at me, I could see the love in his eyes. His whole facial expression changed with it. And the way he held and kissed me was so tender. There was so much potential in the life we could build together. Yet, I felt scared about giving up my nondescript life in Australia. Concern about subjecting myself to a life where I would be regarded so differently, and as an outsider, tormented me. At the same time I didn't want to slip back into a life of comfortable monotony.

I needed to see where this journey would lead. Thoughts of the future eluded me. Aryan and I were effectively jobless and homeless; we'd have to create a whole new life for ourselves. Where would we live? Where would our kids go to school? How often would I get to see my family? And how could Aryan be so confident he wanted to spend his life with *me*? I didn't doubt Aryan's sincerity, but his confidence felt so alien. All I could do was take one step at a time, and believe that things would fall into place if we were meant to be together.

My thirty-third birthday came and went. It was another dry day, so the alcohol shop was closed. Every year, the Indan government announced a list of days prohibiting the sale of alcohol. The dry days usually fell on certain festivals, elections and religious occasions. Added to this, the first day of every month was a dry day in Kerala. It was the day that most employees received their salaries, and the Kerala government wanted to discourage them from drinking. (I could hardly imagine what would happen if the Australian government did such a thing.) We spent the afternoon consuming cocktails at Dolphin Bay and gazing out over the ocean. Thankfully, dry day laws weren't followed on the Cliff, where they served alcohol without permission anyway. I couldn't help feeling I was getting old and that my life was still directionless. It was a new and unpleasant feeling. At the same time, I recognised that I was learning so much. It wouldn't do me any good to be impatient.

The season was drawing to a close. Ken, the African drummer who lived nearby, was keen to know if we intended to keep leasing the guesthouse. If not, he wanted to take it on for the next five years and develop it.

I could see the potential in Ken's plan. In reality, it would be difficult for him to make any money, given the huge capital investment required. What's more, the owner was getting greedy with the amount of rent that she wanted. I didn't see much point in renewing our lease under the circumstances. Emily agreed with me. She was now living in London and didn't have any plans to return to India.

With five months remaining on my visa, Aryan and I were left wondering what to do with ourselves. The weather was getting hotter and humidity levels were building every day.

'Let's go north to Manali,' he suggested. 'Some of my friends have been there. It's a beautiful place in the mountains.'

The thought of fresh, crisp air really appealed, so I agreed. We'd take the train to Delhi, and from there the overnight bus to Manali.

You would think I was now a whiz at packing and leaving, but preparing for our departure brought back feelings of trepidation about moving on, and of leaving the ease of the known for the uneasiness of the unknown. After the relative calm of Varkala, I dreaded being in the deluge of humanity in a large city again – the pushing, shoving, staring and people wanting to sell me things. I felt tense just thinking about it.

'I can only be strong if you are. I don't think we can do this trip with you like this,' Aryan looked at me, worried.

I took a walk along the Cliff to fortify myself. After eight months together, Aryan and I knew we made a good team and complemented each other well. I was useful at planning and he excelled at implementing. He packed our bags while I finalised our travel arrangements. We were in this adventure together.

We said our goodbyes to the people we'd befriended on the Cliff. Most of them weren't emotional; everyone was used to the transient free spirits passing through. Shack owners were packing up their belongings for storage. Many of the seasonal workers also had plans to head to the hills. Sulfi from Dolphin Bay had started to grow a moustache.

'It's the end of the season. Plus, it will help me to be taken seriously by the police around here. It looks like I'm out of my caste without one,' he explained.

Such was the pervasive power of the *meesha* (moustache) in Kerala.

Kama was looking forward to Julie's return from Belgium in a week. No matter how much Daisy and I warned her about what he was really like, she didn't want to believe it. She felt she needed to come back and make up her own mind about him.

Our last meal in Varkala was the most delicious fish *tikka* we'd ever had on the Cliff. I surprised myself by stringing together a sentence in Hindi.

'*Varkala me, yeh machi sabse achhi hai* (this fish is the best in Varkala).'

Perhaps my long hours of study had started to produce results after all.

The next morning, Aryan and I threw our eleven bags aboard the Kerala Express and headed north.

# Revelations in the Mountains

I BREATHED in deeply as I opened my eyes, filling my lungs with the crisp mountain air. Snow-capped Himalayan peaks greeted me through the window. Aryan and I sat on the porch outside our room, drinking hot coffee and admiring the exquisite view. Prem Joshua's uplifting world fusion music played softly in the background, and the smoke from the stick of incense that we'd lit swirled around. We were staying in a small family-run guesthouse on the hill in the tiny village of Old Manali. Orchards of blossoming cherry and apple trees surrounded us. Clusters of small white butterflies fluttered joyfully in the spring sun. The snow had been late coming that year, and had only just cleared by the end of March. Rebuilding was industriously under way for the tourist season ahead.

We'd arrived in Manali on an overnight bus from Delhi. The

sixteen-hour journey had turned into twenty hours, as the windy road was blocked by a collision between two trucks. As I stepped off the bus, dazed, I was surrounded by the usual melee of men offering their services.

'You want taxi, madam?' 'You want rickshaw, madam?'

I discovered they could be readily subdued with an '*ek minute*' (one minute). They repeated it to each other, startled at the sound of Hindi from a foreigner's mouth.

It was in Delhi that I realised what I wanted to do with myself in the future. It came to me unexpectedly, while sitting in the rooftop restaurant of the Shelton Hotel, in the seedy Paharganj tourist district. I was reading the newspaper over breakfast when an advertisement caught my attention: 'Become a writer. Comprehensive creative writing course to get you started,' it announced boldly.

I hadn't considered being a writer. It was such an esoteric profession, but the idea resonated with me. I recalled being in primary school, when my teacher proudly told my parents that I was the only child in first grade who had been able to write a proper story. My previous boss had also admired my ability to write understandable reports that required minimal editing. Writing was the one thing I'd enjoyed about my job. I tore the ad out and kept it, vowing to enrol in the course when the time was right.

As Aryan and I explored our surroundings in Manali, it was easy to see why the area was often referred to as the mysterious abode of the gods. The energy level seemed higher, buoyed by towering pine trees and raging rivers, and the pristine environment was perfect for divine creation. It wasn't long before we encountered three *sadhus* (Hindu holy men) keen to bless us in exchange for money. Well groomed and wearing collared shirts under their crisp saffron robes, they showed little sign of having renounced themselves from society. More likely, they were some of the fake *sadhus* that India was awash with. These *sadhus* prospered by posing for photos with tourists and offering phony prophecies. Still, we took a picture with them. Everything was new and exhilarating.

New Manali was every bit as commercialised as Old Manali was quaint. Cafés and guesthouses intermingled with villagers' homes in Old Manali, and it was common to see the locals herding their animals up and down the steep, narrow road. In New Manali, hotels, shops and restaurants jostled for space, along with the hordes of Indian honeymooners and tourists escaping the summer heat. In the evenings, they flocked to the stalls in The Mall to have their fill of *paani puri* (crispy hollow shells filled with spicy water), fairy floss and other snacks. Newlywed wives could be seen looking coy, their arms covered in *mehendi* (henna) and bangles indicating their transformed role and new position in society.

In contrast, Old Manali was a haven for hippie backpackers, many from Israel, who came to spend their days smoking handmade *charas* (hashish from the resin of cannabis plants).

'Boom Shiva,' they'd chant as they lit their chillums and passed them around. Cannabis plants flourished freely and wildly in Manali, on the roadside and even in front of the police station. In testimony to the plant's omnipresence, there's even a small village named Bhang about four kilometres from Manali.

*Charas* became illegal in India in the 1980s, but still has a sacred role in Indian culture because of its medicinal and mind-altering properties. Lord Shiva, the Hindu god of creation and destruction, was believed to have spent a thousand years in meditative rapture in the mountains high on *charas*. These days, s*adhus* and other devotees of Lord Shiva offer it to the god in worship and emulate him by smoking it. Since I was a non-smoker, it didn't appeal to me. For me, being in Manali was like being a vegetarian in a steakhouse.

Aryan and I set about finding somewhere to live. The driver who picked us up from the bus station showed us some apartments. The first two were located down the back of residential areas also housing cows and sheep. One didn't have a kitchen, while the other had an Indian-style bathroom complete with squat toilet.

The third place was in the newly constructed wing of a guesthouse, tucked away amid the orchards overlooking the Beas River. The walkway to the guesthouse led us past rows of flowering fruit trees and randomly growing cannabis plants. Men and women could be seen toiling in the fields, using buffaloes to pull their old-fashioned plowing equipment. The apartment was perfect and would apparently be ready in five days, after the carpenters had added the finishing touches.

Over a week later, the apartment was still incomplete but we decided to move in anyway. The wardrobe didn't have any shelves or a door, the gas and stove were yet to arrive, the water tank was still waiting to be filled and the Internet cable was dangling from the roof. But we had a home with a magnificent view.

When we went into New Manali to stock up on supplies for the apartment, much to my disappointment, I soon realised that the facilities were more primitive than in Varkala. Supermarkets were non-existent. Items had to be purchased from individual specialty stores where shopkeepers spoke minimal English. There were plenty of 'English Wine Shops' but in curious contrast to what their names suggested, most didn't sell wine; only the demands of the whisky-drinking Indian male was catered for.

Aryan and I decided to tackle getting the kitchenware first. We stood in a small claustrophobically crowded shop, stacked ceiling to floor with steel pots, pans and other household goods. A painstaking process followed: I pointed to each item, while Aryan asked the shopkeeper how much it was. The shopkeeper slowly got each item down, presented it for inspection and quoted a price. It was impossible to browse and make comparisons like I was used to.

Buying food was just as time-consuming and difficult. Armed with the shopping list for *khaane ki cheeze* (things to eat), we decided to split up. It was beyond my ability to face the live meat market with its cages of doomed chickens and carcasses of various animals hanging and lying everywhere, so I chose to get the groceries.

My first challenge was purchasing *channa* (chickpeas). Chickpeas didn't come in tins in India, and in smaller grocery stores they didn't even come in packets. Instead, there were rows and rows of jute sacks filled with varieties that I'd never seen before.

'*Kaun sa wala*? (Which one?)' the shopkeeper asked.

Dismayed, I looked around until I spotted the white chickpeas that I was familiar with.

'Umm, *yeh wala* (This one),' I pointed to the bag.

I stumbled and mumbled my way through the shopping. I didn't want to have to resort to speaking English to the shopkeepers who addressed me in Hindi but at the same time, inexperienced in Hindi, I dreaded sounding foolish. After traipsing through the maze of the market and six shops later, I was exhausted but had managed to get everything we needed.

Wanting to do something constructive with our time in Manali, Aryan and I decided to open a small shop on the corner near the guesthouse. One of his friends from Kolkata had a stock of hand-painted backdrops that glowed under UV light, similar to the one that had been hanging in Aryan's room. We would sell them, along with a range of clothing and accessories that the friend had also acquired from various merchants. I'd often thought about having a shop since I was a child. I've always been fascinated with cash registers, so much so that I insisted on working as a checkout operator at the local supermarket when I was only fourteen years old. I'd even lied about my age so they'd accept me. I continued to work there until I was 21. Most of the time, I loved it.

The day the shop opened, we performed a special *puja* (prayer) for its success. Taking a couple of coconuts, a symbol of good luck and prosperity, we headed to the Manu Temple at the top of the hill in Old Manali. We removed our shoes and stepped inside, rang the brass temple bell to get the attention of the gods and lit a cluster of *agarbatti* (incense) sticks to purify and scent the atmosphere. In a circling motion, we held them up to the statues of each god.

On the floor in front of the shrine we cracked one coconut and, breaking it in half, offered it up to the gods. The ritual complete, Aryan and I placed *tikkas* (marks) on our foreheads at the location of the third eye *chakra* using *kumkum* (red turmeric) powder. At the shop, we distributed sweets to all the other shopkeepers, and broke open the second coconut outside. Inside, we lit more incense and placed a small statue of Lord Ganesh, the remover of obstacles, on a shelf.

While the shop opening got off to an auspicious start, Aryan and I soon discovered our personalities weren't suited to being shop-keepers. In India, the shopkeepers who prospered were those with confidence and the gift of the gab. They attracted the attention of prospective customers, lured them into their shops and success-fully convinced them why they should buy their goods. Being quiet by nature, both Aryan and I found this difficult. We also quickly realised that customers wanted a bargain, and were more concerned about the price than the quality of an item.

We didn't want to sell our stock cheaply, so I decided to put them up for auction on eBay. To my amazement, the demand was solid. Prices that were considered high in India were reasonable elsewhere. As our stock began to run out, I started buying items from the other shops and selling them too.

What wasn't easy was mailing the items to the buyers. I had

diligently researched the postage options and costs on the India Post website before committing the details to buyers. However, I later discovered that the services offered on the website didn't reflect those provided by the Manali Post Office. Crowded and disorganised, without any discernable queues, the post office fitted the model of a typical government-run office in India. It had clunking ceiling fans and towers of mail stacked on all available surfaces. Too many people and not enough fresh air made it stifling inside.

Much to my dismay, the post office was only offering basic services to customers on the day I first visited. This did not include registered mail. According to the staff, they weren't planning on sending registered mail again until two days later.

The elderly moustachioed assistant was unhelpful when I returned.

'I'd like to send this as a registered letter.'

'Sorry, madam, registered parcel post only,' he replied.

'What do you mean? The India Post website says that it's possible to send items up to two kilograms as registered letters. This item weighs less than 200 grams,' I insisted, holding up the envelope containing a folded, lightweight backdrop wrapped in cardboard.

'Not possible, madam. Only registered parcels,' he was adamant.

'If I send it as a parcel, how much will it cost?' I sighed.

'Approximately 400 rupees.'

This was a lot more than the 150 rupees that the India Post calculator online had quoted for a registered letter.

I'd already advised the buyer of the postage cost and couldn't increase it. There was no option but to send the backdrop as a registered parcel, and pay the additional cost myself.

'You'll need to write your passport and visa details on the envelope.'

'Why?' I was becoming exasperated. I didn't have my passport with me. And I didn't want to waste more time and money going all the way back to the apartment to get it.

'Because you're a foreigner, madam. If the mail gets returned you'll have to pay money to the customs department, and we also don't want the mail to sit unclaimed in this post office.'

'Why would customs duty be payable on a returned item that is of Indian origin? And how will my visa and passport details help you in case the item is returned? I've written my address in Manali on the envelope. It can simply be sent there. I've never been asked for my passport and visa at a post office in India before,' I shouted hysterically, fed up and completely overwhelmed by random policies that didn't match official information and demands that didn't make sense.

Why was there no consistency? Why was it so impossible for anything to go to plan in India?

Aryan came over to see what was wrong.

'If he sent the item, would he have to provide any of this extra information?' I demanded.

'Of course not.'

'Fine, then you send it. I give up,' I said to Aryan.

'*Bewakuf!* (Idiot!)' I yelled as I stormed out. 'And everyone else, mind your own business!'

Tears rolled down my cheeks as I sat on the footpath outside the post office, waiting for Aryan. An Indian lady and her mother noticed me, and asked if I was okay.

'Don't be upset. Everything will be fine. You should go to the larger post office in Kullu. You'll be able to send your mail much more easily there,' they comforted me.

I hated myself for letting the postmaster get the better of me and for creating such a scene. Aryan must be so embarrassed. I wondered how he coped. It wasn't the first time I'd become annoyed and shouted at people lately. I was used to feeling capable back in Australia. In India, I often felt helpless and bewildered. And, no doubt, lacking in commonsense.

But right at such an awful moment, India had turned the tables on me yet again, and presented me with two kind people who cared for my wellbeing. I didn't know what to think.

India tested every part of my personality, and brought out positive and negative qualities that I didn't even know existed. I'd felt compassion for people like I'd never felt before, and also rage like I'd never felt before. I considered myself an undemanding and polite person, a people pleaser, but India made me snap in ways that I never imagined I could. It pushed my emotions to the limit, then handed me a peace offering. There was no doubt that India was forcing me to become more assertive and less controlling. But I still had to learn not to let situations overwhelm me.

The ongoing scrutiny that my relationship with Aryan attracted also made me edgy. Locals asked Aryan where I came from and what he was doing with a white girl. Sometimes, they'd get confused as to whether or not I was Indian.

'Is she Kashmiri?' they'd want to know. It was common for Kashmiri Indians to have pale skin and dark hair.

The police troubled us as well. As we were walking along the road from Old Manali to New Manali, Aryan and I were stopped by a policeman in his vehicle.

'Where are you from and what are you doing here?' he grilled Aryan first. Then he turned to me.

'Show me your passport, madam,' he demanded. As he flicked through, his attention settled on my Nepali visa.

'This visa is expired,' he commented, obviously not understanding which country the visa was for. Then, turning back to Aryan, he slyly made a remark in Hindi.

'He asked me how I'd been so lucky as to *patao* (woo) you,' Aryan told me after the policeman had gone.

The reactions of some foreigners were just as biased.

'I also speak some Hindi,' a *gora* (white man) interrupted us at a café one evening. He was sitting on the table next to us and our Hindi conversation had caught his attention. Encouraged by the beer he was drinking, he started sharing his life story.

'I partied so much when I was young. I had fast cars and fast women but I gave it all up when I realised I was no longer getting the highs that I needed. That's when I came to India and lived as a *sannyasin* (someone who has renounced worldly life) for ten years in complete chastity. I even wore chains down there and took pleasure in my self-control.

'However, my downfall came when I returned to the UK. I met a ravishing redhead and completely lost myself to her, along with the evils of alcohol and cigarettes again. I came back to India and now I've fallen in love with a twenty-year-old girl from Tamil Nadu. I thought she might've been 30, and she thought I was 50. But I'm actually 60. Her parents were initially pleased with my interest but when they found out I didn't have any money and didn't want to live in the UK, they put a stop to our relationship. I'm so frustrated because I've realised I'm getting old but I don't feel it. My age is getting in the way of what I want to do,' he lamented.

When I left the table to go to the toilet, the conversation abruptly turned to me.

'You got lucky. How did you end up with someone so stunning? Are you planning to go and live in Australia?' the *gora* bluntly questioned Aryan.

It hurt, the way that people openly and superficially judged us because of the colour of our skin and the countries we came from. It made me self-conscious and led me to constantly and irrationally imagine what people were thinking and saying about us.

A little over a month after we'd arrived in Manali, I unwittingly ended up on the set of a Bollywood movie. Part of the movie was being filmed at an historic castle nearby, where a huge carnival scene was being created. Shopkeepers with eye-catching items were needed to act as stall-holders in the background.

Serendipitously, Aryan had gone to Manali and I was in our shop by myself when the assistant art director stopped by.

'These backdrops are really vibrant. Would you mind displaying them on the set of a movie?' he asked.

If Aryan had been in the shop, he would have said no, but I was curious about how Bollywood movies were made. Plus, we'd be paid for our time. It didn't take much to convince me to say yes.

The next day, Aryan and I found ourselves in a mini-van loaded with Indian shopkeepers who sold everything from wooden masks to furry jackets. The most entertaining was a young artist from Bihar who produced traditional Madhubani paintings. He talked incessantly to us during the journey.

'My name's Himanshu. I'm from Bihar but live in Kerala, Goa and Manali selling my art now. I had a love marriage to a Gujarati, but I've got a girlfriend who's an American yoga teacher. She knows everything about me but my wife doesn't know anything. I love to flirt.' I didn't quite know what to make of his complicated life circumstances, which he seemed to be proud of, and hoped that he wouldn't decide to flirt with me.

We arrived at a set that was an astonishing hive of activity. Hundreds of workers were industriously building, painting and sculpting around the clock. It was fascinating to see so many artisans in action, bringing to life a fairytale with their hands. At a loss as to what to do, we spent most of the day sitting around waiting. The remainder of the shopkeepers, who were due to turn up at 2 p.m., didn't arrive until 8 p.m. Lunch was late. The shopkeepers discovered the food wasn't to their liking and went to eat at a nearby vegetarian restaurant, demanding that the production company pay. As soon as I stepped outside to the lunch buffet, I was pounced upon by a couple of young Rajasthani women on vacation.

'*Didi!* (Sister!) Photo, photo!' they screamed as they pulled my arm.

In the afternoon, the shopkeepers bought a bottle of whisky and drank it behind the set, while Himanshu played Hindi songs on his mobile phone and danced. It wasn't until after dark that the director arrived. A hush swept over the set. He walked in and proceeded to tell everyone where to display their goods.

'Make sure the shopkeepers are on the set at 6 a.m. for filming tomorrow,' I overheard him say.

The set was nowhere near finished. To me, it looked like filming would be impossible. The artisans would be working through the night to get it ready.

At 11.30 p.m., Aryan and I were yet to leave. We'd been told that we should stay there, with the rest of the shopkeepers to keep an eye on our belongings.

'No one mentioned anything about this to me. I don't have a change of clothes or anything. Plus where are we going to sleep?'

Unaccustomed to the Indian ability to slumber surrounded by people and with just a mattress on the floor, I refused. Finally, a car was arranged to take us back to Manali.

We arrived home well after midnight, exhausted. At 4 a.m., the alarm went off. I struggled out of bed, looking like a creature of the night with bloodshot eyes. The sun was rising.

Despite the early start, we arrived on the set two hours late. India, as always, produced the unexpected. The magician who was supposed to be picked up in New Manali wasn't there. We waited for over fifteen minutes before the driver went to retrieve him from his hotel room. When he got into the car, I couldn't help noticing that he had the hairiest ears I'd ever seen. Some strands were over five centimetres long. Just out of Manali, we encountered a broken-down tourist bus that was blocking the entire road.

'*Mera dimag kharab hogaya* (My brain has become bad),' the crew member sitting in the front seat repetitively muttered, as phone calls became more anxious. Time marched on, but we failed to move. A crowd of Indian spectators gathered around the bus and were entertained by a passing stream of locals performing their early morning ablutions. Teeth were cleaned and tongues scraped with sticks, as they openly bathed under taps. At last, the tourists were ordered off the bus and the bystanders pushed it off the road. One guy produced a whistle and blew it keenly while waving his arms around.

Surprisingly, when we finally arrived, the set was complete. We met a subdued Himanshu.

'I had to share a room with seven people and hardly got any rest,' he grumbled.

I rushed around madly trying to get all the stock displayed according to instructions, while Aryan looked at me in exasperation. It was obvious I still hadn't adjusted to Indian time.

Eventually the cast emerged in readiness for the dance scene. The success or otherwise of a Bollywood movie often depends solely on its soundtrack and dance scenes. Interestingly, these dance scenes mostly have no relevance to the movie or real life. They deliberately feature attractive women in revealing costumes, usually dancing in a provocative manner. The lyrics consistently contain over-the-top references to love, life, the heart and romance. With Indian culture being so conservative, such scenes provide an indulgence that people are unaccustomed to seeing every day. To Indians, a Bollywood film without dance scenes would be like curry without chilli – bland and unappealing.

Understandably, a lot of effort and money is devoted to making dance scenes in Bollywood movies. Still, I was shocked to learn that two weeks of preparation and filming would result in only one six-minute dance scene. It was a time-consuming process that required days of work, many costume changes and sets.

The dancing itself was highly choreographed and shot in very small blocks from different angles, and not in sequence. It was mesmerising to watch the set burst into life with great vigour and enthusiasm, only to have the energy dissipate just as quickly as soon as 'cut' was called. With the same song playing over and over for days on end, as each movement was repeatedly filmed, the strength of my grip on sanity was tested.

The set had been transformed into a vibrant extravaganza complete with Tibetan dancers, costumed Tibetan yaks and traditionally dressed locals who had been rounded up from surrounding villages to be extras. The local women were so sweet and friendly. I chatted to them as much as my limited Hindi would allow.

It didn't take long before the director noticed me and came over. 'Your pretty red dress isn't going to be seen if you stay where you are. Stand over here and move these baskets around. Try and avoid being disturbed by the dancing yak, and stop it from biting you,' he instructed. And with those words, my unforeseen role as a Bollywood extra had begun.

The next day, Himanshu's wife arrived from Gujarat. Relieved, I hoped it would put a stop to his attempts to flirt with me. She wasn't at all like how he'd described her. Instead, she was modern, attractive, spoke very good English, obviously understood him and knew how to keep him in line.

'I asked him to marry me, despite the fact that my parents didn't approve of me marrying someone who wasn't from my caste,' she told me. Clearly, she was a strong and determined woman.

I was on the set by myself, as Aryan had a cold and wasn't feeling well. I soon regretted my decision to be there alone. At lunchtime, the crew invited me to join them. With trepidation, I agreed. They seemed preoccupied with their work and very quickly returned to the set, leaving me with the director and assistant director.

After lunch, the assistant director called me aside.

'I just wanted to tell you that the crew is trying to set me up with you. They've chosen me as the victim of their latest prank.'

I wasn't impressed. It was hard enough being the only foreigner on a Hindi-speaking set, without having to deal with people's practical jokes as well. I missed the reassurance of having Aryan by my side, his calmness and instincts about situations to compensate for my enduring naïveté.

I tried to keep as much of a low profile as possible that afternoon but it was difficult with the director deliberately asking me to be in various shots. I counted the hours until I could go home to the safety of Aryan's arms.

It took over two hours for all the shopkeepers to be paid at the end of the day, drawn out by a dramatic argument between Himanshu and one of the crew members.

'This isn't the amount you agreed to pay me. You don't know my worth!' he shouted in front of everyone before storming off. His performance was worthy of being in a Bollywood movie; it was fitting that we were on the set of one.

As a result of the delay, the car that was to take us back to Manali had already left. It looked like it was going to be a long wait for another one.

'Would you like to share a ride with myself and the crew?' the director asked.

Wanting to get home as soon as possible, I reluctantly agreed. After dropping the crew at their hotel, the director climbed into the back of the van with me.

'You're so pleasingly congenial. Good-looking girls usually have attitudes and you never know where you stand with them.'

I wondered where the conversation was headed.

'Will you have dinner with me?' he asked.

I desperately wanted to be back in the apartment with Aryan.

'I'm sorry, I'm really tired. I just want to go home,' I managed to say.

When it was time for me to get out of the car, the director insisted on walking with me back to my apartment.

'It's dark, and it's down a hill,' I protested.

'I want to see the view,' he insisted, not taking no for an answer. Fortunately, Aryan was near the window and saw us arrive together.

'Come in,' he extended an invitation as he opened the door. The situation defused, the director left soon after.

'You're not going back tomorrow,' Aryan said when I told him what had happened.

I had no desire to argue with him. The crew obviously didn't take my relationship with Aryan seriously. But maybe it didn't cross their minds that we were in a relationship. White foreigner and Indian man: more than likely, they simply mistook him as just another shopkeeper and me as another tourist.

I needed to get some space. Hoping that nature would be kind enough to dissolve some of my stress and fill me with energy, I went for a walk in the forested Manali Reserve that connects New Manali with Old Manali. Bordered by the powerful Beas River, its fertile green carpet was peppered with boulders and woven with walking tracks. I lay down on one of the wooden benches and shut my eyes. The sun flickering through the soaring pine trees warmed my face and soothed my mind.

When I awoke, however, the good feelings were swiftly lost. I had an audience – one man was sitting, staring, on a nearby rock. Another was half hidden behind a boulder. Two young guys, gaining confidence from each other, proceeded to strut over and seat themselves right next to me. This inspired the other men to follow. Before long, they were all round me. I tried to remain composed but failed when I realised that one of them was pretending to talk on his mobile phone. What he was actually doing was taking a photo of me.

'*Baysharam*! (Shameless!)' I spluttered, almost speechless with fury. It didn't take long for my anger to turn into pain though. Right when I needed solitude the most, it eluded me. Even worse, it had been replaced by the thing that made me feel most uncomfortable: being ogled at. I didn't want to be an object of anyone's desires. I didn't want intrusions into my personal space. I just wanted to be anonymous and alone.

Tense and burdened, I decided to attend one of the Reiki courses held at the Reiki centre in nearby Vashist. Vashist was fast becoming a popular alternative to Manali, with many travellers staying there to learn yoga and other alternative therapies. The Reiki Master, I discovered, was a tiny, bubbly woman called Ritu. She put me at ease straightaway with her warmth and openness. At last, my teacher had appeared. I was ready. Happily, Aryan also agreed to study with me.

We sat in Ritu's lavender-coloured room, surrounded by crystals and with the Himalayas as our backdrop. There were four of us in the class. Aryan, me and a Spanish couple. We began by learning the theory about energy and the chakras.

'Everything in the universe is made up of energy, vibrating at different frequencies. This includes human beings. The universe is formed out of the energies of five elements, the same as human beings. They are air, earth, space, fire and water. Each element describes the essential qualities of life-force energy. They balance and transform this energy. Each element is also associated with one of the seven chakras, or energy centres of the human body.'

I was most interested in what Ritu had to say about the heart and root chakras.

'The heart chakra is the emotional centre of a person. It's the place where the energies of the three upper chakras and three lower chakras blend. The task when dealing with the heart chakra is to drop expectations, and love yourself and others without barriers. Society and family condition people's minds. We all have ideals in our minds about how a 'father', a 'mother', a 'husband' should be. However, everyone is different. Therefore, we can't judge them against any ideal. We must look at a person as a person. Just because someone is not fulfilling all conditions doesn't mean that they're not a good person. We are always looking through the eyes of others. We are always judging ourselves and others as not being good enough.'

Ritu's words really made me think. It was as if she was speaking to directly to me about my situation. Aryan wasn't tall, white and wealthy – the ideal of what my husband should be, according to the expectations from my old life. Instead, his strengths and what he had to offer me were more subtle.

I'd started noticing how Aryan rarely complained about anything, from the situations he was in to how he was feeling. If I needed something, he willingly got it for me. If I was feeling down, he did little things to comfort me and cheer me up. If I was tired, he offered to do the housework. He was comfortable enough with himself that he behaved the same way around everyone, and didn't feel like he had to prove anything. Maybe he couldn't provide me with material stability, but he could provide me with emotional stability.

We completed each other. He had the unconditional love in his heart that I was so lacking, while I was disciplined and responsible in ways he wasn't. In addition to mirroring the parts of each other that we needed to develop, I also saw some of the negative aspects of my past behaviour in him and got to experience their impact.

'The lowest chakra is the root chakra,' Ritu continued. 'The root chakra relates to the physical body of a person. It's responsible for our physical form. It grounds us to the Earth and opens up for the Earth energies to flow through us. When people can't relax, and are always tense and fearful, their physical body will have a lot of pain and illness. If the root chakra is blocked or weak, a person will lack vitality and even lose the will to live. The past is stored in two places in the body – the root chakra, and the subconscious in the back of the head. The task when working with the root chakra is to strengthen our trust in life and our right to be here. The root chakra also connects a person with their biological mother. One of the best ways to heal your root chakra is to heal your relationship with your mother.'

I did feel an overwhelming need to heal my past, and that included improving my relationship with my mother. Instead of getting frustrated with our differing opinions, like I usually did, I was keen to appreciate her positive qualities and look for common ground between us.

After the theory was complete, we were ready to receive our Reiki attunements. As we sat on the floor and meditated with our eyes closed, Ritu performed the process that would open up our chakras and connect us at a higher level to the universal life energy. It was similar to the process of turning the frequency dial on a radio to find a station. We were being tuned in to a higher frequency, a higher level of vibration.

Although the results of the process could not be seen, they could readily be sensed. I felt a rush of energy in my lower two chakras. Afterwards, I felt dazed. My energy levels felt disturbed and unsettled. My emotions progressed from feeling calm, to teary, to elated, to vulnerable and wanting affection, then to disturbed and wanting to retreat.

That evening, I experienced an intense energy shift. One minute I was overflowing with love and gratitude, and the next minute negative emotions were pouring out of me. I lay down on the bed and buried myself under a blanket. My whole focus went inwards. All I wanted to do was breathe in and out. I felt the negative energy flowing out through the lower chakras. Tears came. I was hot, then cold. Exhausted but in a state of elation, completely charged with energy but in an uncontrollable and unsustainable way.

My attention was scattered. I felt like I was experiencing a different level of awareness. My energy and being seemed to blend with everything else around me. I looked at things and noticed small details in their composition. Objects didn't seem to exist in their usual form anymore. A beetle. A person. A bed. They were simply compositions of energy that happened to look different. Then came warm feelings, like I was blessed with a new gift. One that would always be with me, whenever I needed it. I felt so connected to the universe and a part of all that was around me.

Over the forthcoming days, my body adjusted itself to the new level of energy. My emotions continued to oscillate from one extreme to another. At times, my energy levels were so high it produced a rushing sensation similar to having drunk too much coffee. During those times, I felt like I was being propelled in a whole new direction in life.

In class, we practised giving Reiki treatments to each other, allowing the energy to flow through our hands. We also gave Reiki to ourselves daily. The sensations in our hands, when we placed them over the various chakras, indicated if there were any issues. My hands went cold over my root chakra, indicating a large blockage of energy. However, when I placed them over the heart chakra of another student, I experienced a rush of love and happiness. It was such a dramatic difference. I also found that my left hand became shaky and tingly when energy was flowing through it to repair unbalanced chakras.

During the Reiki treatments, I began to get some uniformity in the emotions that came up. I felt the need to put a wall up, and not let anyone know my thoughts and experiences. I didn't want to let anyone really know me because then I would be exposed and vulnerable. I felt dirty and uncomfortable with myself. I didn't want people knowing me intimately. Then came the thoughts of how people, especially my parents, might criticise my relationship with Aryan. I felt the pain of being judged by everyone, and not being free to be myself. It seemed like so much negativity was being drawn out of me. More tears came.

I realised that I had two related issues. The fear of being judged and the fear of being known. The only way I could get over my fear of being judged was to let myself be judged, and the only way I could get over my fear of being known was to let myself be known. And it was through my relationship with Aryan that I could achieve both, if I was strong enough. The universe had planned it well. If I remained with Aryan and faced up to everyone's judgements about our relationship, then I would receive his unconditional love as a result. This would in turn allow me to feel secure and comfortable enough to open myself up completely. But in order to achieve this, I'd have to have the courage to go against so many of society's ideals about how I should lead my life and who I should be with. I would need every bit of willpower and clarity that I could draw upon.

I did a crystal healing session with Ritu. The pain of my past with Michael flowed through me. There was pain that things didn't work out between us, pain of not being able to prevent it, and pain of being blamed for what had happened.

'You have to forgive him and yourself. Now it's time to move forward and let go of it. Focus on and appreciate your new life, and being with someone who can give you the love that you deserve.'

Aryan came to meet me after the session. He held my hand, and we went walking through the nearby forest to a waterfall. I felt drained but cleansed.

The intense experiences continued as I continued to practise Reiki every day. Sometimes, I felt dizzy like I was going to faint. There was a heaviness in my chest, and a pulling sensation from my heart chakra to my root chakra. The cool, fresh air blowing through the windows smelled like home. I felt so sad, so far away. More tears silently ran down the side of my face. Overwhelmingly, I needed to go home and reconnect with my parents. In recent years, I'd been so absorbed with my life in Melbourne, I hardly saw them. So many visions of us together as a family when I was younger flashed through my mind. I felt like I was starting afresh as a new person, and I wanted to be close to my parents again. It was like my life had come full circle.

As all the emotions and tears came out, Aryan lay beside me and stroked my forehead.

'I can see so much in your eyes,' he said.

The horrible feelings of being vulnerable and exposed surfaced again. Yet, Aryan felt none of it. There was just love, tenderness and acceptance from him, that special quality that made him so different to everyone. Eventually, he turned off the light. The negative emotions dissipated and were gradually replaced with feelings of warmth and comfort. I wanted to be wrapped up in a cocoon, enveloped safely.

'It seems like everything is so quickly moving to a point and converging in my life now,' I said.

'It will only be upwards from now,' he said.

So much was opening up and coming together like the the swirls and strokes of henna being applied. It reached the point where each element started fitting together and it was possible to see the bigger picture.

The Reiki experience changed both of us. We felt inspired about future possibilities, and less inclined to want to party and drink. My energy levels had altered so much that even one glass of alcohol made me tired and depressed. Strangely, it no longer produced the feelings of cheerfulness and relaxation that I was used to.

Despite the challenges, Manali had been a place of transformation for me like it is for many people. Not only sacred but also scenic, it felt alive with the spiritual energy of ancient sages that were believed to have spent time in the area – energy that infused me. The purity and tranquillity of the environment and living so close to nature, where humans and animals existed closely together, was perfect for soul-searching. I thought about the things I was going to miss: waking up to the sight of snow-capped mountains every morning, the rush of the river below our apartment, the fresh scent of the pine trees, the quaint cafés in rambling gardens, fresh fruit from the surrounding orchards, and the cows and sheep that were herded up and down the road.

With time again running out before I had to return to Australia, I started to consider the future. As I browsed the Internet for jobs in India, one unexpectedly caught my eye – content writer for a travel website. It was perfect. I loved to write and loved to travel. The only problem was that I couldn't work in India, and wouldn't be able to readily obtain an employment visa for a job that an Indian could easily do.

But it sparked an idea in my mind. I'd create my own website. Many people made money from advertising and commissions on the sale of products recommended on their websites. Maybe I could too.

Undeterred by the fact that I knew nothing about HTML coding, search engine optimisation or affiliate marketing, I downloaded manual after manual and began to learn. It was complex and involved. Yet, it didn't dampen my enthusiasm. After contemplating a range of different subjects, I decided I'd start with a website on natural health. It was a family interest and I had plenty of information about it. Having a purpose to devote my spare time to made it easier to accept having to leave India and Aryan.

'I've met a lot of girls but none like you,' Aryan declared to me one night close to my departure. 'I feel so much love for you. You're definitely the girl for me, the one I want to marry.'

'How do you know that?' I really wanted to be sure of what he was saying.

'I ask myself questions, and I also notice so many little things that you do for me. You've made all the places that we've lived in a home for us, plus you've helped me become a better person. I'm so much healthier and happier now. You saved me from a lifestyle that wasn't good for me.'

I'd decided to fly home from Mumbai, and we planned to go there together from Manali. He'd stay with his parents in Mumbai and slowly tell them about me. I'd return to my life in Melbourne, and find a temporary job. What would happen after that depended on the reaction of Aryan's parents to his news. He didn't have much hope that they'd view it positively.

The long-distance Paschim Express deposited us in a soggy Mumbai, in the grip of another year's monsoon. Big city life was confronting after the tranquillity of the mountains. Incessant traffic jammed the roads. A motley assortment of standing, sitting and squatting men crammed the streets. I quickly discovered that Mumbai was full of quirky characters.

'I often give people wrong directions, especially to motorbike riders,' the taxi driver happily admitted to Aryan on the way to our hotel. 'Many motorbikes don't have shields on the back of their tyres and they spray water everywhere, all over my windscreen. One day, I told a guy to drive twenty minutes straight in the opposite direction to where he wanted to go, and not to bother to stop and ask for further directions. He would have ended up somewhere near the airport,' the driver chuckled.

At our small hotel opposite Juhu Beach, the manager was keen to find out as much as possible about the mixed race couple who had arrived at his hotel in a taxi overflowing with luggage. I decided to play his game and fired back questions of my own.

'How long have you been working in the hotel?'

'Ten years, madam. But actually, I've been sacked two times in those ten years. This is the third time I've been employed at this hotel.' He smiled and wobbled his head.

I must have looked astonished. 'I can't lie to you about something like this, madam,' he said earnestly.

There was a certain magic in discovering the city by the sea where Aryan grew up. I was filled with wonder that this could be my future home.

Mumbai is known for its extreme standards of living, fast-paced lifestyle and the making – or breaking – of dreams. The suburbs were surging ahead at a rapid rate, filling with shopping malls, department stores and high-rise apartments. On the other hand, south Mumbai still reflected the rule of the Raj with its intricate colonial English architecture. Peppered throughout the city were the slums that also made Mumbai famous, but which most people preferred to turn a blind eye to. On initial impressions, Mumbai struck me as a city with an identity crisis. But its cosmopolitan nature made it more foreigner-friendly and livable than other cities in India.

Aryan and I walked along Juhu Beach and ate fresh *pav bhaji* from the snack stalls, before getting drenched in a monsoon downpour as we ran, laughing, to our hotel for cover. We shopped at the street market on Linking Road in Bandra, and had dinner with friends from Kolkata who had relocated to Mumbai. Refreshingly, nobody bothered us. The city almost felt like home to me already. It felt like I was discovering a new part of Aryan along with it.

My last day in Mumbai was bittersweet. Aryan took his bags home to his parents' apartment, then returned to take me to the airport. The huge smile on his face wasn't something that I expected to see.

'I couldn't help it. I confessed everything to my mum about us. She told me not to worry, that she was my mother and that everything would be okay. She also said that we could marry if your parents agreed. No doubt she'll have so many questions though.'

Aryan was shocked by his mother's easy acceptance. He had expected her to react negatively, like she'd done over his brother's love marriage. Perhaps, more than anything, she was simply happy that Aryan finally wanted to get married.

I couldn't believe her acceptance either. It felt like such a relief. I wanted to know more.

'She was sitting on the floor eating lunch when I arrived. I told her how I'd learned to cook, and showed her some of the things we'd been selling. Then everything just came out. Of course, she wanted to meet you and to know all the details about you, including what you looked like, and what you and your family did. But then she was worried that you'd leave me if you earned more than me. I told her it was nothing like that though.'

'It's true. Love is much more important than money to me. Being loved by you is the best feeling in the world.'

'Oh baby, I really do love you. And, I'll put some love away for you every day while we're apart. Then, we can be together forever.'

We sat in Café Mocha opposite Juhu Beach, sipping espressos and talking as the rain poured down around us. After spending every day together for the past year, neither of us knew how we'd deal with being apart. Our only reassurance was the future we were working towards.

It seemed like everything was continuing to fall into place. I was content knowing that Aryan had a happy home to go to, and that he was in the best health and frame of mind possible. I felt positive and motivated, knowing what I was going back to Australia to achieve.

At the airport, I used the bathroom and surprised myself by reaching for the water instead of the toilet paper. My Indianness had come a long way.

PART THREE

# LANDING

# Destiny Revealed

'YOU look years younger and seem like a completely different person.'

My mum couldn't get over the change when she saw me. I felt different too. More connected to people, with a desire to be open with them. Previously, I would have needed alcohol to facilitate that.

'I've met someone special,' I confided to her. I spoke to her like I'd never spoken to her before, and found her to be unexpectedly receptive.

'He sounds like a gem. It's obvious India has done wonders for you too. You should go back there and keep being creative.'

Her support took me by surprise and gave me confidence. I'd expected to encounter negativity. I was so used to hiding my life from her. Instead, her willingness to be open-minded made me feel closer to her and really improved our relationship.

It was harder to talk to my father. I usually found it easier to relate to him because he was more emotional like me. But I also feared his reaction as he was very protective. Although he didn't try and stop me, I knew my plans worried him. He didn't like the thought of me being with someone he'd never met, and one from a country so far away such as India. Just as Indians had preconceived ideas about foreigners, so too did foreigners about them – the wariness cut both ways.

I announced to anyone who wanted to know that I was going back to India to be with Aryan, and to write. Many people were alarmed. They relayed stories of Indians who had taken advantage of foreigners. Even my Indian friends in Australia were sceptical and concerned.

I was torn in so many directions. I felt more connected to my parents than I had in many years, and was enjoying spending time with them. Yet, Australia felt so strange. There was no spicy smell of incense. No feeling of wonder and possibility. Just a quiet emptiness, from everything being so orderly and in its place. I'd also become used to speaking in Hinglish, sentences that were a medley of Hindi and English, and had to stop myself.

It was worse at my house in Melbourne. My room and my furniture were there, but so were people I'd never met before. My housemate had moved on and friends of a friend were staying there. I sat on the sofa in my study, gazing out the window and feeling dazed and displaced. I now had belongings scattered in three places – my house, my parents' house and in India – but no home to call my own.

I tried to remain focused on getting back to India, but at the same time, I needed to be in the present. Getting a job was a priority. I registered with an employment agency in Melbourne and went for an interview. In the past, I would have been filled with trepidation and dread. This time I went energised and in a positive frame of mind.

The consultants were friendly and helpful, and they found me a position while I was there. It was a temporary role administering community programs at a state government department. Instead of feeling anxious, I went to the interview with an open mind, in touch with everything around me. It didn't surprise me that I was offered the job. The manager held my previous work in high regard and was pleased to have me join the organisation. The only problem was I was needed for five months – longer than I'd planned to stay in Australia, and longer than I wanted to be apart from Aryan, but I decided to let fate take its course.

I returned to work, trying to appreciate rejoining to the professional world. It added structure and status to my life after a year of wandering. I couldn't fault the job or my colleagues, but being confined to a controlled environment, in a high-rise office building all day, left me unmotivated. I felt like I was losing my connection with the outside world. The sense of emptiness returned, along with constant tension in my muscles like my whole body was contracting. I could feel my mind narrowing, shrinking and closing. The life was being sucked out of me.

During my lunch hour, I lay on the soft grass under a tree in the park opposite. Eyes closed and totally relaxed, I let my body absorb the healing energy of the plants and earth. On the train, I read spiritual books about change and how to attract what I wanted into my life. I tried to keep myself inspired and focused, but inevitably, the daily work routine dominated my life and was adept at dragging me back into the lifestyle I'd known for so long. It was comfortable and familiar, and provided me with an assured income. But I knew

I couldn't let it take over; I could feel in my soul that I was destined for other things.

I felt so alive when I thought of my future in India, even though we'd both be starting our lives from scratch in Mumbai. Did I really want to give up all that I'd worked for in Australia to do that? It would be so much easier to stay where I was.

Deep down, I knew I had to keep moving forward. I'd grown so much that I'd outgrown my life in Australia. My motivation came from India. If I didn't go back there I'd lose it.

Aryan's love for me remained steadfast and unconditional. We spoke daily.

'My parents are so pleased with the changes in me. I've been helping out around the house, coming home early and not drinking. I've even started inspiring my friends.

'I was never sure that we'd end up together. I always thought you'd leave and go back home. It was only during our last week in Manali that I realised for sure that we could have a future with each other. Now I'm really serious about us.'

Every day, Aryan's mother asked him a new question about me. Once, it had him phoning me in an anxious state, wanting to know my date and time of birth, and where I was born. His mother and elder sister had decided to get our horoscopes matched.

In India, where Hindus place a great deal of emphasis on Vedic astrology, it is common practice before marriage to find out a couple's compatibility. The technique, which is around 3000 years old, has its roots in Vedic scriptures. Based on the precise positions of the planets at the time a person is born, it assesses 36 *gunas* (attributes) that form an important part of every person's physical and spiritual life. A score below 18 means that the couple is incompatible and the match should be rejected. If the score is between 18 and 25, the match is acceptable. A score of 26 to 32 means that the match is very good. A score above 32 is an issue, as the couple will have the same nature. This isn't viewed favourably for a long-term relationship.

Soon, the results were in. Aryan phoned to tell me.

'My mother came rushing into my room and woke me up early to tell me. The *pandit* said that only 1 in 100 couples are fortunate enough to get a match as good as ours. Our meeting was favourable and destined. We're going to be very happy together.'

'Are you serious? That's amazing,' I was so pleased.

'Even my mother was amazed. She kept wondering how it was possible to get such a good match with someone who isn't even Indian.'

Apparently, we'd scored 24.5, which was average. However, Aryan's animal was a harmonious mouse and mine was an eagle, which supposedly meant that we were great friends (perhaps as long as I didn't decide to eat him!).

It was true. We were each other's best friends.

But an eagle? I hardly considered myself bold enough to be an eagle, soaring above the world. The voice in my head kept nagging and beckoning me to hold onto the past, and keep living a normal and ordinary life. Was I mad throwing away my comfortable life to go and live in India?

Wanting reassurance that I wasn't making a mistake, I went to see a psychotherapist.

'You're definitely on the right track and heading in the right direction,' he offered after listening to me.

He readily recognised my issues. 'The reason why you're holding onto the past so much is that it's known to you and is part of the fairytale you created for yourself. You're scared of moving forward. You're scared of living your life differently, scared of where your life will end up. You may even be scared of how good you'll become.

'It's obvious from your behaviour, and how critical you are of yourself, that you have low self-worth. Your big life lessons are to learn to love and appreciate yourself, and value yourself. Your value isn't dependent on what other people think of you, you know. You need to be assertive and stop basing your worth on the opinions of others.'

He continued. 'Your real fear is coming from the possibility that you might actually succeed in your plans. What if there is a grand new life waiting for you? Then you'll end up at odds with who you currently are. Many people will no longer recognise or relate to you. You'll lose friends. You'll probably feel very alone. But, you'll be tapping into something much greater – the power of doing what you were put on this earth to do. And you'll find new friends in places you never thought you'd look.'

It all made sense. Did I really have the strength and courage to live my life in an unconventional way, the way that my heart told me was right?

Aryan's parents had showed a lot of courage by accepting our relationship. We hadn't expected their support, at least not so soon. Love marriages, especially to foreigners, were still quite rare in India and very much against Indian culture. Traditionally, marriages in India involve the joining not just of two individuals, but of two families. Substantial effort is put into arranging marriages and finding a suitable family from the same caste and of similar social standing. A good match garners much respect in the community. Going against this deeply ingrained tradition can have wide-reaching, even scandalous, implications. Not only can the head of the family lose respect in the community for allowing the marriage to happen, it can also tarnish the family's reputation and affect the future marriage prospects of the other children.

Many people in India are beginning to think progressively. Yet, they're often stopped from behaving in such a manner by the reactions of a conservative community that abhors anyone doing anything differently. Admirably, Aryan's parents had decided to place their children's happiness above community expectations. No doubt, their relief at Aryan finally wanting to get married helped. They were curious to meet the girl who had brought their wayward son back to Mumbai and prompted him to settle down.

I enrolled online in the writing course that I'd come across in Delhi. Each night after work, I shut myself in my bedroom and worked on compiling a website about natural health. Although I was learning a great deal, I was fast ending up with an unwieldy and unpolished website that I didn't really know what to do with.

One night, I came across an advertisement for freelance writing jobs on the Internet for a large article library website. It evoked the same sense of enthusiasm that I'd felt in Manali for the ad for travel writers.

To apply, I'd need to provide details of my background experience and two samples of my writing.

'There's no point. It's all too hard. You're really not good enough and wouldn't be accepted,' the discouraging voice in my head piped up. It didn't take much to convince me. Of course, I wouldn't be accepted. I didn't have any experience.

As I lay in bed preparing to go to sleep, a separate and more soothing voice spoke to me.

'Remember the travel article about India that you had published on the Internet years ago? Find it and submit it. You'll be successful.'

This voice felt right. It was an intuitive voice that came from deep within.

I still needed one more piece of work. After much thought, I decided to write a fresh article about the Sunday market held along Melbourne's St Kilda Esplanade. I immersed myself in the market, noticing and noting down the sights, sounds and smells.

Not long after I submitted my application, it was approved. The website lacked articles about India so I decided I'd write about Indian travel. Perhaps if I was good enough, I'd even be promoted to features. With that resolved, I abandoned my natural health website to focus on travel writing.

A little over a month before I planned to return to India, Aryan's family started looking for somewhere for us to live. Aryan didn't want to keep living with his parents; like me, he preferred quiet and privacy. Plus, his youngest brother and wife were already living with them in their two-bedroom apartment. There wasn't enough room for more people.

I was quite relieved. Although I would have agreed to live with them, it would have been a challenge for me, and made the adjustment process even harder. Aryan's family decided that we should live near his elder sister so she could help me settle in. His mother, eldest sister and youngest brother's mother-in-law took him to inspect apartments.

'It was such a slow process. They kept stopping to look at things and ask the price along the way,' Aryan complained on the phone. I laughed, imagining him being surrounded by a contingent of three constantly chattering Indian women.

They found a suitable one-bedroom apartment but it was in a vegetarian Gujarati apartment complex. These denominational apartments are very common in Mumbai, where people of the same backgrounds cluster themselves together. We were neither vegetarians nor Gujarati. The landlord objected.

'It's okay, my family handled it,' Aryan reassured me. 'They argued with the landlord so much that he finally he gave in and agreed to give us the apartment.'

Only a very brave Indian man would resist a feisty group of Indian women.

'And what did your family tell the landlord about us?' I was curious to know.

'They said I'd be living there with my fiancée, and that we'd soon be getting married.'

I giggled. 'Wait until he finds out your fiancée is actually a foreigner.'

As my departure crept closer, I was inundated with conflicting emotions. Nervousness, dread, sadness, excitement and an overwhelming feeling of wanting to be back there immediately. Again, I was in the all-too-familiar situation of packing up my life and boarding a plane for the unknown. This wasn't going to be just another trip to India, however. I was going there indefinitely, to be with my sweetheart, get married and live my life like an Indian. At one stage, it felt like the time would never come. Then it was hard to believe that it had arrived.

I sat on the floor of my bedroom, surrounded by boxes, dizzy and my mind in overdrive, coming up with as many memories of the past as possible to hold me in Melbourne. It was torture; I was almost paralysed with anxiety at the prospect of stepping out of my comfort zone. Miraculously, in among all the mental turmoil, came a saving grace from a most unexpected and unlikely source. On my last day at work, a colleague gave me a book, *The Dream Giver*, by Dr Bruce Wilkinson. In it was the story of Ordinary, who dared to leave his Comfort Zone in the Land of Familiar to pursue his Big Dream.

Ordinary soon learned that although the Dream Giver had given him a Dream, the road to the future that he really wanted was clogged with greater obstacles than he'd ever faced before. Dream-threatening obstacles. These obstacles caused many Nobodies to turn back. But Ordinary put his faith in the Dream Giver's powers and persisted. And the Dream Giver rewarded him with entry through the gateway of his Big Dream.

Increasingly, I was realising the immense power of the universe. Looking back to when I first arrived in Kolkata a little over two years ago, it was becoming obvious that I was being directed and supported to go down a particular path. What was initially a quest for independence and a new perspective had now turned into my life. On the one hand it made no sense anymore, but on the other I had more purpose and inspiration than I'd ever felt.

Giving into my fear of uncertainty wasn't an option. I reminded myself that comfort is a deceptive dream because it becomes a prison. The more I turned away from fear, the more I'd believe that my comfort zone was where I belonged. And the more time I spent being comfortable, the more I'd become convinced that because I hadn't stepped through fear, I couldn't.

The only way forward was to gather my courage and keep moving down the unknown path to my dream, where my soul was calling me. I wasn't running away. I was actually running towards something.

The book became my constant companion for the days that followed, and during my journey to India. As I sat reading it in bewilderment on the plane, with tears rolling down my face, it comforted me in my grief over leaving my home and my parents. That was the moment when I surrendered my dream to the universe and relinquished controlling my life. My dream was just too big for me to handle alone. If the universe had a special plan for me, if it was asking me to take such a big step for my dream, I trusted that it would bring into my life what I needed.

*

My eyes met Aryan's through the crowd, fenced in behind the barricades at the airport. Everything looked so strange and yet familiar. We sat holding hands in the back of the taxi, shy about how to act towards each other after so long.

I quickly realised the biggest adjustment I'd have to get used to was my new home. Mumbai is the most densely populated city in the world. In some areas, there are up to 60,000 people per square kilometre. Space is understandably at a premium, and it has pushed the price of real estate up on par with New York City. Around half the city's population occupies *chawls,* multi-level tenements with single small rooms and a shared bathroom for each floor.

There are very few houses in Mumbai. The middle and upper classes live in apartments. One-bedroom and two-bedroom apartments are common, with two or three generations of family members living in a single flat. Most of the apartment towers in Mumbai reminded me of the Melbourne's characterless high-rise housing commission estates, which housed the city's lowest income families.

Our 500-square foot apartment was less than a quarter of the size of my home in Melbourne, and it needed decorating. Paint was flaking off the walls but the stingy landlord refused to do anything about it. Mosquitoes and pigeons lurked everywhere, along with all the people.

The apartment was located in a decent middle-class outer sub-urban neighbourhood, but middle class in India didn't translate to middle class in Australia. The building that was our new home was less than five years old, modern enough to have reticulated gas instead of the infamous camp-style gas bottle. Yet, the exterior was already dirty and decrepit. Individuals didn't seem to have an appreciation for property. Rubbish was left lying around. To get to our apartment on the first floor, we had to walk past red *paan* stains on the stairwell – graffiti from people's mouths, where they'd carelessly spat after chewing the substance.

I slept a lot during my first few days back in Mumbai. My head swam. I felt completely overwhelmed and sick with fear. The words of some of my friends kept echoing in my head about the insanity of my giving up my comfortable life and material possessions. I wondered if I had gone mad. I felt like running back to the safety and familiarity of my own country, where I had everything I wanted and could understand everyone. Aryan and I hadn't discussed the possibility of living in Australia though. He'd always been happy in India, with his friends and work. I was in search of transformation. For that to happen I really needed a change of environment despite the appeal of familiarity.

Then, to add to my fragile displacement, I found myself in a situation that left no doubt in my mind that I was now living a country that functioned entirely differently from the one I was used to. An experience involving an insidious, everyday activity that no level of Indian society was immune to – corruption. Perhaps there was such a thing as a 'real India' experience after all.

I had to collect three boxes that I'd sent as unaccompanied baggage from the cargo complex at Mumbai airport. Right from the start, the process was fraught with difficulties. We tried calling the airline responsible for the baggage, only to receive a recorded message saying the number had changed. All the new numbers that were given failed to connect.

More confusion awaited inside the customs compound. A large board, detailing the steps required to complete the customs clearance process, occupied prime position at the entrance. Based on the number of men everywhere, in various states of filling out forms, queuing and waiting, the process seemed every bit as complicated as the board suggested.

A man presented himself to us. 'I'm a customs agent. I'll kindly do the needful for 2900 rupees (nearly $100),' he announced.

There was little alternative but to engage his services. We managed to negotiate the fee down to 2200 rupees and asked him to proceed.

'What do you have in your boxes?' the agent asked.

'Shoes, books, kitchen and household items.'

He seemed satisfied with my answers as he recorded them on the forms. That was, until he saw the itemised packing lists I'd taped onto the sides of my boxes.

'You have electrical items in these boxes!' he confronted me.

'Yes, a used printer, DVD player and toaster. What's the problem?'

'Madam, these are not household items, they are dutiable electrical items! You've made a false customs declaration. This is a very bad matter. How could you do this? My whole family business could be brought into disrepute because of this!' he shouted.

I was shocked. 'I didn't make a false statement. These are household items. How was I supposed to know that electrical items have to be declared separately? I've stated on the packing lists what's in my boxes. Besides, these are used appliances. Surely, duty isn't payable on three used household appliances?' I argued back.

At that point, a customs officer arrived to inspect my boxes. He unceremoniously rifled through and pulled out the contents, while continuing the lecture about my undeclared electrical items. Another customs officer noticed my books on palmistry.

'Madam, you read my hand,' he excitedly extended his hand to me. What I naïvely expected would be a straightforward process of collecting my belongings was turning into a fiasco.

One of the customs officers took me to see the chief customs officer.

'I'll charge you duty on the DVD player and the toaster, but not the printer,' he decided.

The amount of duty payable was agreed to be an arbitrary 1000 rupees ($30). I was more confused than ever.

'Happy?' he asked, as if he were doing me a huge favour.

Of course, I wasn't happy. I became even less happy when I was told it was lunchtime. The clerk I had to pay the duty to wouldn't be back for another 40 minutes. To fill in the time, Aryan and I went to have lunch. The only option was the stuffy staff canteen, crowded with unappealingly aromatic men.

After finally giving everyone their money, I mistakenly thought we'd be able to take the boxes and leave. Not so. While standing under a huge sign, which warned that bribes were illegal, our customs agent blithely asked me for a bribe.

'Madam, please give me 300 rupees ($10). It will take care of the trouble you caused me and the other officers by making a misleading statement.'

I was incredulous.

'Madam, kindly be a little generous,' he insisted.

'You should be giving me money to cover the cost of the medical treatment I'll need to recover from this ordeal,' I retorted. 'I should also report you to the appropriate authority as this sign says!'

Sensing that the matter could cause the day to drag on even longer, I offered him a deal.

'100 rupees, take it or leave it.'

After much debate he took it. 'You drive a hard bargain, madam.'

Was this the Indian way of making me feel better about his win and my loss?

Corruption is extremely common and well tolerated in India, despite the occasional public outcry. The reason is often hard for foreigners to understand. In a country where there's such a scarcity of resources, many Indians are more concerned about the end result rather than the means to get there. Western notions of morality rarely apply. It's considered bad if someone has to pay a bribe, but good if the bribe yields the desired outcome. It hurts my head, too, when I try to figure that out.

The prevalence of corruption proliferated in the years after India

achieved independence. Politicians indulged in all manner of corrupt acts, unpunished by deficient legislation that produced no
conclusive reprisal. Bureaucrats, noticing the corruption at the highest levels, started following the example themselves, justifying that
if India's leaders are doing it, it cannot be wrong.

As corruption spread through the administration, ordinary
Indians increasingly felt like they were living in an atmosphere
of corruption. They began to see nothing wrong with it either. It
became something that was simply necessary in order to get ahead
and get things done.

It took me around five days to start settling in. I realised the
cause of my anguish: while my heart was in India, my head was still
well and truly back in the western world. Not only was I imposing
my western standards on everything, I was looking externally for
my happiness and focusing on what I'd given up, not what I'd be
gaining. I'd again developed attachments to so-called 'luxuries' and
'wants', and was struggling to let them go.

'Remember how you said you felt, being stuck in the office every
day in Melbourne,' Aryan gently reminded me.

Oh, so true! I'd hated it to the point I wanted to run out of there
screaming. But it's easy to forget those feelings when you are totally
consumed by what's in front of you. Rather than letting my dream
of the different life I wanted play out, I was struggling to control
exactly how it should be. I was reluctant to give up anything, such
as my comforts, to achieve it. Again, the dreaded western mentality was lurking. I wanted everything and wanted it immediately. In
India, everything takes time and it's extremely difficult to control
the outcome of anything. The easiest way forward is acceptance and
surrender, and appreciation of the idea of impermanence.

The troubled feelings wouldn't last forever, I told myself. Nor
would the situation always be the same. Aryan and I were establishing

our lives in Mumbai; it was bound to be difficult in the beginning. We were, after all, starting from nothing. It would get better.

I had to trust in my dream and the outcome. It was also apparent that the more I sat around thinking about what needed to be done, the longer the dark cloud would continue to hang over my head and overwhelm me.

I threw myself into daily life to absorb myself, and to make a home for us – cleaning the apartment, shopping for decorations and food, unpacking my belongings and cooking. All this gave me back some control over the smaller things in my life and made a huge difference.

The apartment started looking bright and cheery, and just seeing all my books on the shelves was comforting. I began noticing and appreciating the little things: a sparrow on the window ledge, the way the apartment lit up in the midday sun, the quiet from not being located on a main road, the groovy chandelier and the smooth feeling of the Indian granite benches in the kitchen. Back home, I would have overlooked these little things in pursuit of the bigger, perfect picture.

The thought of meeting Aryan's family terrified me, but it wasn't something that I could avoid for long. They'd graciously given me time to settle in but were very eager to meet. I was petrified! I had absolutely no idea what I was supposed to say or do, and I so badly wanted them to like me. There were no western customs and manners to fall back on in such a situation, plus there was the further complication of Aryan's parents not speaking English. Aryan's idea of moral support was to warn me that his dad was scary, didn't talk much and that he probably wouldn't even say anything to me.

I was alarmed, but greatly curious about the people who had made Aryan the loving man who had captured my heart.

I dressed in a *salwaar kameez* for the occasion. Aryan's eldest sister,

Maliha, and her husband came in their car to take us to the family apartment. Maliha was tiny with huge, sparkly brown eyes. I felt like an odd, white giant standing next to her. Despite Aryan's reassurances that she spoke English, Maliha addressed me in Hindi. I struggled to find any words in reply. We were both as unsure and as nervous as each other. Her English had failed her, just as my Hindi had failed me.

I sat trembling with unease in the car, wondering what was in store. Even though it took well over an hour to travel to central Mumbai where Aryan's parents lived, I wished the journey would never end.

'*Baitho*,' Aryan's mum invited me to sit after we arrived. She was much taller than I expected, and wore her long dark hair tied back in a bun at the nape of her neck. Her delicately woven Orissa-style sari, in shades of blue, purple and pink, caught my eye.

'*Yeh sari sundar hai* (This sari is beautiful),' I complimented her.

She smiled and laughed happily. Aryan's dad also greeted me and smiled. He was diminutive, but with a body made strong from work. Could this really be the scary man Aryan referred to? I found it hard to believe. He definitely didn't act that way towards me. Perhaps Aryan felt the adversity between father and son that came from his inappropriate career choice and failure to live up to family expectations.

The fact that I spoke minimal Hindi saved me from the direct inquisition I would have otherwise encountered. When meeting the parents for the first time in India, it's usual for all manner of questions to be asked. Instead, much to my relief, Aryan's mum brought out the family photo albums. The pictures of the latest family wedding were so bright and colourful, capturing the joy of the occasion perfectly.

Aryan's second eldest sister, Amita, who was tall like his mother, displayed none of the shyness I was feeling. She chatted animatedly with me in perfect English about what was going on.

Later, we sat together on the floor in the living room to eat, while Aryan's mum waited on us. It was a delicious home-cooked dinner of chicken curry, rice and *daal*. We ate with our fingers. I couldn't help wishing that Aryan's mum would join us. But as is common in India, she only had her meal once everyone else was satisfied. It was her honour to make sure everyone was well fed and content. After dessert, Aryan's dad spoke to me.

'*Aur kuch chahiye?* (You want something more?)'

The question was unexpected. I froze.

'No, no, *nahin chahiye. Main khatam ho chuki* (It's not needed, I've already finished),' I stammered.

'It went great. You handled everything so well. Even my dad was smiling, and he hardly ever smiles. And see, my mum is taller than my dad, just like us,' Aryan said afterwards.

Comfortingly, Aryan's family reminded me of an Indian version of my own. Being from the country, my parents were genuine, simple and creative. Aryan clearly got his sunny nature and lack of pretension from his family. It was obvious how much love he'd received as a child and how secure that had made him feel.

Yet, he was very different from them. They were very traditional where he wasn't. I could see why he'd resisted his mother's attempts to arrange his marriage. His life experiences were worlds apart from a good, middle-class Indian girl of the same caste, especially one from the village. What would they have in common?

The day that Aryan's mum announced she was coming to see our apartment threw me into a major panic. As is the Indian way, she only informed us a couple of hours before she intended to arrive. Aryan wasn't even going to be there as he had some important errands to attend to.

'Can't you tell her to come another day? I'm not ready to be alone with your family,' I pleaded with him.

I felt so unprepared. I knew she wanted to find out how well I'd made the apartment into a home, and more importantly, how well I was looking after her son.

'It's impossible to tell family not to visit, especially parents,' Aryan insisted. There was no option but to deal with it as best as I could. I was terrified. All my fears about not being good enough and not being Indian surfaced. And how was I going to talk to her? My unreliable Hindi deteriorated rapidly when I was nervous.

I quickly tidied the apartment as much as possible before the knock on the door. My heart skipped a beat and I took a deep breath before opening the door. Aryan's mum was standing there with Maliha.

'*Andar aaiye* (Please come inside),' I said. A broad smile, which didn't reflect my inner turmoil, was plastered on my face.

'*Machi* (Fish),' his mum said, handing me a container. She'd kindly brought me some fish, marinated in her special homemade *masala* (spices) and ready to cook.

The inspection of the apartment commenced. It started with a thorough look at the contents of the kitchen cupboards and refrigerator, before a tour of the rest of the rooms. Aryan's mum then turned and spoke to me in a rapid string of Hindi. As I'd dreaded, I didn't understand a word. I stood there blinking dumbly as my mind tried to process the words.

'Cookbooks. She's asking if you have Indian cookbooks,' Maliha came to my rescue in English. She did speak quite a bit of English after all, it seemed, now that she was feeling more comfortable around me.

Relieved, I rushed into the kitchen and gathered a suitable collection of cookbooks.

'*Arre wah!* (Oh, wow, great!)' Aryan's mum was impressed.

Having gained some approval, I started to relax. I felt surprisingly comfortable in her presence. She wasn't at all intimidating. In fact, she joked a lot and was very funny. She merrily told me how she'd learned to say 'come here' in English. But then a friend had asked her what if she needed to tell someone to 'go there'. Her solution? She'd go there first and then tell them to come! Somehow, I managed to understand what she was saying.

By the time she left, I was sad to see her go. I knew the fear I felt about Aryan's family wasn't justified. Even though they didn't expect me to be Indian and weren't at all critical of me, I was hard on myself and judged myself more harshly than others did.

I'd been in Mumbai for almost two months when the universe rewarded me for being brave enough to leave my comfort zone. It showed me, via an unexpected and unusual email from a stranger, the gateway to my big dream. The sender was an Australian who wrote for the same website I did. She didn't get in touch merely to compliment me; she told me to apply for a position with an organisation that was part of the New York Times Company. They wanted someone to write and manage their Indian travel website. Preferably someone who was living in India, and had experience writing for the web and using content management systems.

I was stunned. A stranger had gone to the effort of writing to me to tell me about a job she thought I might be interested in! Not only was it a job that would suit me perfectly, it was one that combined everything that I was aspiring to: my own website and Indian travel. This job had both. And I'd be able to work from home.

The application process looked intense. The company wanted professional travel writers with published clips. They intended to select five candidates to take part in a two-week online preparation program, the outcome of which would determine who'd get the job. I'd have to learn about the company's editorial standards, prepare a sample website, write sample articles and blog posts, and publish them on the sample site using the company's templates and publishing tools. An editor would evaluate my work and decide who to hire at the end of the process.

For some reason, I was oddly undeterred. I sent in my application and was accepted into the program in a matter of hours. I would start in a week. Meanwhile, the company sent me hundreds of pages of instructions about how to use their publishing tools and what they wanted me to write. Hotel reviews, restaurant reviews, walking tours, lists of attractions, photo galleries – all of it original.

Madly, I sorted through all my travel photos, roamed around Mumbai compiling interesting walking tours and racked my brains to create appealing articles about the places I'd visited, stayed and eaten in. Twice, I worked through the night. Once, I worked continuously for over 24 hours with barely any breaks. I didn't even have a desk, so I sat with my laptop in a beanbag on the floor, papers spread out all around me. I'd never worked so hard or put so much effort into anything in my life. Somehow, from somewhere, energy kept flowing into me to allow me to continue.

When I received the email telling me that I'd been selected for the position, it felt like two years of wandering around India and questioning myself had culminated in something worthwhile. As the Dream Giver had promised, I'd been rewarded for my courage, and in a way greater than I could ever have imagined. I could hardly believe that I had been so blessed. I felt like weeping tears of relief and joy. I told my parents the good news, and they shared my excitement.

What I later discovered astounded me even more. The company usually gets hundreds of applicants for its positions, especially in the popular travel channel. And I was the person who got the job – I couldn't help feeling like the universe had manifested a miracle. I may have attracted the opportunity into my life with my thoughts and actions. But, like a genie in the fairytale creation process, a greater force had conspired to deliver it to me. There was no other way to view what had happened. I hadn't even been searching for a job; I was humbled and touched.

The event was indisputable proof that it really was possible to create my own reality. It was one thing to read about the power of attraction, but another to have it take place in my life. All I needed to do was persist and have faith in the power of the universe. The job couldn't have come at a better time. It provided us with a much needed source of income and kept me focused when the wearisome trials of daily life in Mumbai became too much.

Aryan had decided to prove to his family that he was responsible by working with his sister Maliha and her husband in their manufacturing business. It was expanding, and they were importing a computer-operated wire-cut machine to make engineering parts out of metal. Aryan would learn how to operate the machine, oversee the workshop and visit clients. The machine took months longer to arrive than expected. In the meantime, he did random DJ gigs when openings came up. There was no point looking for a permanent job as no one knew exactly when the machine would arrive. I also didn't want him to be out working late in clubs every night, while I was alone in our apartment.

Pieces were being moved around, and it was a period of great transition. I couldn't wait for some quiet, and for when things would settle down. But first, I would have to adjust to life in Maximum City, a city that seemed to have minimum middle ground. A city that's both addictive and repulsive at the same time. A city that takes so much, and yet gives so much.

Hiland Park, my first home in Kolkata, was the city's first luxury high-rise development. Located on the outskirts of the city, its gleaming white towers rose starkly from the vacant grassy surroundings.

The kitchen in my mostly unfurnished apartment was barely functional. It had no cupboards, no cooking utensils, no hot water, and no microwave oven to warm my food. The stove, as is common in Indian homes, was a portable silver cook top that looked like something you'd take camping.

I spent most of my free time with other volunteers who were staying in the neighbouring apartment, Tara (left) and Claudine (right).

Where I volunteered, the irrepressible Lakhi taught me how to reprimand people in Bengali. We were always laughing about something.

There were many open air markets in Kolkata, where fruit and vegetable vendors sold produce spread out on the ground before them or heaped onto tables. In the background, decrepit local buses trundled by. Here, underneath the Howrah Bridge, an arresting wholesale flower market overflowed with piles of bright yellow and orange marigold garlands.

My second home in Kolkata was an apartment on the first floor of a small residential building in Deshapriya Park, a typical Bengali middle-class neighbourhood. Unlike Hiland Park, it didn't have air conditioning, and I had the additional challenge of shopping at the local markets. In the evenings as the sun set, Aryan and I would sit on the terrace, drink beer, and talk about our lives.

Aryan and I took the train from Kolkata to Varkala, a two night journey. Train stations were hectic, as people fought their way aboard with steel trunks and jute sacks.

The guest house that I was managing in Varkala consisted of three bungalows on a large block filled with palm trees. We lived in one of the bungalows, and bought a small scooter to get around. It was a simple life.

Varkala Cliff featured a long winding stretch of cliff, with views that extended over the Arabian Sea. A paved footpath ran along the length of the cliff, bordered by coconut palms, touristy shops, beach shacks, hotels and guesthouses.

Kerala, proclaimed as 'God's Own Country', is like a world where time and tradition have stood still. The palm-fringed canals of the backwaters offer a kind of tranquility that's difficult to find anywhere else.

Many locals in Kerala are involved in the seafood industry. Fish is still caught by hand using nets, cast into the water by fishermen who go out into the water in rickety wooden canoes.

Aryan had no trouble finding work as a DJ in the beach shacks. There were many hot and sweaty nights, dancing under the stars. In the evenings, we often headed to the beach at the bottom of the Cliff to relax.

Our dog, named Scooby, kept away the intruders. He came to us as a small puppy but grew very big in the end. I still loved to pick him up though. Thankfully, the guest house owner was happy to keep him after we left.

When the season was over, Aryan and I took another long distance train from Varkala to Delhi. We'd accumulated an extra bag and now had eleven bags to transport with us. So much for travelling light!

Manali was very soothing to the soul. The small family-run guesthouse that we stayed in when we arrived, in the tiny village of Old Manali, was surrounded by blossoming cherry and apple trees. The snow had just cleared, but could still be seen on the nearby hills.

New Manali was every bit as commercialised as Old Manali was quaint. The main street was always filled with Indian holiday-makers, honeymooners, and snack vendors.

I couldn't handle the local meat market, with its cages of doomed chickens and carcasses of various animals hanging and lying everywhere.

Strangely enough, probably due to my country upbringing, live snakes didn't bother me. I wore them draped around my neck like fashion accessories, courtesy of the snake charmers that came to Manali from Rajasthan every year to make money from tourists.

The view from our apartment in Old Manali, which overlooked the Beas River, was magnificent. It was blissful to wake up to snow-capped peaks every morning.

After arriving in Mumbai from Manali, Aryan and I ate fresh *pav bhaji* from the snack stalls on Juhu beach. It was my first introduction to Mumbai street food, and it was yummy!

Different to Kolkata, in Mumbai generations of families are all crammed together in towering apartment buildings due to the lack of space. Our apartment building, in the middle-class suburb of Kandivali West, was less than five years old but like most buildings, its exterior wasn't well maintained. (Our apartment was the bottom left hand one.)

Inside, our apartment was decorated in bright but modest Indian style, with traditional low-to-the-floor seating. The grills on the windows, a feature of most Mumbai apartments, made it feel a little like being in a prison though.

Black and yellow auto rickshaws, which looked and sounded like giant bees, ruled the roads in the Mumbai suburbs. They could often be found bumper to bumper in the unyielding traffic. Going out in it, especially on the back of Aryan's motorbike, usually gave me a headache within half an hour.

The Mumbai local train can be impossibly crowded, reducing people to uncivilised behaviour in a bid to get on and off, as there's no room for movement.

I loved the Sunday Sundown Session at Aurus, a bar and restaurant on Juhu beach. Aryan loved the step there, which dramatically reversed our height difference much to the amusement of our friends.

At our Hindu wedding, my mum welcomed Aryan and put a red *tilak* (auspicious mark made out of *kumkum* powder) on his forehead.

I chose an Arabic design for the henna (*mehendi*) on my hands and arms, consisting of swirls and floral patterns.

Aryan looked very handsome in a turban. It was the first time I'd seen him wear traditional Indian dress.

I never imagined that on my wedding day, I'd look like Lord Jagannath during the Rath Yatra festival in Orissa, with a huge ornamental gold crown on my head.

As part of the wedding ceremony, Aryan dabbed red *sindoor* on my forehead as a mark of me being a married woman.

After the ceremony had finished, people threw flowers at us. It was a jubilant moment where we felt so relieved and happy.

*Right*: A complete change of clothes was required for the reception that followed straight after the wedding ceremony.
I put on the traditional red sari that I was so looking forward to wearing. Jewellery hung off almost every body part, and a packet of sparkling *bindis* had been stuck onto my hair. Less is definitely not more in an Indian wedding!
*Below*: One of my favourite wedding photos.

*Below*: The Taj Palace Hotel in Mumbai was one of the buildings under siege during the 26 November 2008 terrorist attack. Most of the heritage wing, including the dome, was destroyed by fire. It took two years to rebuild it. The incident left me, like many others, feeling tense and traumatised.

High altitude Spiti Valley, in northern Himachal Pradesh, was like a world within a world. The arid and barren landscape was scattered with small villages and monasteries.

The highlight of my trip to Spiti was a yak safari from village to village. A stocky, shaggy beast, the yak must be respected for its strength and temperamental nature. (Just ask my safari partner who was thrown off one, lost his turban in the mud, and damaged his ankle so badly he had to be transported back to a Delhi hospital!)

Hitting the road on the rickshaw challenge – driving an auto rickshaw from Chennai to Mumbai over two weeks – revealed some unexpected highway traffic. Overburdened bullock carts were a common enough sight.

However, the real surprise was two *sadhus* (Hindu holy men) and their elephant, on a pilgrimage by foot from south India to the holy town of Haridwar in the north.

Out of all places I'd been to in India, it was Udaipur, city of famed lakes and palaces that really captured my heart. The City Palace Complex, which the royal family still occupies, looks over Lake Pichola.

My room at the Shiv Niwas Palace hotel, which is part of the City Palace Complex, faced Lake Pichola. The view of the Lake Palace Hotel, a former summer palace of the royal family, was like out of a regal fairytale.

Ganesh Chaturthi is my favourite festival in Mumbai. All over the city, canopied roadside tents house immaculately and uniquely crafted displays of Lord Ganesh. The energy inside is tangibly powerful and calming. Devotees place piles of coconuts, fruit, and sweets at the Lord's feet to gain his blessings. On the last day of the festival, the statues of Lord Ganesh are carried from their podiums and given an exuberant send-off before being immersed into the ocean. There's music and dancing in the streets all night.

Buddhism is the dominant religion in many areas of far north India close to the Tibetan border, and Tibetan prayer flags are a common sight. Prayers and sacred mantras are written on the flags and when blown in the wind, it's believed that the energy will bring happiness and good health to everyone who sees them.

In Kerala, temple festivals are held all over the state from February to May. The feature of these festivals is the elephants, and some festivals have thirty or more on display.

# Maximum City Mayhem

MUCH to my dismay, the first thing to be taken away was our ceiling fans. A few months after we'd moved into our apartment, our landlord decided to repossess them for his new home. There was little we could do. Our rental agreement didn't include a list of fixtures and fittings, plus the landlord held our security deposit. Property rental laws are archaic in India, and full of pitfalls for tenant and landlord alike. While it's difficult for a landlord to remove an overstaying tenant, it can be as challenging to get the security deposit back from a landlord. Even if contracts are legally enforceable, it can take years or even decades for this to happen. A landlord has the right to set the amount of the security deposit payable by the tenant. In Mumbai it's often equal to the total rent for the whole eleven-month term of the agreement.

The rent on our apartment was 9000 ($220) rupees a month, and the security deposit a whopping 100,000 rupees ($2500). We'd also paid the standard one month's rental to the real estate broker for finding the apartment.

'I'll come and get the fans on Monday,' the landlord informed us. Monday came and went, and there was no sign of him. On Wednesday evening, he phoned again. 'I'll come and get the fans tomorrow. Call me after you've removed them and got them ready.'

It prompted familiar feelings of indignation. 'Not only has he not bothered to turn up when expected, he wants us to do his work for him and at short notice too,' I muttered. Surely these things shouldn't surprise me anymore. Where was my Indian commonsense?

Aryan just wanted to get the inevitable job done as soon as possible. At ten-thirty that night, we were surrounded by disassembled ceiling fans partially hanging from the ceiling and spread all over the floor. Dirt and dust sullied the tiles that I had freshly washed that day. I'd have to do it all again tomorrow. At least at that moment, I was spared from knowing that there wouldn't be any water to clean with.

The water supply was the second thing to be taken away. The watchman delivered the bad news to us the next morning when he knocked on our door.

'The water supply will be turned off in half an hour,' he informed us. Apparently some repair works were needed and the outage would only last two hours. Ten hours later, at 8 pm, the water supply was finally restored.

The next day, it was turned off again. The same routine continued for four days. Little did we know that it was the beginning of the end of our 24-hour water supply. The water mysteriously continued to go off at irregular and unannounced intervals. Various excuses were given by the watchmen, who were custodians of the water supply in the apartment complex. The tanks were being cleaned, a pipeline was being repaired, the municipal council wasn't supplying enough water.

Eventually, the water supply settled into a regular pattern. We got water for a few hours three times a day, and never any to flush the toilet. The water supply to the toilet had been completely cut off.

Having a 24-hour water supply was something I'd taken for granted all my life. I found this new way of living hard to fathom, especially in India's most progressive city. My whole day had to be planned around the water supply, and we had to fill large buckets full of water to pour down the toilet. I was even more perplexed that the landlord didn't seem particularly concerned about the problem.

I sent him disgruntled emails. 'We're paying you rent on an apartment that's supposed to have 24-hour water supply, and we're barely getting six hours of water a day. Please investigate.'

One evening, he turned up at our apartment unannounced.

'The municipal council isn't supplying enough water to the apartment complex,' he declared. 'The council has been diverting water away to new developments in the area. This is because the housing society registration formalities are yet to be completed, and the apartment complex doesn't have its own pipeline.'

The booming number of new real-estate developments in Mumbai had put further pressure on Mumbai's already scarce water supply. As a result, the municipal council didn't provide new apartment complexes with full water supply until their housing societies were properly registered. Never mind that the apartment complex had been built almost five years ago. The application for registration was still sitting in a notoriously inefficient council office somewhere.

'Once all the formalities are complete, the *paani ka* problem will be solved forever. It won't take much longer, just a few more months,' the landlord reassured us.

My tenuous Indian commonsense told me not to believe him.

'Anyway, you should be thankful you have a water storage tank. It's an excellent solution. Your apartment is the only apartment in the whole complex to have one,' the landlord enthused.

Our apartment did indeed have an overhead water storage tank, which could be directly filled from the water supply, when it was available, just by turning on a tap. However, its only outlet was a small tap in the far corner of the bathroom. It wasn't much use for washing dishes in the kitchen or taking a shower. I'd assumed that every apartment in our complex had one of those water storage tanks.

'Really? Why doesn't everyone install a water storage tank?' I asked.

'Oh, they're not allowed to. Overhead water storage tanks are not permitted in the apartments. I used to be a member of the housing society and I actively implemented a rule that banned the installation of overhead water storage tanks. But I installed a tank in my own apartment,' he concluded proudly.

'So how do the other residents store water?' I wanted to know.

'They have to put it in big drums and buckets.'

The outcome of the landlord's actions was predictable.

'An angry mob of residents gathered at the door of this apartment. They hammered on the door and threatened to beat me up. However, in reality, they couldn't do anything. I was a member of the housing society and had all the power,' he gloated.

I couldn't believe not only the unfairness and hypocrisy of the situation, but also the landlord's self-interest. He wasn't at all concerned that he'd deprived all the residents of an important convenience. Instead, he was supremely satisfied that he had something that they didn't.

For decades, Mumbai had been a magnet to Indians from all over the country who were seeking a better life. Her arms wide open, she'd generously welcome anyone who had a dream and find a place for them in her fold, even if it was merely a patch of pavement. She adjusted. But overburdened, she now harshly forced them to fend for themselves, in any way they could. One person's loss was always another's gain.

Just ask anyone who's ridden the 'Mumbai local'.

I'd thought India's long-distance trains showed an unfettered part of humanity, but Mumbai's local rail network exposed me to a very raw and uncompromising side of the city's citizens, where the mentality of scarcity caused self-interest to reign supreme. For the harried and tense passengers, missing a train meant wasted precious time. Time that could be devoted to some other important task.

The Mumbai local transports around eight million commuters a day, making it a lifeline as well as a source of loathing. Not for the faint of heart, it has the ability to make people shudder merely at the mention of its name. Trains can be impossibly overcrowded, the doors never close and constantly have passengers hanging out of them. People even travel sitting on the roof. It's the cheapest and quickest way to get from one end of Mumbai to the other, about 50 kilometres from north to south. Keen to feel independent, capable, and a part of the city, I was undeterred from becoming acquainted with it.

Mumbai's train stations are worn and unkempt, sullied by the multitude of passengers who traipse through them every day and the homeless who dwell on their platforms. The fragrance of sweat, urine and ubiquitous spices is unmistakable. On my first train trip to Churchgate in south Mumbai, Aryan delivered me to the correct platform at the station, to a place where a large group of women had congregated.

'This is where the ladies' compartment will arrive. Make sure you get on here, and be prepared to push,' he warned.

The Mumbai local had separate compartments for women to spare them from the unwelcome advances of misbehaving men. However, being a woman certainly did not make one a lady in the inaptly named ladies' compartment. As the train ground to a halt, the crowd grouped together and surged towards the doors en masse, screeching like parrots. Passengers who were trying to get off were unceremoniously pushed aside as the unruly mob forced its way on, before again separating and scrambling for a seat. An elderly woman sitting on the floor was trampled in the process. She shouted out, but was completely ignored.

As I stood, barricaded by bodies in the aisle, I watched a fight unfold between two women. One had claimed a seat by placing her handbag on it, but the other had removed the bag and sat down. It was a bold move, and one that brought swift reprisal. A shouting match ensued, but the offending woman refused to budge. The other woman flew into attack, pinching the woman's arms and scratching her neck. The spectacle had me transfixed, and I blatantly stared like the most curious of Indians. Finally, another passenger intervened to prevent a brawl.

The lack of etiquette wasn't just restricted to overburdened facilities such as the local train or to the less privileged part of the population. Absence of manners was also prevalent at the shopping mall where I bought my groceries. Hefty Indian housewives overlooked me in the queue at the vegetable weighing counter. They waddled past me and attempted to hand their single items to the clerk as if I didn't exist and without any acknowledgement or asking if I minded. On occasions, I even saw mothers deploying their children to do it for them.

Venturing out was like going into a battlefield, where I constantly had to fight to get ahead. When hoards of women barged onto the train and jammed the exit, without allowing anyone to disembark first, I ruthlessly grabbed them and shoved them aside so I could get off.

'*Tum paagal ho,*' they shouted at me, calling me crazy. To me, the way they'd forced themselves aboard without any regard for disembarking passengers was crazy. I shouted back at them in return. The city made me as harsh and as unforgiving as it itself could be.

Meanwhile, at back at the apartment complex, occupants on the upper floors of our building seemed to mistake our balcony for a large garbage bin. They carelessly threw their garbage out their windows and onto it. Empty food packets, drink bottles, and even old magazines ended up there.

We obviously weren't the only aggrieved residents. An amusingly worded notice appeared one day, taped to the lift and noticeboard in the lobby:

> It has been observed that flat owner in B wing are throwing waste material like plastic bottles, Plastic Bags, peace of Bread, other dirty things throw Window. They are also splitting in Corner of Staircase. It is a request to all Flat owner to behave like educated, qualified, and civilised person. Let us keep our Building clean then Mumbai and then Country. From: A humble request from Flat Owner of B Wing.

Unfortunately more than a mere notice was required to get people to change their habits. The paradox is that Indians aren't as unclean as they appear to be. It's just that for many, what constitutes cleanliness – or lack of it – is very different from the west.

According to Hindu scriptures, cleanliness is necessary for spiritual advancement. The body and mind must be kept clean, like a temple. Any substance that comes out of the body is considered polluting. As a result, Hindus try and expel as much as they can from their bodies. The chorus of gagging sounds that can be heard across India every morning as people clear their sinuses and bronchial passages reveals how enthusiastically they go about it.

Inside the home, the kitchen is traditionally considered sacred, as food from the kitchen is offered to the gods before it's eaten. So care must be taken to wash and purify the body before entering the kitchen and cooking in the morning. In very conservative households, people of a lower caste aren't permitted to enter the kitchen. Women even refrain from entering it when they're menstruating.

As can be expected, people are fastidiously clean inside their kitchens, paying as much attention to its cleanliness as they do their bodies. Utensils are scrubbed until they're sparkling and rubbish is quickly removed. That's where it ends though. Once all offending substances are outside the body and the home, they're no longer of concern.

To get me out of the apartment and distract me from my frustrations, Aryan took me around Mumbai on the back of his motorbike. Aksa Beach was only ten minutes away from where we lived, and it soon became my favourite place to go. During the week, it was relatively deserted, the shore dominated only by a resort and a few snack stands. We sat on the sand eating *vada pav* (spicy fried mashed potatoes in a bun, otherwise known as the Indian burger) and drinking fresh lime soda.

In Bandra and Juhu, we staked out the homes of India's Bollywood stars. As unfamiliar with them as I was, I was still fascinated by the huge part they played in people's lives and how the glitzy movie industry contributed so much to making Mumbai the city of dreams. Every Sunday evening for almost two decades, fans gathered outside iconic actor Amitabh Bachchan's house, *Jalsa*, in Juhu.

Whenever he was home, he routinely appeared on his balcony to greet them, causing a mini traffic jam in the process.

Yet, for most of the part, suburban Mumbai lacked the charm of south Mumbai. Auto rickshaws weren't allowed in south Mumbai, but in the suburbs, they ruled the roads. The sheer volume of the incessant traffic spewed out noise and pollution.

The refined residents of south Mumbai (or south Bombay, as they still preferred to call it) very rarely crossed the invisible border into the suburbs. There was little to attract them. South Mumbai catered to their worldly wants with foreign-replica restaurants, designer stores and exclusive clubs. But, at the other extreme, it also provided opportunity for those less fortunate, such as the barely literate *dabba-walas* and *dhobi-walas,* who were vital for the city's functioning. It amazed me how rich and poor existed alongside each other, their lives intertwined in many ways.

The thousands of *dabba-walas,* men who carry containers, delivered around 200,000 tins of freshly cooked food to the city's office workers for lunch, at the same time every day. Rather than eat out, workers prefer to have home-cooked lunches made by their wives or mothers. Every morning, with precision, the *dabba-walas* collect the tins from residences and return the same tins empty in the afternoon, travelling by bicycle, on foot and by train. I marvelled at the skill of these dedicated men, decked out in crisp white *kurta pyjama* suits and caps, for whom the usual concept of Indian time proudly didn't apply.

The *dhobi-walas* also had a remarkable system in place at their huge open air laundry, the *dhobi ghat* which borders one side of Mahalaxmi railway station. Their job is just as arduous, if not more so. They spend most of their waking hours standing knee-deep in seemingly endless rows of concrete troughs filled with chemicals, manually scrubbing and beating the dirt out of close to a million items of laundry every day. The *dhobi ghat* has become a popular tourist attraction, offering a fascinating glimpse into the inner workings of the city. One day, I was brave enough to venture down from the viewing spot on the bridge above it and sneak a peek inside. Hundreds of families live and work there, in the colourless grey interior, surrounded by mounds of sheets and shirts. Instead of toys, a group of three barefooted youngsters played with a chicken. When they saw me, they ran over and, smiling, offered it to me to hold in a heart-warming gesture.

There is no doubt that life in Maximum City can be brutal for those without resources. They toil endlessly just to survive, with very few pleasures as we know them in life. However, even those who are better off can't completely escape the city's foibles. Although I'd been blessed with a job that gave my life meaning, Mumbai refused to yield to my love of order and control. After welcoming me, it was apparent that the city was determined to test me and my worthiness to be there. It did it slowly by confounding me in a different way on a daily basis, pushing me closer and closer to the brink of insanity.

Just when I'd finally accepted the absence of our water supply, the *kachra-wala* (cleaner) knocked on the door wanting to hook a hose up to the tap in our toilet and use the water to wash down the first-floor landing and stairwell. Pouring water everywhere then brushing it away with a broom is a common method of cleaning in India.

'*Lekin paani nahi hai* (But there's no water),' I tried to tell him. I'd barely had time to finish washing the lunchtime dishes before it was cut off.

I was wrong though. The *kachra-wala* connected the hose to the tap, turned it on, and water came gushing out. From where, I had no idea. Another of the landlord's illicit storage tanks? He spent the next fifteen minutes hosing down the landing and stairwell.

Water poured down the stairs and out into the lobby. A couple of hours later, I went outside. The stairwell and landing were still wet, but dirtier than ever from the mud off people's shoes where they'd walked. I shook my head in dismay.

It was the Internet that actually troubled me the most, particularly because I constantly needed it for work. Most days brought a different issue with the connection. If not the cable, then the server. Or maintenance work. Or outages that would last from a few hours to a whole day, the duration of which could never accurately be predicted.

'Half an hour, madam,' I was invariably told when I called up to complain.

To add insult to injury, the service provider deliberately disconnected the Internet once a month while the account was settled. Instead of issuing a bill that we could pay, they sent a representative around to collect the cash. Once, it took days for someone to come and get it, and therefore for the connection to be reinstated. I had to go to an Internet café on a number of occasions to meet deadlines. The ongoing connectivity problems made me so enraged that I stormed into the company's head office and demanded an explanation.

I hardly recognised the angry person I'd become at times. It felt like I was embroiled in a twisted, dysfunctional relationship. Deep down, I did love India. But on the surface we continued to wage war on each other. There was yelling and sulking, and a desire to part ways. Coming from an orderly country that valued courtesy, I found it difficult to reconcile myself to the messy way that the city operated and thoughtless manner in which people behaved. I really struggled to make sense of it all.

Yet, I didn't want to give up on India. Her whims were part of her appeal. She was untamed. A land of mystery and possibility, where something different and interesting happened every day. There was only one way forward, and that was to bear with the daily trials and tribulations. Eventually, hopefully, I'd notice them less. I'd become accepting and detached. Then, maybe India and I could reconcile and reach common ground.

# When Strangers Call

NO doubt I would have dealt with the daily challenges a lot better if our apartment was a sanctuary I could retreat to. For me, home is a place to escape from the outside world, a peaceful haven where I can relax and rejuvenate myself. But not in Mumbai. I didn't live in a fashionable, foreigner-filled suburb such as Bandra; I lived in conservative, middle-class Kandivali West. Very rarely was a foreigner seen there. As a result, I was a spectacle.

I'd accepted that unwanted attention would be a part of life in India when I went out, but I'd always been able to close the door on it. When I was safely ensconced inside, I could dress how I wanted and be myself, away from prying eyes. Yet, at the apartment complex, a constant and steady stream of people knocked on our door.

Children wanted to collect cricket balls and shuttlecocks that regularly landed on our balcony. Tradesmen wanted to collect tools that they'd accidentally dropped from higher levels. The newspaper, cable TV and Internet providers wanted to collect payment. The landlord wanted to collect his mail.

As is the case with many people in India, the landlord was disconcertingly fond of unannounced visits and not turning up when he was supposed to. The informal and open nature of Indian culture, along with the ancient Sanskrit phase *Atithi Devo Bhava* (A Guest is like God) that's ingrained in Indian minds, means that visitors have been dropping in on each other unannounced for centuries. In big families with blurred boundaries, unannounced visits keep alive the sense of kinship. They also provide interest for bored housewives with nothing to do all day apart from cook and watch *saas-bahu* (mother-in-law and daughter-in-law) serials on the TV.

One hot day, I was in the middle of washing the floors while the water supply was on. There was a knock on the door. Dressed in shorts and a singlet, sweating profusely and showing an indecent amount of leg, I opened the door to the landlord. I had no option but to invite him in.

'Please sit, I'll be back in a minute,' I told him while I dashed into the bedroom to put on something more appropriate. Not being a tea drinker, I didn't have any tea or biscuits to give him. The only thing I could offer him was water.

The landlord's mother also dropped in unannounced once in a while. The first time she did so, she headed straight for the kitchen like every other Indian woman. There was some bread sitting on the bench.

'What do you eat for breakfast and lunch? Do you eat this bread for both meals? It's not healthy. You should have *roti* (Indian bread) only,' she informed me.

'But it's so much trouble to make it,' I said. Aryan's second eldest sister, Amita, had given me a demonstration. I'd tried it a few times but found the process messy and painstaking, as dough got under my nails and stuck to my rings.

'No, no, no, it's quick once you know how to do it properly. I will show you.'

She went over to my shelves and started searching for the ingredients.

'These shelves are very badly organised. Look here, I will sort out all your containers for you.' She started pulling them down, taking out their contents and changing them around. I could hardly believe it. Here was a stranger completely rearranging the containers on my shelves – never mind if I approved!

Although I preferred that they let me know when they were coming, I didn't mind the occasional presence of the landlord or his mother too much. He was a young engineer with an interest in spirituality and compelling things to say, despite his staggering self-interested behaviour. She was a warm and intelligent school-teacher who often brought me clothes.

The landlord's wife, however, possessed none of these graces. The first time I met her was during an unannounced visit. I was still in bed, so Aryan answered the door and let her in.

'Where is your wife? I want to see her,' she demanded.

'She's not up yet.'

Undeterred, the wife opened our bedroom door and barged in. I was stunned. I was half-asleep and half-dressed in bed, with a woman who I'd never seen before standing in front of me.

The wife's second unannounced visit was as bad as the first. It happened on the day my grandmother's funeral was taking place back home in Australia.

'You get the door,' I told Aryan as I ran for the bedroom.

I'd been crying and really didn't want to see anyone. Again, she came looking for me. When she opened the door to the bedroom and entered, I could barely even manage to smile at her. Feeling terrible, I later explained to the landlord what had happened.

'She must have been coming to offer her condolences,' he joked. Then he added, 'She's a little less cultured in her mentality.'

The landlord's excuse was a legitimate one. Unfortunately, many of the people living in our apartment building had the same mentality as his wife. There were six apartments on our floor, including ours. One was vacant, and one was a childcare centre. I very rarely saw the people who occupied the apartment next to ours, so was never sure who lived there. However, the remaining two apartments housed a rotund man who roared like a bull when he fought with his wife, and an elderly Maharastran lady and her husband.

The elderly lady who lived in the flat at the end of the hallway liked to go on frequent walks around the complex. It didn't take her long to come and investigate who we were. If she saw us returning home, she'd follow us back to our apartment and then come inside. Although she only spoke a few words of English, it didn't deter her from talking to me.

She took to knocking on our door at all hours of the day and night. It wouldn't have been so bad if her visits had a beneficial purpose. Rather, she sat and looked over my shoulder while I tried to write, or walked around the apartment and snooped. Nowhere was off limits, even our bedroom where my desk was located.

During one visit, she pulled me aside.

'Eat lots of pomegranates to have a baby. Shhhh, don't tell your husband,' she whispered conspiratorially.

I didn't dare mention to her that we weren't even married yet.

She was very persistent. Another day, I was deep into my work, trying to finish an article so that I could go out and do the grocery shopping. There was a knock at the door. Aryan let her in, and she promptly came over to my desk.

'You like the Big B, Amitabh Bachchan?' she started chatting to me about the Bollywood actor. I nearly screamed in annoyance.

Aryan was about to go out and leave her with me.

'No way! You're not going anywhere,' I shouted at him in rapid English.

She didn't understand what I said but it was obvious that I was tense. She turned to Aryan and asked him what was bothering me.

'Aunty, I have to go out and do the shopping, so I have to get ready,' I insisted to her. She made no move at all to leave, and just sat there talking to Aryan.

Aryan didn't feel like he could tell her to go away because she was an elderly woman. It was a matter of respect. I had no idea how to handle the situation because it was something I'd never experienced before.

The intrusions gradually started bothering Aryan as well. Early one morning the neighbour's knocking got him out of bed. She was standing at the door with a group of workmen in tow. They needed access to our balcony. Hours later they returned and came marching through our bedroom. I'd just gotten up and was still in my nightwear. I had no chance to make myself look respectable at all. Apparently, they'd dropped a tool and it was lodged somewhere below our window. They came back a third time, again unannounced, carrying a huge magnet to retrieve it.

'I can't stand this any longer. How am I supposed to live like this?' I fumed to Aryan.

I couldn't relax. I felt I had to be appropriately dressed at all times, ready to receive whoever came knocking. There was no privacy and no solitude. In a country where modesty was important, and where I was constantly the centre of attention, I felt extremely awkward if someone dropped by and I wasn't dressed to Indian standards. Yet, the weather was so hot, I didn't want to cover my legs and shoulders at home like I had to when I was out. I also needed to be left alone to do my work. The problem was that people couldn't fathom that I had a proper job and worked from home.

'It's your home, you should dress how you want. Don't worry about the people who come to the door,' Aryan said.

He was very casual about what he wore in the apartment. I didn't have the same freedom, particularly as it was often men who knocked on the door unannounced. I didn't want to further add to the common perception that foreigners were indecent. As it turned out, all these intrusions were small annoyances compared to what was in store. I really got to experience what an uncultured mentality was like when new neighbours moved into the vacant flat next door.

They first made their presence known by knocking on our door to borrow matches for the *puja* (prayer) they were performing to bless their apartment. A couple of days later, they returned. I heard a commotion coming from their side of the building. When I opened the door to see what was going on, I realised it was the new neighbours having a heated altercation with a real estate broker. There were at least six of them, and they were all yelling loudly at the broker. The only words I could understand were *'paisa'* (money) and *'chabi'* (key).

They moved in a few days later, and I became acquainted with them very quickly because they knocked on my door almost every ten minutes.

*'Andar se yeh darvaza bandh karo, aur yeh aur yeh nikal do* (Close this door from inside, and remove this and this),' they ordered in Hindi while pointing to the doormat and rubbish bin. Their furniture was being delivered and space needed to be cleared.

Then they wanted to borrow a small table so that their electrician could stand on it to install their ceiling fans. Then they wanted to connect a cable to our power supply and use our power until theirs was turned on a day or two later.

My Hindi wasn't that good. Had I understood properly? They wanted to use our power supply? Disbelieving, I phoned Aryan, who was at work. It was exactly what they wanted. And Aryan, being such a kind-hearted guy, agreed. Never mind the fact that it's illegal.

Not long after, there was another knock on the door. The new neighbours wanted to borrow a portable fan to cool themselves until their ceiling fans were installed. I really didn't understand what they were asking for this time, so they came inside our apartment to look for what they wanted. All our rooms and possessions were thoroughly examined and exclaimed upon, even after it was apparent that we didn't have a portable fan.

'*Yeh kitne ka hai*? (This costs how much?)' they frequently and brazenly asked.

My privacy totally invaded, I started feeling anxious. It was exacerbated by the fact that 'forbidden' items were sitting visibly on our kitchen bench – a collection of wine bottles was lined up on display. This was a Gujarati building, and the neighbours were Gujaratis. Besides meat, alcohol was taboo in most Gujarati homes because of the puritan influence of Mahatma Gandhi, who'd lived in the state of Gujarat. In fact, Gujarat was a dry state. The sale of alcohol was banned there. The last thing I wanted was to be on the receiving end of any disapproval or complaints for sullying the apartment building.

'I'm going to look inside your apartment now,' I announced to the neighbours, to get them out of our apartment. They seemed delighted at the prospect.

I was astounded when I reached their kitchen. It was engulfed in a sea of silver. Every surface was occupied by a silver tin. And there were more silver tins, of various shapes and sizes, still waiting to be unpacked out of very large boxes. What could they possibly keep in so many tins? My dismay must have been apparent, because everyone started laughing.

I discovered that there would be four people living in the apartment. Two parents, their son and his new wife. The son and his wife slept in the only bedroom, while the parents slept in the living room. Wanting to be friendly, I bought some *ladoos* (sweets) to welcome them while I was doing the grocery shopping. Very innocently, based on my experience with neighbours back home, I thought that this would draw to a close my interactions with them. New neighbours were usually greeted, offered assistance and rarely seen again.

Little did I know that my goodwill gesture was like inviting my new neighbours into my life at any time of day or night. It earned me an immediate request to join them in their apartment, where the usual questions were asked.

'What are you doing in India?'

'Can you speak Gujarati?'

'Can you cook?'

'What can you cook?'

'Have you cooked dinner yet?'

'Do you have children?'

Exhausted from the inquisition, I was glad to retreat to my apartment.

Early the next morning, the knocking recommenced. The new neighbours wanted to warm some milk for their *chai*. Apparently, as well as electricity, they didn't have gas either. Or hot water.

It was very bad timing. I was in the process of reheating some leftover chicken for Aryan's breakfast. Quickly, but not quickly enough, I tried to put the chicken back into the fridge. The wine bottles were still on full display where they couldn't help but be noticed.

Later that day came a request for ice.

When family members came to visit the new neighbours, they wanted me to individually meet every one of them.

'*Aao, aao* (Come, come),' they insisted, almost forcibly dragging me out of my apartment. After being examined and questioned by five family members, I was told that more would be arriving the next day. Where could I possibly escape to?

But that wasn't all. As I was going back to my apartment, the mother cornered me and started talking to me animatedly in Hindi. I would like to give her the benefit of the doubt, but I do believe she told me to clean the dirt on the floor in the hallway. I could understand her references to cleaning and how dirty the floor was, and the pointed way in which she looked at me.

'*Kachra-wala aaega* (The cleaner will come),' I tried to tell her.

I certainly wasn't going to clean a mess I didn't make. Besides, I'd become aware of The Rule: the only dirt that matters in India is the dirt that's actually inside the home.

My thoughts about what the mother might have said became more believable the next morning. By 10 a.m. we'd received three knocks on our door. The first came at 8 to tell us our newspaper was waiting on our doorstep. We were well aware of that; it was there every day. On the second knock, she told us to keep our rubbish bin inside because it looked dirty. No matter that everyone kept their bins outside. The third knock was from the daughter-in-law, who wanted me to go to their apartment.

'Not possible, she has work,' Aryan replied.

I'd made him answer all the knocks on the door, including one while he was shaving. I hoped the new neighbours would see that they were inconveniencing us. I thought that if I refused to show my face, they'd get the message that I was unavailable and didn't want to mingle with them.

'You need to start making up excuses. Tell them you have guests coming or that you have to go out or have other plans. Anything to stop them from bothering you,' Aryan advised.

He was telling me to adopt what I had termed the Indian lying technique. This was the same technique he'd used to deal with prying passengers on our long-distance train trips. At its worst, people in India agreed to things that they had no intention of doing, and gave misleading answers. I struggled to accept that lying was a survival tactic in India, and that it wasn't considered immoral or unethical. In contrast, many Indians believed that having a boyfriend was much more immoral than not telling the truth.

When the new neighbours' kitchen became functional, they were kind enough to deliver some freshly cooked vegetarian Gujarati food to us to eat. I was wary about showing too much gratitude, though.

'You need to be careful,' Aryan's sister Maliha had warned us when we told her about what was going on. 'If you're too friendly, they'll ask you to accommodate their guests if there's not enough room in their apartment.'

I was incredulous. Surely that couldn't be true? They would ask us to accommodate strangers in our small one-bedroom apartment?

Aryan confessed to the elderly Maharastran woman down the hall how much the new neighbours were troubling us. She didn't like them either.

'Rumour has it that they used to live in a *chawl*,' he reported back to me. 'That's why they don't know how to behave properly.'

The knocking on our door declined markedly. The reason why wasn't pleasing though. The neighbours had started leaving their apartment door wide open. As they sat in their living room, they had a direct view of everything that went on outside their apartment, including when I went in and out of mine.

'*Kyaa karti hain*? (What are you doing?)' they asked me as I placed heavy bags of groceries on the floor while trying to quickly unlock my door.

On one occasion, they were adamant that I go into their apartment. They wanted to show me how they'd decorated it. As I looked around, it was obvious that they'd been busy acquiring garish and kitsch items. They were terribly proud of them too. The centrepiece was a sparkly light fitting on the ceiling that changed colours. It looked like they were planning on having a disco in their apartment.

I began to form my own theory about them.

'You know what I think?' I said to Aryan. 'They've come from a *chawl*, and they're spending all the dowry money that they got from their son's wedding.'

He laughed. 'You could be right.'

What other reason could there be for them to move into a rented apartment, and spend large sums of money on adorning it in such an ostentatious way?

Finally, the day came when the unwanted attention pushed me over the edge. The son knocked on our door, for no apparent reason apart from the fact that he and his family were going into their apartment. The mother came over and quizzically looked me up and down. I stood there unwashed, dressed in cargo pants and a T-shirt.

'*Kyaa karti hain*? (What are you doing?)' she asked, as usual.

'What are YOU doing? Why are you asking me that?' I wanted to shout at her. Instead, I stood there stunned, like an animal caught in the headlights. What could I possibly say? I'm at home, dressed comfortably, minding my own business. Then I'm disturbed for no reason, looked at strangely and asked what I'm doing. Maybe she thought I was dressed in men's clothes or something.

I made up my mind not to answer the door anymore. The resolution wasn't so easy to put into practice. Only hours later, I was washing clothes in the bathroom, semi-undressed and drenched. I had put on psychedelic trance music at high volume. Over the music came a banging on the door at an equally loud volume. I tried ignoring it but it wouldn't stop. Exasperated, I put a towel around myself and yanked open the door. It was the daughter-in-law's sister. She just wanted to say hi. It was all too much for me.

'Please, can't you see that I'm busy?' I exploded and slammed the door shut. Surely no Indian would have to put up with being such a constant source of attention?

After I calmed down, I deeply regretted my rude behaviour. I cursed myself for failing to deal with the circumstances better. The vexing contact with the new neighbours had become the focal point of my life, and it was making me feel miserable and even more out of place.

It was only when I shared my burden with an American friend, Justin, that I got some light-hearted relief. He was living and working in Mumbai. Back in America, he'd taught yoga to Linda whom I'd met in Kolkata.

'They're just not cool,' he summed it up. 'But they're only doing what they're used to as part of their culture.'

The more I thought about it, the more I realised he was right. If I lived next door to a Bollywood celebrity and hounded her day and night, dragging her into my apartment to meet my relatives and constantly knocking on her door to see what she was doing, no doubt she'd soon become irritated. Such behaviour would definitely not be cool. My neighbours were acting the same way towards me. Forget fame, I'd much rather have fortune!

Thankfully, just as night follows day, Aryan had many friends in Mumbai and they were cool. Most of them were in the music industry and, accustomed to foreigners, they treated me the same as they did anyone else. Being out with them in Mumbai's vast nightlife helped me stay sane. As too did the neighbours gradually losing interest in me while I increasingly ignored them.

# A Social Chameleon

THE familiar smell of cigarette smoke wafted down in greeting, as Aryan climbed the stairs to the second floor of Leopold's Café in Colaba. Behind him, the doorman attempted to control the mob that had gathered, impatiently waiting and hoping to be granted entry. It was so packed inside that people were milling around in the stairwell. Bodies also lined the black-and-white chequered walls, and occupied the matching black-and-white chequered chairs. The crowd was diverse. Foreigners, Indians, upper class and middle class all mixed together. The year was 1990. Leopold's had evolved into one of the most fashionable bars in Bombay, as it was still called then.

Aryan edged his way through the masses to the DJ cabin, located behind the bar that bordered one side of the room.

'How's everything?' he smiled and acknowledged the bar staff, as they poured his usual pint of draught beer.

Joining the existing DJ behind the console, Aryan started flicking through the rows of cassette tapes stacked all around the cabin. He pulled out a tape of the Bee Gees. Not wanting to lose the energetic vibe the DJ had created, he chose to open his set with 'Stayin' Alive'. Retro and rock were extremely popular then. Bollywood music was still unheard of in clubs.

After putting on his headphones, Aryan slotted the tape into the cassette player. Holding down the play and rewind buttons together, he listened through the headphones for the brief silence that would indicate the end of each track. Having found the desired one, Aryan took out the tape, rewound it a little with a pencil, and placed it back in the player. It was now queued up and ready. When a break came towards the end of the current track, he stopped it and pressed play on the other cassette holder. The short but unavoidable gap in the music was enough to send the crowd screaming with longing.

Despite the crowd's enthusiasm for the music, DJing was a little known profession and certainly not a respected one. Most people associated it with seedy dance bars, where women provocatively entertained men while they drank.

There were only half a dozen reputable nightspots in the city, and barely as many DJs. Cellar at the Oberoi Hotel and 1900s at the Taj Palace were the main playgrounds of the city's privileged. The Indian economy, however, was on the brink of a revolution. The License Raj, an elaborate licence and regulation system that restricted free enterprise in India, had just been abolished. The result would produce a rapid mushrooming of chic bars and clubs in Mumbai over the forthcoming decade.

By 1995, the transformation was well under way. A growing western influence was felt, and themed venues with creative concepts were opening up across the city. An international artist had remixed an old Hindi song, spearheading the Bollywood music craze. The track was a huge hit. DJs played it over and over again to appreciative audiences. Local DJs started remixing Hindi songs and people began to take note of DJing as a profession. The nightclub culture also spread to other cities in India. Kolkata's first real disco, called Anticlock, opened up at the Hotel Hindustan International. Aryan left Mumbai to work there. When he temporarily returned to Mumbai in 2000, the city's nightlife was almost unrecognisable.

From dusk until dawn, any night of the week, pubs and night-clubs overflowed with people. The whole city seemed to be partying. Lofty industrial warehouses had been transformed into upmarket nightclubs. Standalone superclub Fire 'n' Ice dominated the scene. The DJs there introduced trance music to Mumbai and the club-bers embraced it. New nightspots were opening up every month and loyalties were fickle. Older establishments were forced to either reinvent themselves or go out of business.

The crowd had also changed. Call-centre employees with gener-ous paycheques became regulars on the party circuit. There were pubs and clubs to cater for everyone. College hangouts, such as Waves and Madness, were open from the afternoon. It was common to see drunken youngsters congregating in front of their entrances.

The way that DJing was perceived had also dramatically altered by 2000. With Bollywood remixes skyrocketing in popularity, DJing had become associated with the Bollywood film industry. DJs regularly attended celebrity events and appeared in newspapers alongside celebrities. Everyone wanted to become a DJ. Schools quickly sprang up to meet the rising demand. This new generation of DJs came from rich and influential families who supported their career choice. The proliferating number of DJs meant that there were more of them than there were jobs, so it was essential to be well connected in the industry. Mumbai's older generation of DJs either retired, reinvented themselves along with the clubs or diversified into music production.

I sampled Mumbai's nightlife for the first time in 2002, at the nightclub of the moment called Athena. Hidden down a dusty back lane in Colaba, it had succeeded in drawing the moneyed crowd away from Fire 'n' Ice. The prohibitive 1000-rupee cost of admission (equivalent to around $30 or twenty curries at a family restaurant) per couple *or* single – for those unfortunate enough not to have a partner – made it a selective, ritzy and glitzy world. A world that was palpably surreal.

Inside, I was surprised to find myself in a place of minimalist décor and almost devoid of the usual Indian peculiarities. Except for the haze of Indian faces, bouncers and bar staff resplendent in bow ties, and Bollywood music scattered through the classic Euro trance, the nightclub could have been anywhere in the world. Stepping out from the club's slick interior and onto the road where the homeless slept, however, served as a glaring reminder of where I really was. It was India at her most extreme.

Athena later metamorphosed into Prive, an even more exclusive members' only club with an annual membership fee of almost 100,000 rupees ($2500). But those who *look* like they belong inside may still be granted entry if they can flash imported American designer jeans, watches, shoes and belts. And the ladies? Forget jeans. In Mumbai, glamorous women wear the shortest of dresses and highest of heels, and carry designer handbags and notable males as accessories.

When I moved to Mumbai, I quickly learned that Athena wasn't the only thing about the city's nightlife that had changed in five years. No longer was Mumbai the city that never slept. In fact, come midnight and it was beginning to yawn. A 1.30 a.m. curfew had been introduced, forcing bars and clubs that weren't part of luxury hotels to close early. It was the start of a move that would be repeated across India.

While India had broken free of the economic constraints of the License Raj, the country was still held back by stringent social constraints. Mumbai's burgeoning nightlife had become accessible to more people, but it didn't reflect the conservative views of traditional middle-class India. Politicians saw it as a great opportunity to appeal to the masses of middle-class voters. And thus, curfews were born.

Nowhere is the dual India so starkly revealed than in social situations. I was caught between extremes, requiring a schizophrenic modification of the way I behaved depending on the occasion. I felt relaxed in India's clubs and lounge bars. I'd also been at ease at the upper-class parties in Kolkata, with their distinctly western ways. Men and women openly interacted and chatted in English over glasses of alcohol. When the food was served, everyone helped themselves and ate together.

The common standard of conduct of India's middle class is entirely different however. At gatherings in middle-class homes, men and women tended to remain segregated. The women carry out their conventional responsibilities of cooking and waiting on the men. Hindi or other regional dialects are the main languages. If any alcohol is consumed, it will be by the men only.

I was honoured to be invited into the homes of Aryan's family and their friends, who openly and curiously welcomed me, but it was often an uncomfortable experience for me. I found it unnatural to be relegated into the domain of the women, where I floundered without Aryan's support. Usually, it was because of my inability to hold a conversation and understand everything that was being said in Hindi. Although I enjoyed being among everyone's happy and animated interactions, a lot of the time I could do little more than sit there and dumbly smile. Nevertheless, I respected and willingly abided by the customs. More than anything, I wanted to adapt to the culture and fit in.

One night, lifelong friends of Aryan's sister Maliha and her husband invited us to their apartment for a seafood dinner. I had promised I'd be there. They were a kind and gracious couple whom I genuinely liked. When the night arrived, I felt unwell. I wanted to go to dinner, but I didn't want to leave the cosy cocoon of our apartment and be confronted by the chaos outside. Not wanting to disappoint anyone, I made the effort to attend. Although I didn't regret it, halfway through the night I wanted to run away and jump on the first plane to Melbourne. I felt so lonely and like I didn't belong there.

As soon as we arrived, I was called into the kitchen with the other women while the men remained in the living room. Dinner was yet to be cooked, so the women set about preparing the trays of fish and prawns that were laid out on the bench.

'*Kyaa bana rahe hain*? (What are you making?)' I asked the lady of the house, trying to attempt conversation.

She happily chatted to me. Being a Maharastran, Hindi wasn't her first language either, so we shared something in common as we lurched along. Since I had to be in the kitchen, I decided to learn as much as possible about the cooking. I could only remain in there a short time though.

Despite the open window, as the fish was fried, the kitchen soon became hot and smoky. There wasn't a rangehood to remove the fumes. I gasped for breath, as my eyes stung and sweat began to blanket my face. At that very moment, the man of the house started serving beer to the male guests.

'You'll have?' he encouraged me.

I was surprised. Obviously aware of the western way of life, he wanted me to be at ease and enjoy myself. Appreciating his thought-fulness, I yearned to accept his offer and indulgently grab the beer from his hands.

'No, *nahin chahiye* (No, it's not needed),' I instead replied. Know-ing that the women didn't drink, I felt compelled to decline. This was confirmed by Maliha, who shook her head as I looked question-ingly across at her.

Soon, the heat drove me out of the kitchen. It wouldn't have been appropriate for me to join the men, so I was shown into another living room. There I spent half an hour alone while the women tended to dinner and the men. Most of the time, I spent gazing out the window and into other people's apartments. Groups of men sat lounging around in singlets and shorts, watching TV. I appreciated that it was a rare opportunity for me to observe people and not be observed in return.

After a while, I began to feel sorry for myself. I missed the uninhibited ease of my social life at home. I missed free-flowing conversation, where I wasn't limited to understanding only 25 per cent of what was being said and giving one-sentence responses.

The man of the house kept trying to persuade me to have a beer. In India, it's customary to ask again, even if the offer has been turned down the first or even second time.

'Take it,' Maliha finally said to me.

Even she had started to feel sorry for me. I declined. Where's the fun in sitting and drinking alone?

I didn't have a bad night. Some parts of it were fun, and I even laughed from time to time. For most of it, I just felt very, very lost.

I confronted Aryan when we got home. 'Why didn't you be more helpful and supportive towards me? Why couldn't you have come to check on me and be with me?'

'I thought you were fine in the kitchen with the women. Plus, the serving of food started early and it would have been rude for me to get up and leave the room. Just like you feel obligated to behave how the women do, I also feel obligated to behave how the men do, especially when elders are around. That means staying with the men. Did you notice how none of them left the room?'

'But I wasn't feeling well! And I can't hold a conversation in Hindi, let alone Marathi, which they were also speaking! How could I be okay?' I shouted at him, distressed.

Sometimes I just wanted to throw aside good Indian manners. And, sometimes I thought Aryan didn't realise all the sacrifices I'd made for the sake of good Indian manners.

It wasn't only in middle-class homes where mixing with Indian men was an issue. I uncovered further perils when I went with Aryan and one of his male friends to meet a male friend of ours who was visiting from Kolkata. We planned to go out for dinner and stopped by his hotel to collect him. To my surprise, the staff at the front desk objected.

'Sorry, but you can't go up.'

'What?'

'Yes, we're sorry, but we can't allow you to all go up to the room. You'll have to wait here,' the manager singled me out.

'What's the problem?' I inquired.

Our friend was paying over 3000 rupees per night for his hotel room. Yet, he wasn't allowed to have other people in his room for five minutes?

'We are sorry madam, but it's the rules.'

Ah, the rules.

'Well, show me where it's written then.'

Dealing with India's daily quirks had continued to bolster my assertiveness, but it was an assertiveness that stemmed from irritation and injustice. I argued when there was no adequate explanation for the way things were. I became mad when there was no consistency from day to day. In the end, I blatantly defied anything that wasn't defensible in this country of contradictions.

The staff failed to produce any explanation as to why I wasn't allowed in the room, so I proceeded to go up. They did nothing to stop me.

'Jason, do you know what a fight I had to go through to get into your room?' I greeted him, jumping on his bed.

Seeing him brought back memories of how much fun we'd all had in Kolkata. After I explained what happened, he was so annoyed that he went straight down to the lobby and scolded the staff for their indiscretion.

It left me wondering what must have taken place in the past for the hotel to introduce such a rule. Could it be that I appeared to be a foreign prostitute, going to the room with a group of Indian guys? A further incident sometime later confirmed that it was indeed the case.

Ash, another friend of Aryan's, who used to work with him at Anticlock in Kolkata, visited from Delhi. He had become part of a prominent Indian electronic dance music group. He had a DJ gig at a nightclub in Mumbai. After it was over, Aryan and I headed back to his hotel room, along with his brother, to continue the party. Three Indian men and me. I had an idea of what was coming.

Just as the night manager behind the reception desk was about to protest, Ash intervened.

'This is my brother, and this guy is like a brother to me,' he said pointing to Aryan. 'And this is his wife. I haven't seen them for a long time. The room was booked for me by the event organisers, so please don't let there be a problem.'

'Okay, okay, go up. Everything is fine,' the manager conceded with a smile and a wobble of his head.

As we moved towards the elevator, we were intercepted by a tubby male hotel guest who'd been lingering in the lobby. He beckoned Ash to go outside with him.

A minute later, Ash came back, enraged.

'He wanted to know if she was a prostitute and where he could get one like her. I nearly punched him,' Ash referred to me, as he spat in anger.

It turned out that the tubby Indian guy had an Indian prostitute and intended to take her to his hotel room. Obviously, he thought a white one would be better.

Was that how it really looked to most people? Why else would a white girl be with a group of Indian men? I wasn't doing anything wrong by western standards but in India it looked extremely suspicious. The thought lingered even when the room-service waiters entered the room. I wanted to hide myself away from assuming eyes.

Two things brought a dose of normality into my life in Mumbai: Sunday brunches and sunset parties on Juhu Beach. Lazy Sunday brunches had become a huge craze in Mumbai, with many upmarket restaurants and hotels offering unlimited buffet and drink deals. My favourite venue was Vie Deck and Lounge, right on the Juhu beachfront with a panoramic view straight out to the water. I loved it as a substitute for picnics by the bay in Melbourne, and for the indulgent sense of escapism that it gave me. We sat under a huge white umbrella, breathing in the salty air and looking out to sea. As we kept filling our plates high with Mediterranean food, the waiter kept filling our glasses with wine. My mind was happy to be distracted by this gentle and soothing side to Mumbai.

Late in the afternoon, when lunch was over, we walked along the sand towards Aurus where the regular Sunday Sundown Session would be held. The beach, devoid of the usual bikini-clad sunbathers that could be expected on a western beach, resembled a curious circus scene. Cows roamed freely. Monkeys performed tricks. People frolicked fully clothed in the water and vendors intermingled with the crowd. There were coconut sellers, balloon sellers, a guy with wooden flutes, and women peddling cheap bangles and henna stamps. An artist was hand-crafting a crocodile and scorpion out of sand on the shore. The beach came alive like this every Sunday.

The sun was close to setting when we arrived at Aurus. A little more seductive in its appeal than Vie, it was decorated with chandeliers and candles, and a canopied bed. The sun lit up the beach in magical hues of orange, purple and red as it set, drawing the crowd to the railing. The music started off chilled and built up as the evening progressed. More and more people poured in; some were people I'd met before, others were new faces I hadn't seen, all of us dancing in the warm night air. The party had started early so it ended early, returning everyone to their beds before the week began. It didn't end in the laidback way that I'd anticipated though.

Waiting in the auto rickshaw at the traffic lights on the way home, I saw a familiar shape approach. The peace in my head was about to be invaded. It was a beggar woman and she was fixated on me. I sighed. The last thing I wanted was for such an enjoyable outing to end with harassment.

'*Abhi nahin* (Not now),' I tried to discourage her politely.

It had no effect.

'Madam, madam,' she continued, tapping my leg with her dirty hand and revealing a disfigured limb. The sight moved me a little, but irritated me more. If my skin was brown, in this patriarchal Indian society she would be asking Aryan for money, not me. There was no point in giving her anything anyway. Beggars worked in gangs in Mumbai, with all the earnings going to the leader before being distributed.

'*Bas! Mujse paisa nahin milega* (Enough! You won't get money from me),' I spoke more forcefully.

She responded with further moaning and tapping. Any sympathy that I had felt was now replaced by anger. I can deal with beggars' whining, but I get aggravated when they keep poking and prodding for attention.

The auto-rickshaw driver also told her to stop. He moved the rickshaw forward a little. She refused to give up.

'*Naraaz mat karo!* (Don't irritate me!)' I warned, before turning away to ignore her. No longer able to reach my leg, she started tapping me on the head. The line was crossed and I finally cracked. The alcohol that I'd consumed made my mind blur.

'Didn't I tell you not to? Now get lost and leave me alone!' I screamed at her in English and harshly slapped her away. I reached a new low – I'd hit a beggar.

'I can't stand this,' I howled to Aryan. 'Why can't you protect me from it all? You should have stopped her from bothering me. I just want one day of peace.'

Aryan, on the other hand, couldn't understand why I was so upset. He was, no doubt, just as horrified by my behaviour as I was.

He had no idea how it felt to be constantly stared at, questioned, hassled and even mistaken for a prostitute because of how I looked. I faced the same hurdles that other foreigners did, but I lacked the protective barrier of being able to wind up my car window, closet myself away in a plush apartment and console myself that I was above it all. I didn't aspire to live like that. I had chosen to be with an Indian man, and to make India my home. I wanted to feel like I was a part of India. But India, and the way people treated me, made it difficult for me to do so at times.

At my home, the neighbours eagerly awaited my presence with their door open. Even if I dressed like an Indian, talked like an

Indian and behaved like an Indian my skin colour kept giving me away. Those who saw me would most likely think that I was just another foreigner in India, perhaps an expat on a well-paying contract, or the wife of an expat on a well-paying contract.

In Kolkata and most other places in India, I'd lived a foreigner's life. I felt like a foreigner, my friends were foreigners and we mostly behaved like foreigners. All that had changed now. I lived among Indians, without a foreigner in sight. I made an effort to adopt Indian customs and dress in Indian clothes where necessary. I didn't have either the money or luxuries that foreigners did, and sadly no longer felt like I had much in common with them. I lived my life in a way that was often impossible for them to understand and appreciate. I couldn't blame them either. I often found my life difficult to understand too.

I struggled to find my identity and where I belonged in Mumbai. Just as how there are many extremes to India, I felt like I was living extreme, multiple lives but didn't fully fit any of them. As tourists looked for the 'real India', I looked for the 'real me'. I was determined to adapt. Perhaps the secret was not trying to be Indian, but rather, an Indian version of me. Just as the 'real India' had many facets, I needed to recognise that there could also be many facets of the 'real me' as well.

# Two Weddings and
## a Headache

PLANNING a wedding is stressful in any circumstances, but trying to do so in a foreign country without fully grasping the culture and the language is even harder. I was at a loss with where to begin. In hindsight, it was probably a good thing that I didn't know what was involved, otherwise I may never have agreed to let Aryan make a respectable woman of me.

As the months passed, the issue of our marriage – or rather, the fact that we were still unmarried – magnified. We couldn't keep living together like we were and get away with it. An outrage was brewing. The landlord kept asking when our wedding would take place, and the housing society wanted to see our marriage certificate. My visa would also expire soon.

I hadn't spoken to my family much about the possibility of getting married before I moved to Mumbai. I didn't want to prematurely concern them, in case something went awry. Back home, my dad was concerned. He wasn't comfortable that I was so far away and in a serious relationship with Aryan. A combination of work commitments, intense dislike of crowds, and an ear problem prevented him from coming to Mumbai to find out for himself what was going on. Having contracted tinitus from ongoing exposure to loud noise at work, his ears were very sensitive. No doubt he'd struggle to cope with the constant din of the traffic in Mumbai. I did, and my ears were fine.

It wasn't very surprising when my dad's sister Patricia and her husband Nick announced that they'd be visiting Mumbai on their round-the-world trip. My aunt would report back to my dad. My cousin Virginia also came to visit. And then my mother.

All of them took to India in the best spirit possible; they were adventurous and bold. My cousin and mum even rode the Mumbai local train.

'Is Aryan always this peaceful and happy?' my mum asked. 'He seems to be really good for you.'

She noticed and appreciated his sweet, easy-going nature, just as I did. And the way he balanced out my episodes of stress and anxiety. Aryan's family was delighted to meet my mum. They lavished her with gifts, and were thrilled to see her dressed in a sari.

My mum went home content that I was in the hands of a caring family, and excited about the opportunities that India was bringing me. I let her break the news of my impending wedding to my dad and other relatives. It was cowardly, but I didn't want to deal with any disapproval. I was finding it difficult enough coming to terms with the life-changing decisions I was making, and only wanted to keep positives in my mind.

Aryan's parents suggested that we get married on their fiftieth wedding anniversary. We planned a simple Hindu ceremony, followed by a reception. We'd also need to have the formality of a registry wedding. Since I wasn't a Hindu, the religious ceremony wouldn't be enough. It would be meaningful to us though, and the day we'd choose to celebrate as our wedding anniversary.

Aryan and I decided to get the civil ceremony over and done with as soon as possible so that we could meet India's moral requirements and get my visa sorted. I reeled at the thought of two weddings, especially the rambling process that would be involved in getting married at a government registry office.

I was still struggling to feel secure in Mumbai, let alone get married. Aryan also marvelled at the direction his life had taken. When we met in Kolkata, neither of us had any intention of getting married, least of all to each other. A few years later, here we were, on the brink of tying the knot. I'd only recently come to terms with being single again – did I really want to risk getting married again?

The fact that Aryan had no qualms about marriage was reassuring. He'd had plenty of time to have fun and explore being single. He'd lived his life without any regrets. He knew who he was and what he wanted – he was never going to need to go off and 'find himself'. I could trust him to be committed. That, combined with my faith in the bigger picture of my goals in India, helped me feel confident in our decision.

Aryan wasn't concerned that I had been married before. Having had a number of prior relationships himself, he was as accepting of my past as I was of his.

We decided to view the civil ceremony as a procedure rather than a wedding. Our idea of starting our future lives together was not in a dim and decaying government office, crowded with impatient couples and disinterested public servants.

The Mumbai Office of Registrar of Marriages, located behind the Old Customs House in the Fort District of south Mumbai, certainly was a typically run-down government office. It had flaking paint, a decaying ceiling, plastic chairs, reams of stacked papers and a stray cat running around. Two gold-and-red velvet thrones sitting near the entrance were small concessions to the austerity, and hinted at the importance of what went on there.

It took us four hours to submit our Notice of Intention to be married. The process was hampered by one particularly unhelpful officer, who either provided us with no answers or misleading answers to our questions. Getting the photocopies of my documents notarised was another challenge. The notary public from the Magistrate's Court next to the registry office refused to do it because they were a foreigner's documents. He didn't want to take the risk of them being fake, even though he could see they were all the originals.

The only option was to take a taxi to the High Court a short distance away. An agent waited out the front.

'How can I help you?'

'We need to get these documents notarised.'

'No problem,' he assured us as he took the photocopies.

'Wait! Don't you want the originals as well?' I called out to him.

'Not necessary, madam.' He returned the photocopies to us within five minutes, with the addition of arresting big red seals and numerous other official stamps. All for 50 rupees ($1.20) per document.

A little over a month later we returned to the registry office, this time to solemnise our intention to be married. Both of us wore jeans. It was another lengthy process involving more forms, photocopies, three witnesses and waiting. At last, our names were called. The marriage officer handed us each a piece of paper with our vows on it, stating that we would be each other's lawful husband and wife. We recited them. Then, it was time to sign on the dotted line. Slightly baffled and bewildered, Aryan and I were pronounced married.

Afterwards, we sat on the thrones and exchanged wedding rings while fascinated strangers, who were also there to be wed, took photos of us with their cameras. But the process wasn't over yet.

'Come back again only after two weeks to collect your marriage certificate,' one of the officers told us.

Relieved to have gotten the biggest step out of the way, we headed to Leopold's Café and opened a bottle of champagne.

Next came the process I'd have to go through to be able to remain in India. As the initial step, my tourist visa needed to be extended and converted into an entry visa. Permission for that could only be obtained from the Foreigner's Division of the Ministry of Home Affairs in Delhi. I turned up to locked gates at 8.30 a.m., on a hot Delhi morning, in order to get a good position in the queue when the compound opened. Two hours later, the waiting room was about to overflow with the masses that continued to stream in.

I gazed around at some of the more interesting characters. There was a Sardar (male follower of the Sikh religion) sporting a fluorescent pink turban and a disgruntled American. No one had been able to tell the American the proper process for submitting his visa application, or even if there was a number system in place. He was about to reach boiling point when someone finally pointed out the number on the top of his blue form. People from the Middle East surrounded me, many with whole families in tow. With no *babus* (government employees) in sight, they lounged all over the unattended interview desks.

The process moved surprisingly quickly after the staff filed in. They cleared the interlopers, sifted through the piles of forms and commenced calling applicants. My interview took less than ten minutes.

'Come back at 5 p.m. to collect a letter with instructions to be submitted at the Foreigner's Registration Office in Mumbai,' the unexpectedly friendly *babu* told me.

In a country of more than one billion people, what were the chances that I would encounter two foreigners from Varkala in Delhi at the same time? But that's exactly what happened.

'I saw Lucy in the Visa Facilitation Centre,' Aryan mentioned as we left. Sure enough, she was there again in the evening when I went to collect my letter. Lucy, from England, was a long-term resident of Varkala.

'I've come to Delhi in the hope of getting some final advice on my visa renewal. It's been dragging on for over eight months and has become too involved to be dealt with in Kerala. So over 130 phone calls later, I've ended up here,' she sighed.

'Varkala has changed a lot since you were there,' Lucy continued. 'So many foreigners have been forced out by locals who've been complaining to the authorities. They either haven't had their business visas renewed or have been deported. Some are even up on drug charges.'

That evening, Aryan and I also encountered the *Little Book, Big Secret* man in Delhi's grungy Paharganj backpacker's district. He was, of course, spreading the word about his conspiracy theory. Like Lucy and me, he'd come to Delhi with a greater purpose.

'My family and I don't have visas. We've been doing the rounds of the Ministry of Home Affairs to find out if we'll be allowed to stay in India. No one seems to be able to give us an answer though. We've been called back there three times already.

'Something big is going to happen in the town of Bowen, Australia, in September,' he gravely called out to us we departed.

As it turned out, our registry wedding was much less stressful than our real wedding. A combination of a family crisis, Indian time frames, hectic lives, travelling away from Mumbai and not knowing what was involved in arranging an Indian wedding soon had me at my wits' end. Two weeks before the wedding was due to take place, the venue (a groovy roof garden in Bandra) and entertainment had been organised, but nearly everything else was still outstanding. Even the wedding invitations were still being printed. I'd notified close friends and family in Australia of the wedding, but wanted to send them their invitations in advance too.

People in India didn't make plans weeks in advance however. They acted spontaneously. This meant that guests only needed to be formally invited a few days ahead, particularly as we were keeping the guestlist small. The invitations would be personally hand-delivered by family members. There was no way I would be able to send the wedding invitations to Australia in time for people to receive them.

My friends and family were due to arrive in India around five days before the wedding. Most of them had never been to India before and would need looking after. I wanted to have plenty of time to spend with them and take them sightseeing. I didn't want to have to worry about last-minute wedding plans.

I tried to get as much as possible organised for the wedding before they arrived, but I was so helpless. Everything took longer than expected. I didn't know where to get things or even how I should dress. An Indian wedding was completely out of my realm of expertise. There wasn't even one style of Indian wedding to guide me. What took place and what people wore depended on the community they belonged to. Not only that, two outfits were required: one for the wedding ceremony and another for the reception.

Oriya weddings are known to be simple and modest affairs. The attire for the wedding ceremony would be more conservative and traditional, while the bling would be saved for the reception. Unlike weddings back home, wedding ceremonies in India are private affairs, usually only attended by close family members and friends. It's understandable, as these ceremonies can take the whole day. The remainder of the guests, often hundreds and sometimes thousands, turn up for the wedding reception lured by the promise of an extensive buffet of food. More guests mean more importance, and more prestige. It's a huge contrast to weddings in Australia, where numbers are often kept as low as possible to save money, and it can be viewed as rude to attend the party (and the free feed!) without attending the ceremony. Despite our minimal guestlist for the reception, around 150 people were still expected. A substantial-sized wedding by Australian standards, it was considered small in India. Only a dozen of the guests were from my side. Many people I wanted to be there couldn't travel because of the global financial crisis.

Aryan's mother had stashed away a red-and-gold sari from Orissa for my wedding ceremony. However, I didn't have my reception sari or jewellery. I was beginning to get upset about everyone's lack of concern about the wedding arrangements. Even Aryan had become tired of my nagging about needing to get everything done. He was obviously clueless about what remained to be done and how long it would all take to finalise. I started to resign myself to the wedding being a disaster.

Then, early in the morning ten days before the wedding, Aryan received a phone call. It was his eldest sister, Maliha. It seemed that people had at last woken up to the fact that it wasn't long until the wedding. Orders were given. Aryan had to collect the invitations from the printer that evening. I had to go shopping for my sari that afternoon.

It took four hours of looking, comparing and dressing up to find a suitable sari for the reception. Maliha and I both agreed the sari should be red. It should be practical enough for me to wear again in the future, but still formal enough for the wedding. It also had to be made out of lightweight material and not too heavily decorated, because it would be the middle of summer. Richly decorated saris are surprisingly hot to wear.

That's where our agreement ended.

'One of the signs of a good sari is the embroidery work around the border. It should be heavy and hand stitched,' Maliha told me.

I liked simple patterns. To my mind, which was used to relatively plain western dress, the saris that we looked at appeared overdone and garish.

The salesman at the first store showed us dozens of saris. Two interested me but Maliha delivered the verdict: 'The border work on this one isn't good', 'This one isn't made out of good material'.

The saris she liked all had big patterns or too many different colours on them. I wanted something delicate.

At the next store, a further twenty saris were duly pulled out from behind the counter. Our opinions continued to differ and I was starting to lose hope. I almost resigned myself to settling for something that I was less than happy with. Then the salesman showed us another sari. We both looked at each other and smiled. It was made out of georgette, and had an unusual but striking hand-stitched border. The rest of the sari was quite plain, which also appealed to me. I tried it on over my jeans, and we agreed it was the one.

Days later, bad news awaited, though.

'I'm sorry, but I don't like it,' my youngest sister-in-law, Radha, informed me when she saw the sari. A fashion designer, she was married to Aryan's youngest brother. She was also in charge of designing Aryan's wedding outfits. Radha thought it was too plain.

'It doesn't have enough embroidery on it. It looks too casual to be worn as a wedding sari.'

I was devastated. I was so far out of my depth that I couldn't even choose a decent wedding dress for myself. She did have a point, though. The more I looked at the sari, the more I agreed with her. It was impossible to take the sari back and exchange it as it had been hemmed and the blouse stitched. There was only one thing left to do – get more sequins sewn onto it.

Five days before the wedding, only chaos reigned. Cars, flowers, lights, decorations, menu, *mehendi* (bridal henna on the hands) were all still in the process of being organised. There had been, on average, four hours of shopping every day. Most of that time had been spent looking at items and comparing them. I felt constantly besieged by the number of choices to be made.

The previous day I'd been taken shopping for the jewellery that I'd wear to the reception. I needed to cover myself in many ornaments, the bigger the better. Items would be adorning almost all parts of my body – forehead, ears, nose, neck, arms and feet. This round of shopping was followed by another four hours of shopping the next day. I had no idea it would take so much effort! Bangles, *bindis* (forehead decoration), gifts for my sisters-in-law, gifts for me and the most important thing, the *mangal sutra* (meaning 'auspicious thread', it's made out of two strings of black and gold beads, joined by a gold locket).

To buy this necklace, which would be my Hindu equivalent of a wedding ring, Maliha and I had to venture into the fray of Indian gold-shopping. As Indian families favour investing their money in gold, it's serious business. Most families have a preferred jeweller, and Aryan's family was no exception. Like any good Indian gold store, it was perpetually busy. The daily prices per gram of gold were listed at the entrance to the shop. Inside, there were no fewer than twenty shop assistants tending to the flock of women who crowded the counters.

All kinds of gold jewellery were being placed on scales and their prices calculated according to weight. The bright yellow colour glittered charismatically. It wasn't 18-carat gold, which was widespread at home. This gold was 24 carats, as pure as it's possible to get.

As I had fair skin, I'd always preferred silver to gold. However, that was going to have to change. Despite my attempts to choose a small and delicate necklace, Maliha forced a substantial gold locket upon me.

'People will be looking at it and commenting. We don't want to appear cheap,' she insisted.

Indian weddings, I learned, were about showing off. Families spent lavishly, even if they couldn't afford to. Poorer families took out huge loans to finance the expense.

'I know of weddings that have cost 40 lakh rupees ($100,000),' Maliha said. India was far from the impoverished country that some people thought it to be. A home could be purchased with that amount of money.

The expense comes from the number of events in a Hindu wedding. A typical wedding consists of an exhausting six parts over three days – *sangeet* (evening of singing and dancing performed by female family and friends), *mehendi* (application of henna designs to the bride's hands), *haldi* (cleansing application of turmeric to the bride and groom's skin), *baraat* (marriage procession featuring the groom riding on a horse or elephant), *pheras* (wedding ceremony where the couple walks around a fire) and the reception.

Aryan and I wanted our wedding to be memorable, but not costly. We decided to keep the wedding as simple as possible and leave out the *sangeet*. We also planned to give the reception a Punjabi twist in the form of a *bhangra* band. The aim was to break the ice and get everyone, both foreigners and Indians, up and dancing together. It was impossible for me to participate in a *haldi* ceremony.

'Have you seen how turmeric stains my fingers yellow? My whole body can't look like that on my wedding day!' I was alarmed.

Aryan was also especially keen not to have a *baraat*.

'Oh come on, it would be hilarious to see you riding a horse,' I coaxed him.

'No way!' he was adamant.

To add to the tension, a problem was brewing over the selection of a *pandit* (Hindu priest) to perform the wedding ceremony. Radha had concerning things to say about the Oriya *pandit* who'd performed her wedding.

'The ceremony went for over six hours. He went on and on, and I could hardly even understand what he was saying. I wanted to pay him to finish fast. I was so hungry and dizzy by the end of it that I fainted.'

Aryan and I wanted a short ceremony that didn't take longer than two hours.

'Let's get that *pandit* that your sister uses for *pujas*,' I insisted.

To me, a *pandit* was a *pandit*. However, he was a Gujarati *pandit*. As I was to later discover, Gujarati wedding rituals, although Hindu, differed from typical Hindu ones. Only four rounds (*pheras*) of the sacred fire are performed in Gujarati weddings, instead of the usual seven. Nevertheless, he would have to do. Our wedding was going to be a blend of cultures anyway. He would merely add to it.

The shopping continued after my family and friends arrived in Mumbai. They didn't want to risk their health by drinking anything other than mineral water. This led to an elaborate mission to find and buy as much mineral water as possible.

'We got lost and ended up in a slum. The people there were so warm and welcoming, though. They invited us in!' my mum exclaimed.

I was relieved that everyone seemed to be enjoying the random delights of India. More shopping continued. Everyone wanted to buy Indian clothes and jewellery for the wedding. Led by Aryan's sister Amita, we converged on a wholesale market near Dadar railway station. Within ten minutes, she was as stressed as me. People had headed off in all directions, leaving us wondering how we were going to keep track of them all. Five hours and much confusion later, everyone had found something.

Most of my friends and family were staying in a serviced apartment in Bandra, near the wedding venue. It was filled with women, as the husbands had all let their wives come in a group to the wedding. My dad had remained back in Australia too. Although there was an understanding that it was for the best, it created another issue, because someone had to perform the role of my father in the ceremony. Not only that, I didn't have a brother, who was apparently required to escort me to the *mandap* (stage).

Only one – brave? – male family member, an uncle, was attending the wedding. He and his wife, who was the sister of my uncle Nick, had been to India previously, and they intended to spend more time travelling around India after the wedding. I roped him in to take my father's place, and thankfully he was gracious about accepting his honorary position. Justin agreed to take the place of my brother.

My *mehendi* party was to be held in the apartment two days before the wedding. That same day, I also had to collect my cousin from the airport.

'My luggage isn't here,' Justine said when she finally emerged nearly two hours after her flight had landed. Apparently, it hadn't been loaded onto the plane and was still in Sydney. The airline didn't know when they'd be able to deliver it.

We arrived back at the apartment to find restless and hungry occupants, two fretful male *mehendi* artists and no bed for Justine. The Indian guests were an hour late for the *mehendi* party and the food that we'd ordered came two hours late. Despite my repeated requests to the staff, the spare bed couldn't be located.

'I can't handle this responsibility anymore. Nothing is going right. I can't deal with it. I'm worn out and have had enough,' I sobbed. The control freak in me never did cope well under pressure.

While I'd become accustomed to the idiosyncrasies of India, my friends and family hadn't. By now, they'd grown impatient and needy. They weren't used to eating dinner late in the night, as invariably happens in India, at a time that they were usually going to bed. Food is normally served as guests arrived at parties in Australia. In India, it was served later, before guests departed. Their angst was understandable. But India ran on India time, and always would. It struck me that this was how Aryan must feel when I got fed up with the many small things I encountered. The party was salvaged when Aryan's family arrived with a bag full of saris and began giving everyone an Indian makeover.

Then we got down to the serious business of *mehendi* application. The Mughals are believed to have brought the art to India thousands of years ago. Although there's nothing spiritual or sacred about applying henna to a bride's hands before a wedding, it serves as an important mark of transformation and fortuity. The Arabic design, characterised by swirls and floral patterns, still remains in India, but a distinctly Indian design has also emerged. It commonly encompasses detailed lines, lotus flowers, paisley patterns and peacocks, and usually extends most of the way up the bride's arm.

Of course, *mehendi* wouldn't be an Indian tradition without some superstitions attached to it. The darker the henna stains the bride's skin, the more her husband is supposed to love her. The new bride isn't expected to perform any household chores until her *mehendi* has worn off, so brides like it as deep and as dark as possible. A bride's *mehendi* design also includes a hidden inscription of the groom's initial on her palm. It's believed that if the groom fails to find it on the wedding night, the bride will dominate the couple's married life. The use of henna isn't restricted to weddings though. Women in India also apply it to their hands and feet during festivals and special celebrations, as it's considered to be very auspicious. Henna has even been elevated to the status of body art, worn to make a decorative statement.

I selected an Arabic design for my *mehendi* as it was less concentrated. I didn't want to look like I had two black hands and arms. The *mehendi* artists were fast in their work. As with most occupations, India's *mehendi* artists traditionally belonged to a particular caste and the skill was handed down from generation to generation. Called Nai, it was a caste that incorporated barbers, hairdressers and midwives. The caste was deemed a lower class one due to impurity from touching customers' hair, feet and blood. In contrast, in modern-day India, talented contemporary henna artists train at beauty colleges and command high fees.

Soon, over a dozen pairs of hands and arms were elaborately decorated. While we waited for it to dry and stain our hands, we practised some Bollywood dance moves. I left the henna on overnight, so that it would be as dark as possible. In the morning, my bed was filled with crumbly flakes, but to my delight the design emerged a deep brown colour that remained on my hands and arms for weeks.

Although the wedding day dawned peacefully, it soon resumed the chaotic pattern of the previous few weeks and remained that way until the end. Aryan rushed to his parents' apartment early in the morning for his *haldi* ceremony, where all the married women applied turmeric paste to his body to cleanse it.

I knew so little about what was going to happen to me that I found it hard to believe that I was actually getting married. But, eager to experience a new ceremony in a different tradition from my first wedding, I figured it would truly be the fresh start to married life that I needed.

I was supposed to go with Maliha to the Bandra apartment to get my hair and make-up done. Radha had arranged a professional make-up artist to meet me there. Maliha had a lot to do, however, and was running late as usual. In the end I went without her. With me came the *pandit*, who was in a hurry to get to the wedding venue and start the preparations. We loaded the car with bags full of coconuts, rice, fruit, betel nuts, garlands, ghee, sweets, red *kumkum* powder, brass pots and numerous other items required for the elaborate wedding rituals.

After my hair and make-up was done, a row of sparkling bridal bindis was placed above my eyebrows and I was slathered in gold jewellery. I could hardly recognise myself. An Indian bride. My heavily kohl-rimmed eyes registered astonishment when I looked in the mirror. At the wedding venue, Aryan was also almost unrecognisable, dressed in a delicately woven gold tunic and dhoti, red scarf and turban. It was the first time I'd seen him in traditional Indian clothes and he looked so handsome.

As I was hurried inside, my mum welcomed Aryan. She greeted him with a garland and *aarti* (traditional Hindu prayer with a lamp placed on a platter), and put a *tilak* (auspicious red mark made out of *kumkum* powder) on his forehead. She then led him to the stage where two red thrones had been placed. Meanwhile, the soles of my feet were anointed with red dye, and a red-and-gold veil was affixed to my head. Justin held my hand and walked me to the stage. The wedding was ready to commence. A conch shell was blown loudly to attract the attention of the gods and herald the start of the proceedings.

Aryan and I exchanged garlands to signify the acceptance of each other as husband and wife. Then a long thread was placed around our necks by my family to protect us from evil influences. Next it was time for me to be given away, by my substitute father, to Aryan in the *kanyadaan*. My right hand was placed in Aryan's right hand, and filled with betel nut, flowers and money. Our hands were tied together, sacred mantras chanted and blessings given. The joining of our hands, as well as the knotting together of my veil and Aryan's scarf, symbolised the union of our souls in holy matrimony. Next, the holy fire was lit. Ghee and rice were poured into it as it crackled.

If I'd had any idea of what my Indian wedding might look like, it certainly didn't include having a huge ornamental gold crown placed on my head like Lord Jagannath during the Rath Yatra festival in Orissa. Shaped like a betel nut, it was embellished with coloured beads and fabric. Yet, it was an important and unavoidable part of the wedding ceremony. With crowns on both our heads, it was time for Aryan and me to do our laps of the holy fire to confirm our marriage.

The four rounds, as per Gujarati custom, symbolise the basic human goals of *Dharma* (duty), *Artha* (earning wealth and livelihood), *Kama* (love) and *Moksha* (liberation from suffering in life). Aryan and I also helped each other touch seven betel nuts with our right toes. The betel nuts represent the seven vows of married life, incorporating nourishment, courage and strength, prosperity, progeny, happiness, harmony and commitment. Next, we fed each other sweets four times as we recited the vows in Hindi. I promised to serve Aryan first and to give food to any holy men who came to the door. Aryan promised to provide for me and come home early so we could eat together.

As a mark of my being a married woman, Aryan dabbed *sindoor* (red *kumkum* powder) on my forehead. Then came the time for him to give me my *mangal sutra*. Except it was nowhere to be found.

The chaos had finally caught up with us. The *mangal sutra* was back in the apartment. A replacement was quickly borrowed, the *pandit* blessed it, and Aryan put it over my head. At last the wedding was over. People threw flowers at us, and we touched everyone's feet.

The whole ceremony took around two hours. It was noisy and full of disarray. Guests arrived late because of the traffic. I misplaced the toe rings I'd been given. The conch shell continued to be blown throughout the ceremony. Rice was poured on our heads and went everywhere. All the foreigners, including me, had no idea what they were supposed to be doing, and required ongoing instruction and explanation. There was constant chatter. I struggled to recite the vows in Hindi and understand what I was saying. But it was a happy occasion and utterly memorable. I couldn't stop smiling.

As soon as the wedding ceremony was over, Maliha rushed me back to the apartment to get ready for the reception that would directly follow. A full change of clothes, hair and make-up was necessary. It was time to put on the traditional red sari that I was so looking forward to wearing. Despite having jewellery hanging off or attached to almost every body part, from head to toe, the Indian women thought I still looked too plain. A packet of sparkling *bindis* was swiftly located and they began sticking them in my hair. They were on a mission, and none of my protests would stop them.

Back at the reception, Aryan waited for me, wearing a rich brown Sherwani suit with a long jacket and hand embroidery on the front and sleeves. We took our positions under the flowery canopy of the stage and prepared to greet each of the guests and receive their good wishes. If it's a large reception, this can take all night.

After lining up and wishing the couple well, the guests usually proceed to the buffet to start eating. The arrival of the *bhangra* band interrupted the formalities and produced an instant transformation. One minute, the guests were sitting sedately and talking among themselves, in the next, they were up and breaking out in the most incredible dance moves I'd ever seen. Arms punctured the air, shoulders rapidly shrugged, hips swivelled and legs leaped. It was just like in a Bollywood movie.

The reception was a surprising success, which was such a relief for Aryan and me. We were concerned there'd be a divide between east and west, and disapproval from some people. We needn't have worried. The day brought everyone closer together. Many fears and misconceptions melted away that night of our wedding reception, as both families connected.

Aryan's family had gone out of their way to make sure my family was comfortable and enjoyed themselves. It couldn't have been easy for them, particularly as they hadn't been around foreigners before and knew very little about western customs. My family had been open-minded towards India and all its tribulations. It gave me hope that with the right attitudes, two cultures can be blended.

After the night was over, I collapsed at the table where my mother-in-law was sitting to finally have dinner.

'*Khaana kaisa hai*? (How's the food?)' she asked.

The unfamiliarity of the day receded with the familiarity of her question. I was a real part of the family now. An Indian daughter-in-law and wife. Along with the role came new responsibilities, customs and traditions; traditions steeped in legends that I knew nothing about, yet all were to be learned and followed.

# White Indian Housewife

A LONG time ago, in the days of mythical India, there was a courageous but childless king called Asvapati. The king desired a child so badly that he devoted himself to spiritual practice, in the hope of pleasing the goddess Savitri enough that she would grant him a child. The goddess finally appeared and honoured his wish. The king and his wife had a girl as beautiful as the goddess herself. They named the child Savitri in honour of the goddess.

Princess Savitri grew up to be so radiant, accomplished and wise that men were intimidated by her presence. No one was brave enough to ask the king for his daughter's hand in marriage. The king was distraught.

'Dearest daughter, the time has come for me to choose a husband for you, but you have no suitors. I will fall out of favour in the eyes of the gods if I don't get you married. You have no choice but to go out and choose a husband for yourself. Choose someone who is virtuous and deserving, and who will appreciate you,' the king told Savitri.

Savitri left the palace and went searching far and wide for a suitable husband. She visited other kingdoms and even hermitages in the hope of finding someone pious and worthy. Eventually, she came across Satyavan. He was a handsome prince who lived in the forest with his father, who'd been driven out of his kingdom by his enemies. His father was blind, and Satyavan chopped wood and cared for him devotedly. Savitri decided that Satyavan was the man she would marry.

The king opposed the arrangement. He found out from a sage that Satyavan was cursed and destined to die in a year. Despite this, Savitri remained adamant.

'He is the only man for me. I will only choose my husband once,' she insisted to her father. Eventually, the king conceded and the couple got married.

Savitri went to live in the forest with Satyavan. He cherished her dearly, and they were very happy. But Savitri grew more and more distressed as the predicted day of Satyavan's death drew closer. As he didn't share her knowledge, it was a huge burden for her to bear alone. Three days before her husband was due to die, Savitri began to fast. Early on the day of his death, she performed the Laxmi Narayan *puja* for protection and good fortune. Then, when he went into the forest to cut the wood from the banyan tree, she convinced him to allow her to accompany him. After a while, he grew dizzy and laid down to rest. At that moment, the forest turned dark and ominous. A tall figure materialised. It was Yama, the God of Death.

'I have come to take your husband,' he told Savitri, as he yanked Satyavan's soul from his body.

Savitri refused to accept her husband's fate, and followed Yama as he carried Satyavan's soul away.

'You must turn back. Your time has not yet come,' Yama ordered Savitri.

She paid him no heed. 'Please, bring my husband back to life or let me die too.'

Yama began to feel sorry for her. He was aware that she had married Satyavan despite knowing he only had a year to live.

'It is impossible for me to return your husband to you as it's against nature's law to give back the dead,' Yama told her. 'However, I will grant you three wishes as long as you don't ask me to restore your husband's life.'

'Oh, thank you so much. I will accept whatever you can give,' Savitri replied. 'First, please restore my father-in-law's kingdom so that he may lead and protect his people. He has suffered enough already. Secondly, please grant my father the son that he always longed for.'

'It is done,' Yama agreed.

'Lastly, good Yama, I would also like to bear sons.'

'Granted,' he replied.

'But I am faithful to my husband and won't have children by any other man. How can a dead body make me a mother? Therefore, you must return him to me.'

Yama realised that he had been tricked. He remained silent for a minute, then smiled.

'I appreciate your persistence. But what I like more was your readiness to marry a man you loved, even though you knew he'd only live for a year. Go back to your husband's body, he will soon wake up,' Yama said, as he released Satyavan's soul.

Savitri returned to the banyan tree where her husband's body lay. She devoutly began walking around the tree, in a traditional Hindu form of worship called Pradakshina. As Yama promised, her husband came back to life. And, as stories go, they lived happily ever after.

This tale, from the ancient Hindu text the *Mahabharata*, forms the basis of Savitri Brata. A day of fasting and prayer for the wellbeing of husbands and a happy married life, it's observed once a year by married women from Orissa and other parts of eastern India. The wives in my new Indian family undertook it ardently.

Not being religious myself, I'd never understood the reason why people ritually fasted. Why willingly deprive the body of the important food and nutrients that it needs? I reacted apprehensively to my in-laws' invitation to participate in my first Savitri Brata. Fasting, let alone subserviently fasting for my husband's wellbeing, wasn't something I could readily see the benefits of. Being non-traditional, Aryan also knew and cared little about the occasion. But my desire to learn about Hindu customs led me to do it.

On the morning of the occasion, I ate only fruit. As I dressed, I dabbed a line of red *sindoor* between the part of my hair, stuck a round *bindi* between my eyebrows, lined my arms with bangles and placed my *mangal sutra* around my neck. I already wore a nose ring, ankle and toe rings. Adorned with all the symbols of marriage, I was ready to leave the house.

'I'll expect a great gift from you for this,' I jokingly told Aryan.

I'd discovered that it was customary for husbands to reward their wives' devotion and sacrifice with gifts.

Maliha had bought new saris and prepared *thalis* (platters) containing a variety of fruits, some flowers, a coconut and a selection of items reflective of a married woman. There were bangles, *sindoor*, *bindis* and other cosmetics. We each took a sari and *thali* to the temple where, covering our heads, we offered each item to the gods to have it blessed. We lit incense and gave the flowers to the gods, placing them around their feet.

Behind the temple was a large banyan tree. Its root, stem and branches symbolically represent the holy trinity of Hindu gods – Brahma, Vishnu and Shiva. On the day of Savitri Brata, the banyan tree also represents Savitri and the story in the *Mahabharata*. As we walked around the tree like Savitri once did, we made offerings and tied cotton threads to it. The thread, which holds a sacred place in Hindu rituals to evoke the blessings of the gods, also becomes a symbol of strength when wound around a tree.

At Maliha's home after the *puja*, we ate the fruit and put the cosmetics on each other.

'This is the fun part of the day,' she explained to me.

I believed her, because I was actually having fun.

'Back in Orissa large groups of married women will get together, sing and recite the story about Savitri,' she further elaborated.

Later in the afternoon, Aryan arrived with my gift.

'You have to touch his feet to receive his blessing first,' Maliha told me.

Touching a person's feet, considered to be the lowliest and most unclean part of their body, is a great sign of respect. Aryan looked on with amusement and disbelief as I did as instructed. He handed me a lovely earring and necklace set.

Participating in the ritual provoked unexpected feelings and realisations in me. Far from the day of deprivation I had expected, it was instead a day of female bonding and enjoyment. Eating only fruit for the day cleansed and purified my body, while the legend and ritual guided my mind towards the purpose to be achieved.

What woman didn't want her husband to live a long time and her married life to be happy? It didn't matter if Savitri's story was real or not, it gave meaning to the ritual, and the ritual gave focus to my abstract thoughts. For that short time, I was able to detach myself from the world, raise my consciousness and be part of something much larger.

The experience and my greater understanding led me to think more about religion, particularly Hinduism with its rich mythology, millions of gods and multiple pathways. On the surface, it seemed like an unfathomable fairytale. Yet, deep meaning resided within, which really resonated with me. That is, the notion that everything is actually an aspect of a greater, infinite and omnipresent whole. Just like the one sun has many rays, the whole has many manifestations. Each Hindu deity represents a particular energy. This includes Krishna, who embodies joy, freedom and love; Kali, who represents the realities of life and death; Durga, the divine mother goddess who protects mankind from the evil of negative emotions such as greed, hate and envy; and Rama, who is the model of right action and virtues. And Hinduism encourages followers to worship that which appeals to them, depending on their circumstances and what they need in their lives. There is no set path.

When I first visited India, I saw many colourful pictures of Hindu deities. They are immensely eye-catching, and beloved of tourists. But did people seriously pray to these weird and wonderful characters with animal heads and multiple arms?

I was always attracted to the graceful white woman, albeit with four arms, who was accompanied by a swan and strummed a *veena* (string instrument). I later found out she was Saraswati, the goddess of creativity and learning, and partner of Lord Brahma who created the universe. Her whiteness is a symbol of purity and simplicity. Her four hands represent the four aspects of human personality involved in learning: mind, intellect, alertness and ego. She plays the music of love and life with two of her hands, and in the remaining two, she holds sacred scriptures and a lotus, the symbol of true knowledge.

Although Hinduism interested me, I still baulked at the superstitions that many Hindus believed in. As a married woman there were many odd customs to follow that contradicted my own.

'Once you're married, you shouldn't say your husband's name,' my sister-in-law Amita told me.

This was again, due to folklore and the desire to prolong the husband's life. There's an ancient belief that saying the husband's name shortens his lifespan, and many traditional Hindu wives still follow it. Other pious Hindu wives choose not to say their husband's name out of respect for him as head of the household.

'How am I supposed to get his attention then?' I asked.

'You say *suniye!* (Please listen.) If you want to be really respectful, you can also say *aji sunte ho.*'

'What's that?'

'It means "dear, can you hear me?"'

It all sounded so unnatural and unnecessarily formal to me.

'And what about if I'm referring to him in conversation?' I wanted to know.

'You should call him "my husband", "he" or "him". It's okay, you can also call him by a nickname, just don't say your husband's name,' Amita advised.

I usually called Aryan by a nickname when I was speaking to him, as he did me, so it wasn't much of a problem when we were alone. However, when I was talking about him to his family, his name invariably slipped out. They were kind enough never to reprimand me, but I really didn't want his parents to think I was shortening their son's life by saying his name.

My efforts not to say Aryan's name carried into daily life as I tried to make a habit of it. Gradually, it became ingrained and I grew less aware of it. But others noticed. One evening before our Hindu wedding, Aryan and I were having dinner with my friends and family from Australia.

'Why do you keep referring to Aryan as "him" all the time? He's sitting right next to you, why don't you say his name?' an outspoken family friend commented, implying I was being rude. Another clash of cultures!

'I'm not supposed to say his name,' I started to explain.

Everyone was astonished. Back in Australia, names were important but in India they're shunned. In India, elders are called 'aunty' and 'uncle', and peers 'sister' and 'brother', even if they're not related in the literal sense.

Besides new customs to follow as a married woman, there were also numerous ornaments to wear. Much as I admired them, as a person who wasn't fond of wearing a lot of jewellery, I also found them cumbersome and constantly worried about losing them, or scratching them, or dropping them. In contrast to the western wedding ring, most Hindu women will usually be adorned with at least five – and often more – signs of marriage: red *sindoor* between the part in their hair, red *bindi* on their forehead, nose ring, *mangal sutra* necklace, bangles, anklets and toe rings.

Just as wedding rings are exchanged in a western marriage ceremony, Aryan had placed the *mangal sutra* around my neck and *sindoor* on my forehead when we'd gotten married. I'd also been given bangles, toe rings and anklets by my new Indian family. Traditionally, the ornaments are meant to awaken the divine feminine energy, protect against evil forces and serve as an obvious reminder of the woman's married status. Their origins, like many things in India, are steeped in mythology.

For Hindu women there's no finer example of a devoted wife than Parvati, partner of the all-powerful Lord Shiva. After the death of his first wife, a devastated Lord Shiva apparently turned his back on the world and retreated into a life of solitary meditation. Without his energy, the cosmic order became unbalanced, allowing the demon Taraka to overrun the heavens and earth.

Parvati was the only woman capable of luring Shiva out of isolation and into marriage, eventually resorting to becoming an ascetic herself to get him to notice her. Their ensuring sexual union and love story is legendary, making Parvati a source of power for all married women. Red *sindoor* and *bindis* are associated with her female energy, and it's believed that she protects the marriages of all women who wear them. Many ancient Hindu texts also mention the use of red *sindoor*.

The *bindi* is strategically placed on the forehead between the eyebrows, where the third eye *chakra* is located. Wearing it at this latent location of wisdom and intuition serves as a focus for spiritual growth. It's also believed to help retain the potent kundalini energy that rises up through the *chakras,* from the first *chakra* at the base of the spine.

The Hindu equivalent of a wedding ring, the *mangal sutra,* doesn't have as long a history as the *sindoor* and *bindi*. It's not mentioned in any scriptures either. Instead, in ancient Hindu weddings, a yellow thread (called a *kankana bandhana*) was simply tied onto the wrists of married couples to protect against evil energies. The design of the *mangal sutra,* however, is steeped in folklore. The strings of black beads, which the necklace is made from, are believed to absorb negative energies before they reach the bride and her family, thus providing protection from the evil eye. Hindu women are very superstitious about the *mangal sutra,* and consider its loss or breakage to be very inauspicious.

Unlike gold, which is most popular in India, my bangles were made out of deep red glass, while the toe rings and anklets were silver. There were reasons for this. The glass and the sound the bangles emit as they clink together are believed to provide protection from negative energies. It's easy to spot a newlywed Hindu woman: she's the one with rows of bangles extending most of the way up her arm. Married women continue to wear at least a few glass bangles, and will smash them when their husbands pass away. Accidental smashing of the bangles requires immediate replacement, lest their broken state brings about the husband's misfortune or death. Some women even gather the pieces up and kiss them three times to ward off any untoward impact.

The lesser metal of the toe rings and anklets reflects the belief that gold, a symbol of status associated with the goddess Lakshmi, should only be worn above the waist. As a result, the lowly and impure feet are never adorned with gold.

My toe rings had an ornate Oriya design with three small bells attached to them; I was to wear them on both of my second toes. They were exotic and I adored them. I really did have rings on my fingers and bells on my toes. My anklets were also decorated with small bells. Like the sound made by bangles, the noise is believed to offer protection from negative energy.

I also wore a nose ring. I'd had my nose pierced in Melbourne, even before going to Kolkata. It was always something I'd felt like doing, but it had never been appropriate while I dressed in suits and worked in an office. My mother put nose piercing in the same category as tattoos, and along with most of western society, associated them with rebellion. It didn't take her long to see my new adornment sparkling under the light at the kitchen table soon after.

'What's that on your nose? Your nose isn't pierced, is it? What did you do that for?' She was suitably aghast.

Her only consolation was that I could at least take it out, unlike a tattoo. Poor Mum!

In India, the reaction to my pierced nose was entirely different. I'd always worn a discreet diamond stud in it.

'Now that you're married, you must wear something bigger. This is too small,' my in-laws commented, referring to my tiny diamond.

Feeling encouraged, I went out and bought myself an actual nose ring, with a row of little diamonds. It was noticed and accepted immediately.

'This looks beautiful. Very suitable,' people admired.

I constantly wore my wedding ring, toe rings, anklets and nose ring. Sometimes, I added a *bindi*. The other items, I reserved for festivals and when visiting my in-laws. I was scared of something happening to my expensive *mangal sutra*, and I'd accidentally broken some of my bangles (no doubt shortening poor Aryan's life span again!) as I was so unused to them. I didn't want to break more.

Admittedly, there was another reason why I didn't want to wear so many visible signs of marriage. I'd thought that being married would put a stop to people's curiosity about my relationship with Aryan. I thought wrong. If anything, it aroused more curiosity. And, as a bonus: perplexity. Our marriage made a mess of India's strict social hierarchy.

In Indian culture there exists an overwhelming compulsion to classify and rank people based on certain qualities. The way a person is treated in India is very much based on their position in society and the power it affords. Upon meeting someone, the first thing an Indian will usually do is determine that position, and act accordingly. This is one of the reasons why they ask so many intrusive questions.

'What does your father do?', 'where do you live?', 'are you married?', 'do you have children?', 'what's your qualification?' and even 'how much do you earn?' are all questions aimed at uncovering a person's social standing. Caste, which is usually revealed by a person's surname, has, in the past, been the overarching factor. These days, it's not enough to make an accurate assessment. Other factors also taken into consideration include occupation, relationship status, skin colour, ability to speak English and whether the person has any important connections. Ultimately, it's money and looks that count the most. A good-looking unmarried man with fair skin and a professional occupation, but with only medium English, would still be placed higher than a married man with good English but dark skin.

This system of social stratification is most absorbingly reflected in the matrimonial ads for arranged marriages. (Admittedly, the classified ads in *any* paper are a wonderful repository of human emotion, from hope to delusion, but whatever floats your boat.) It's in the matrimonial columns of India's newspapers that the preoccupation with status is dramatically revealed. The credentials of potential brides and grooms are audaciously listed and suitable alliances are invited. A typical ad may read:

> Delhi based reputed Medico family seeks alliance for their beautiful, fair, smart, slim daughter 23/5'5 MBA (U.S.), pursuing CPA from US, and working in respected bank in US. Looking for tall, handsome, below 28, well placed professional. Preferably qualified Medico. Match from Status family only.

Before about 1990, it was families with connections, grooms in the government service and English-speaking brides who were most sought after. It's a huge contrast to the 1930s and 1940s, when a typical matrimonial ad consisted of a desire to find a 'Handsome, healthy, virgin girl. Western fashioned, highly educated need not approach'.

Of course, hierarchies exist everywhere. The movie industry has one, schools have one, companies have one. What's incredible about India's hierarchy is the sheer volume of people, a population of over one billion, that it incorporates and how it's managed to remain intact for so long. Its future is uncertain though, as external forces such as the intrusion of the west, have been slowly putting pressure on the hierarchy.

Although I was a casteless foreigner, my white skin and the perception of wealth and power that came with it unwittingly catapulted me to the top of the tree. Hundreds of years of British rule had left its mark on India: above all, they succeeded in creating an elite group of English-speaking Indians who copied them and tried to be as British as possible.

Many Indians gave up their dress, speech, mannerisms and style of living to acquire that of the British. In return, they were rewarded with a place in the new hierarchy of power, status, upward mobility and greater income. By measuring their worth in terms of how well they were able to imitate the British and be accepted by them, these Indians set a difficult standard for those who followed in their wake. It seemed to have created a school of thought where anything Indian was inferior to anything western.

Not surprisingly then, the fact that I was married to an Indian was greeted with shock by many people. When strangers saw us, they had difficulty believing we were married, or *could* be married. No doubt, the height difference of around 10 centimetres had something to do with it. Yet, it was more than that. It was about perceived status and placement in the social hierarchy. Aryan was neither high caste nor professionally qualified, nor did he have a forceful demeanour or commanding presence. He wasn't perceptively powerful. Hence, people either thought I'd married 'below myself' or wondered what was wrong with me because I hadn't snared a doctor or engineer.

The fact that I wasn't from a 'status family' and the suitability of our personalities didn't come into it. Such things were overridden by my appearance. It was automatically assumed that, because I was white, I had money and influence. Doors opened for me, invitations flowed, staff fell over themselves to serve me and if I complained about something, people took me seriously. Not being anyone noteworthy, it felt very odd to be treated that way. It was also a curious notion because the west certainly isn't respected for its moral behaviour, or rather, its perceived lack of morality. The explicit sex scenes on television and in films have led Indians who have little contact with the west to think that white women are ready to have sex with anyone who comes along.

Interestingly, it was the increasingly status-obsessed middle class who put up the most resistance to our relationship. This rapidly burgeoning group of people has struggled and worked hard to have more money, and mobility, than ever before. They're determined to achieve a higher position in society. Just like my new neighbours splurging on the most ostentatious furnishings for their apartment, to the middle class, outward displays of riches and success are important evidence of having 'made it'. Therefore, why would you not marry a prestigious doctor or engineer if possible?

In contrast, the poorer sections of Indian society often found my marriage more amusing than anything. My toe rings were invariably noticed when I went to the local beauty parlour.

'Ooooh,' the girls working there marvelled.

'Indian husband,' I explained, as they giggled with glee.

Although I still felt inadequate about my place in Aryan's family, they treated me well. They appreciated me for appreciating their culture, and found me and my bad Hindi amusing. What they liked most was the impact I'd had on Aryan. He'd finally returned to Mumbai, settled down, joined the family business and become responsible. The future was a weight off their minds.

'Thank God we have you in our lives now. We were so worried about Aryan,' Amita once said to me. 'He's changed so much for the better since he's been with you. You're the only one who's ever had this effect on him.'

# Sink or Swim

BEING married brought with it the comforting feeling of belongingness and security. I delighted in being a part of Aryan's family, and having a future overflowing with possibility. Yet, we both continued to grapple with our existence and the adjustments that were necessary.

Change did not come easily. The humidity, coupled with consistently high temperatures, along with the ongoing water problem, was sapping. We altered our routine, thinking we'd get up early and catch the first instalment of water to wash clothes and do the cleaning. Our erratic sleeping pattern had been okay when we didn't have much responsibility in our lives. But now, it was a burden.

The working day in Mumbai generally starts late, around 10 a.m., and ends late, around 8 p.m. Aryan wasn't left with much time in the evenings, after coming home from the family business and having dinner. His heart was still in music and he wanted to continue to learn new production software and work on music projects. I needed to sleep because I had to write the next day. As money was being reinvested into the family business, it meant I was still earning most of our income. With that responsibility, I felt like my needs were more important. When Aryan didn't alter his routine, I felt unsupported and resented the fact that I was the one who had to do most of the gruelling work of adapting.

The four walls of the apartment began to feel like a fishbowl. I didn't have an outlet for how I was feeling, so Aryan bore the brunt of my frustrations. I expected things that Indian wives probably wouldn't.

Friends of his would sometimes be in the neighbourhood, and he'd go out to meet them.

'I'll be back in half an hour,' he'd tell me. Three hours later, he still wasn't home and I had dinner ready to serve. He was used to the flexible concept of time in India, whereas to me, half an hour meant half an hour. I was used to people calling if they were even going to be ten minutes late, and the fact that he saw no need to do this left me feeling like he had no consideration for me.

I also found it hard to sleep when Aryan stayed up late. Noise travelled in the small apartment, and I hadn't developed the ability of most Indians to readily doze anywhere and anyhow, despite what was going on around them.

These elements made me yearn to be back in Australia living my old life. During moments of weakness, I felt I'd sacrificed so much for Aryan and wanted to always be the first priority in his life. But I knew, when push came to shove, that we couldn't leave India. I finally had my dream job, and that, I wasn't prepared to give up.

Just when I thought things couldn't get any more trying, Aryan announced he needed to go to Kolkata and Bhutan for three weeks. He'd landed a DJ gig in Bhutan, and wanted to get together with a small group of friends in Kolkata to collaborate on some music.

'Let's take a short holiday before you leave,' I suggested. 'It's really getting to me in this city, and I can't stand it anymore. I need a break.'

We decided to go to Matheran for a few days. The closest hill settlement to Mumbai, Matheran was a popular summer retreat for the British. Although it provided a cooling respite from searing temperatures, the most appealing thing about it was that all vehicles were banned, even bicycles. Horses and hand-pulled carts are the only means of getting around. After Mumbai's manic traffic, I wanted complete serenity.

An historic toy train slowly crawled its way up the hill, across bridges and through forests, and two hours later deposited us in the heart of town. The unsealed roads revealed rich red soil underfoot, and the presence of many horses made it feel like we'd been transported back to colonial days. Even our hotel, a rambling place with villas by a pool, had a distinct colonial ambience to it. We spent our days walking along the nature trails, riding horses into the sunset and fending off monkeys. In the night we drank beer, burned incense and talked.

It was such a welcome contrast to our wearisome bickering in Mumbai. Not surprisingly, I bounced back, and felt free, blessed, energetic and filled with love. The high was better than any drug, and natural.

'I'd ask you to marry me, if we weren't already,' Aryan said to me one night.

I decided I had to support his planned trip, and stay in Mumbai by myself – and make the most of it. I'd challenge myself to be independent and prove I could look after myself in that heaving, chaotic city.

From the hills, my actions in Mumbai seemed like those of another woman: the hiding in the apartment, the ranting and raving, the storming off and wanting Aryan to fix everything that didn't work. Most of all, the fear. Of being stared at, of being misunderstood, of being taken advantage of. I felt like I had to dress like an Indian, talk like an Indian and completely change myself to fit in.

How can one make a new life like that?

I'd been taking myself way too seriously.

I had misgivings about being alone, but when we got back I vowed I'd focus on what I wanted to achieve in Aryan's absence.

The first task was the bank and post office. I hadn't set foot in an Indian post office since the disastrous episode in Manali. It was about time. Blessedly, the post office near our apartment was nothing like the post office in Manali. No one told me I had to send my item by parcel post in order to have it registered. No one asked for my passport and visa details. The transaction was effortlessly completed with a smile. For once, I was glad about the lack of consistency in India.

The bank proved to be more of a trial. I needed to make a deposit into someone's account. I knew where the bank was, but I didn't know the best way to get there from the post office. I insisted that the rickshaw driver take me the long way that I was familiar with, which totally confused him. When we arrived, he shouted something at me in Hindi that I didn't understand, but I was quite sure he was calling me an idiot.

'Sorry, madam, we're not accepting deposits today,' the bank clerk informed me when I reached the counter. 'The computer network is down at this branch. An Internet problem apparently.'

'When will it be fixed?' I knew it was pointless asking, but I couldn't stop myself.

'Don't know, madam.'

'Are there any other branches around that are working?' I was determined not to let the situation get the better of me.

'Maybe, madam. Try Borivali.'

'Can you call them and find out?'

'Sorry, madam, I don't have their number.'

He wasn't keen to go out of his way to be of assistance. Followed soon by this: 'Madam, can I interest you in this excellent combined investment and life insurance product that we currently have on offer?'

I was gobsmacked. 'What? No, I don't even have a bank account in India or any documents! Please just tell me where I can make this deposit.'

The scene attracted the attention of the other employees.

'Madam, the Kandivali branch is operational. You can go there,' one finally advised me.

These seem like such little steps, but to me, they were Everests. That I managed to conquer them reinforced in me that I was capable.

My mother-in-law never interfered in our lives, but she was worried that I might be lonely in Aryan's absence and that I might be committing that terrible Indian sin of not eating properly. Then Maliha rang and told me her mother was going to come over on the train and take me home with her.

Although it was such a caring gesture, and one I was grateful for, I was still irrationally scared of my in-laws. I was scared of not understanding anything, of not being understood, of having to speak mostly in Hindi for days.

What could I do? The only way forward was to keep pushing through the fear. I was never going to learn Hindi quickly unless I spent time speaking it, and I was never going to get to know my in-laws unless I spent time with them. I knew they liked me, and I loved them back.

'Don't worry, they're happy with any effort you make,' Aryan had reassured me.

Just like when my mother-in-law first visited our apartment, my fears melted away when I saw her.

'*Is ke liye, thank you* (Thank you for this),' I told her as we climbed into the taxi at Dadar station, after our train trip.

'*Kyon?* (Why?)'

By thanking her, I was implying that her deed was excessive and uncalled for. She'd simply done what any caring family member would do.

'*Yahan se bahut lamba hai* (It's a very long way from here),' I fumbled to convey how much I appreciated her going out of her way for me.

Our short conversation in Hindi was enough to prick the ears of the taxi driver. He started giving my mother-in-law the third degree as he drove. Although quite bemused by the attention we received, my mother-in-law is very talkative and answered the questions as they arose. 'I came from Orissa 40 years ago. My husband has a furniture shop here . . .'

There was the staring as well. I'd become better at blocking it out, but it was novel for my mother-in-law, who was used to going about her business unobserved. As soon as we reached her apartment, she said to my sister-in-law, Radha, 'So many men staring.'

'Don't speak to any of them. Just ignore them,' she instructed me. There was a time when I did tell the starers to *udhar dekho* (look away), but I'd given up on it long ago.

I was glad Radha was there. Not only did she speak excellent English, so she could translate where necessary, conversations with her were fascinating. Aged in her early twenties, her marriage to Aryan's youngest brother had been one arranged between two families that knew each other. She'd given up her career as a fashion designer to have a baby. There was a sense of relief in both families that their children had upheld tradition.

'I did want to concentrate on my career a bit longer, but I'm content that it's turned out this way,' she assured me. 'I can always go back to work later on. I'm really glad that I've married into a family that is okay with me working. They allow me to be myself. I can still even wear jeans if I want.'

That was the beauty of Aryan's family. Although they were traditional, they had adjusted to city life and become more open-minded. I felt the same acceptance from them as Radha did.

As a guest, I was pampered. At my mother-in-law's insistence, I quickly fell into a lazy routine of eating, sleeping, watching TV, day after day.

'*Abhi khaoge*? (You will eat now?)' she'd ask me during most waking hours. Then, when I'd finished eating, she'd tell me to sleep.

Used to being constantly offered food, I was therefore confused when none was forthcoming one morning at breakfast. I'd been enjoying lounging around in my nightwear and drinking my coffee, as I usually do at home. Everyone was getting piping hot *palak parathas* (Indian bread with spinach) and coriander chutney. My mouth watered; I wanted some.

But *Abhi khaoge* had been replaced by *Abhi nahane*.

My mother-in-law wanted me to take a shower. Something wasn't right. Why wasn't I getting any food?

'Should I have a shower now?' I finally asked Radha.

'You don't have to if you don't want to, but we always do. Hindus consider it to be unclean to eat before bathing in the morning,' she said.

This was a revelation. Aryan had never showed such concerns. And everyone in his family had been too reserved to tell me how to behave. Sure enough, as soon as I'd showered, a steady stream of food flowed to me from the kitchen.

Spending time with my mother-in-law was very inspirational. I helped her with the cooking, and she helped me with my Hindi. I sat on the floor in front of the TV with Radha, and cut up vegetables. Then I watched her prepare the dishes. She chatted to me in Hindi the whole time she was cooking.

'*Is me daalo. Tel, rai, jeera, pyaaz* (Put it in this. Oil, mustard seeds, cumin, onion).'

Her patience, no doubt garnered from bringing up five children, was endless.

I was amazed to learn how she taught herself to speak and read Hindi when she came to Mumbai from Orissa. If she can do it, so can I, I thought. I was also encouraged that her Hindi wasn't perfect, that she spoke as if everything were masculine, and addressed everyone as if they were male. No one was ever bothered by it.

Determined, I sat down and practised writing the Hindi alphabet over and over again starting with the vowels: *a, aa, i, ii, u, uu*. And then moving on to the consonants: *ka, kha, ga, gha, cha, chha*. I did it again and again, row after row, until I started remembering the order. Next, I tried to write people's names. Much to everyone's amusement, I put vowels in the wrong place and got the letters wrong. I thought it funny too.

'Practise little by little. Start with reading the signs on shops and in the trains,' my mother-in-law advised.

From observing her during my stay, I learned to play the role of a good Indian housewife. I brought the men water when they got home from work, served their meals and cleaned up after them. I noticed my mother-in-law's sense of pride over always having plenty of food ready for them. She never grumbled when anyone came late. Rather, she was happy that they'd come home to eat.

Seeing this made me recognise that perhaps I'd been too forceful in my judgements about Aryan's behaviour. This was normal in his mother's house. A constant stream of people came and went, often unannounced, and my mother-in-law always had food ready for them.

I was also enlightened by what everyone wore while at home. Radha lived in long shapeless nightdresses called maxis. She donned a different one every day and only dressed up if she was going out. Maids came and went, as did numerous people who knocked on the door. Yet, she was unconcerned about her appearance. It was a huge contrast to how I fussed over being seen if I wasn't properly groomed. Inspired, I resolved to go shopping for some maxis.

I loved spending time in my in-laws' apartment, sitting on the window ledge next to their *tulsi* (holy basil) plant, and gazing down at the ever-changing street below. The apartment that Aryan had grown up in had a soothing energy about it. No doubt this had a lot to do with its location on the lane behind Siddhivinayak Temple. The lane was filled with *sadhus* (Hindu holy men), flower sellers and people on the way to see the resident deity, Lord Ganesh. By the end of my stay, their home had become my home.

When I went back to my own apartment, I felt like I knew and understood Aryan's family so much better.

Aryan returned to a slightly more Indian wife.

'I can read Hindi,' I proudly announced.

He looked at me in disbelief. It wasn't what he expected at all and I couldn't believe it myself. Reading Hindi was painfully slow, like putting the pieces of a puzzle together. I was used to recognising words on sight, not having to sound them out like a child. But a whole new world had opened up to me. I was more confident in my ability to communicate with people and be independent. I didn't feel like I had to act so conservative and be inconspicuous all the time. And I was much less self-conscious.

Unfortunately, my newfound optimism about living in India

didn't last long. On 26 November 2008, at around 10 p.m., Aryan and I were sitting in our living room. His sister Maliha, her husband and her mother-in-law were with us. I'd prepared a full Indian meal (*daal*, vegetables, fish curry and rice) upon request, to satisfy her mother-in-law's doubts that an educated white girl could in fact cook. We were just about to eat when a news report flashed across the TV screen.

'There's been a gang-related shooting in front of Leopold's Café,' Maliha remarked.

It didn't sound very serious. Unfortunately, the reality was much more sinister. As we later discovered, Mumbai was under siege. A group of Muslim terrorists had arrived on a boat from Pakistan. Using guns, grenades and bombs, they went on a rampage, slaughtering people at the Chhatrapathi Shivaji Terminus train station, Leopold's Café, Taj Palace Hotel and the Trident Oberoi Hotel. They also took over Nariman House, an important Jewish building. Hostages were held for over 48 hours. Many were killed, foreigners in particular. The death toll reached more than 200 people. Shocking report after shocking report filled the Indian media. Newspapers contained gruesome pictures of bloodied dead bodies.

From the peaceful safety of our apartment, it was hard to believe that such horrific events were occurring. Yet, media reports and concerned messages from my friends and colleagues confirmed it. That's when reality really started sinking in, and the attacks felt a lot closer to home and personal. The places being attacked were all so familiar to me. I'd walked through the Taj Hotel with my family, met friends there and admired its grandeur. Aryan's first job as a DJ had been at Leopold's Café. Now, these former places of pleasure had become places of mourning. I cried when I read that the general manager of the Taj Hotel lost both his wife and children in the attack; they'd been trapped inside the hotel and viciously killed.

How can anyone ever recover from losing their whole family in such a violent manner?

There had been other terrorist attacks in India while I was there, but this one sheeted the closest to home. Perhaps it's because I now had a family to call my own. Safety is taken for granted in Australia. The possibility of a terrorist attack is unheard of, whereas in India it's accepted as a part of life. Minds are numbed by constant tragedies. Life goes on as usual. It can't be any other way, because there are so many people in India, all with things that they need to do and money that they need to earn. There is no scope for pity and misery.

This time, however, the events of the terrorist attack weren't simply brushed off. People were still going about their business but there was a definite air of gloom. Flights were cancelled. Bars and clubs remained closed. I tried to write, but my head throbbed and my shoulders ached.

The year had been filled with extreme highs and lows. It had rewarded me more than I'd imagined possible, yet challenged me just as much. I was looking forward to bidding it farewell and moving ahead.

Just over a month later, as the clock struck midnight on New Year's Eve, Aryan and I danced outside on the dusty earth as lasers illuminated the sky and sparkling confetti rained down on us. We were at a friend's party at a bungalow by the sea on Madh Island, just off the coast of Mumbai. He'd hired it for the occasion. The music continued unabated through the night and into the next morning, interrupted only when a group of Christians arrived to conduct a sermon at the neighbouring bungalow.

The New Year marked a new beginning for me. I'd finally found some peace and resolved to let go of the numerous fights and battles going on in my mind with the last of the old year.

'I'm only just starting to accept you as my wife for real. I've also seen how much closer you've become to my family since my trip away,' Aryan admitted.

Strangely, it made me realise I'd been feeling exactly the same way about him as my husband. Our wedding ceremony was merely the starting point for the life we'd live together. The transformational henna on my hands had paved the path. Where we went now was up to us. I just had to *accept* that being married meant we would be spending the rest of our lives together, through all of life's ups and downs.

'My biggest problem has been feeling that you're not happy with India, or me being Indian, and that you'll go back home,' Aryan continued.

My complaining and outbursts had unnerved him; the threat of my leaving constantly hovered over our relationship. I could see that I'd created a far from pleasant home for us when I felt under siege. Aryan had the sweetest heart, and deep down I knew he loved me so much, but sometimes I just didn't want to believe it. I had to learn to give him the gift of the same security he had given me, and appreciate him as the stabilising influence in my life, the person whose love had given me so much courage.

My New Year's resolutions therefore centred on change. There would be no more living in limbo. I would commit to living in India fully. This meant packing up my house in Australia and selling off my remaining possessions. My last link – perhaps my security blanket even – would be gone.

And in its place would be my new Indian life, and new memories.

# Making Mumbai Home

IT was almost dusk, my favourite time of the day in Mumbai. I turned on the lamps and burned some incense to encourage Lakshmi, the goddess of wealth and prosperity, into our home. It was a sacred evening ritual that Aryan encouraged me to do. The light was soft, and the heady notes of the sandalwood incense trailed warmly through the rooms inside. Outside, children enthusiastically played cricket in the courtyard. The ball made a clunking sound as it landed and bounced off the cement, and cheers rose up as runs were made.

'*Chal, chal, mar, mar* (move, move, hit, hit),' they shouted encouragement to each other.

The area around the apartment building started to come alive. The warm glow from the shops and the smoky smell of oil and *jeera* (cumin) from the samosas being fried by the roadside drew people into the streets. After living there for two years, I still saw Mumbai as an exotic fusion.

There wasn't a lot about my old life that was same as it was five years ago. Not my job. Not my relationship. And not my home. Being a foreigner in a foreign land makes you so much more aware of how the universe, and life, alters.

'*Sab Kuch Milega*' means 'You'll get everything'. This Hindi saying is especially popular with backpackers in India, who often have it emblazoned all over their T-shirts. Indeed, it usually *is* possible to get everything in India. What you want may not always be available, but it's definitely possible.

I returned to Australia early that new year and piece by piece, step by step, tidied up the loose ends. Aryan stayed in India. I had a lot to sort out and needed time to myself to do it. When I came back to India a month later, it was with an open heart and mind. I'd missed India while I was away. Yes, there were obstacles and inefficiencies, but there were so many things I undeniably liked, too. When I stopped noticing how difficult it was to get some things done in India, I started appreciating how easy it was to get other things done. No matter what happened or what I needed, there was usually someone nearby to conveniently fix it or provide it. And for a very reasonable price.

When the sole of my sandal broke, Aryan took it to the *chappal-wala* who had a small stall on the footpath at the end of our road. He glued and stitched it back together while I waited. Cost: 5 rupees (15 cents).

When our lamp stopped working, Aryan fetched the electrician from one of the small shops in the street outside our apartment building to come and repair it. Cost: 40 rupees ($1).

A tailor sat with his sewing machine on the ground floor of our apartment building. He quickly mended and adjusted the seams of our clothes. Cost: 10 rupees (30 cents).

A *dhar-wala* often visited on his bicycle, which he would put on a stand, and pedalled to rotate a sharpening stone to sharpen our scissors. Cost: 20 rupees (60 cents).

When my laptop played up and refused to stay on for more than a couple of minutes, Aryan reassured me that we'd take it to the computer store nearby. The technician phoned us a few hours later. 'Your laptop is fixed. All the viruses have been removed. You can come and collect it.' It was fully operational again, and for only 250 rupees ($10).

The air conditioner clunked to a halt one hot, steamy evening. It was just over a year old, so the warranty would have expired. What's more, I didn't know where the receipt was. I envisaged an expensive repair bill. Aryan and I returned to the store where we bought the air conditioner.

'We'll send a repairman to take a look at it within two or three days,' the shop assistant assured us.

Not even a day later, two repairmen arrived at our door. Unannounced, of course. They pulled the air conditioner out of the wall and lifted the top off. Both the repairmen and I looked down in horror.

'*Yeh kyaa hai*? (What is this?)'

I was particularly aghast. The unit was filled with pigeon feathers and excrement that had fallen through the grille.

The repairmen were obviously amused by my reaction. Very diligently, they proceeded to clean the air conditioner. When it was reassembled, they plugged it in and it started to work again. I was overjoyed. But I was even more impressed when they went to the effort of sweeping the mess off the floor.

Then came the moment I was dreading. One of the repairmen pulled out a service form.

'What date did you purchase the AC, madam?'

'I'm not sure, I can't remember,' I replied honestly.

'Okay, I am writing this date down,' he said as he made up a date. The repairs were free. It was a welcome surprise to have India 'kindly adjust' in my favour. The lack of proper procedures and processes that had maddened me so much had finally balanced in my favour. Was this what they call karma?

The more I was reminded what an intriguing country India is, the more I rediscovered my interest in it. As I sat at my desk working one day, I happened to glance out the window. A massive, decorated Brahman bull accompanied by a drum player strolled into the court-yard of the apartment complex. The bull had bright orange-painted horns, and wore a colourful blanket on its back and a long necklace hung with bells. The drum player started yelling something that I couldn't understand. Within seconds, both he and the bull were escorted off the premises by the watchmen.

What had just gone on? Definitely something mysterious that only happens in India. My inquiries revealed that it was a Bholanath bull – a bull that can predict the future. Ask it a question and it will shake its head in either 'yes' or 'no'. Also known as the Nandi bull, the bull is the companion of Lord Shiva. Bholanath, one of the 108 names of Lord Shiva, is associated with him in his most innocent form, pleased by simple prayers and eager to grant wishes.

Innovative ways of making money can be found on every corner in densely populated India. Even if no one really believes in the sup-posed powers of the Bholanath bull, it still provided a great source of entertainment for children.

Small things also made me laugh. Simple, everyday things I'd never encountered before. I bought a light bulb from the local super-market. As I was unloading my trolley at the check-out, I heard 'Madam, madam'. One of the shop assistants was trying to get my attention. When I turned towards him, a light bulb shone brilliantly in my face, almost blinding me. After I recovered from the shock, I realised it was my light bulb. The shop assistant had plugged it in and was demonstrating to me that it worked.

My website had become an obsession. When each day was over, I fell into bed exhausted, but the end result was satisfying. Not only was I writing about a place I loved, I was sharing it with people. It was easy to put my heart and soul into it. As the website grew in popularity, businesses in India began taking notice. Invitations flooded in, as did offers of travel from one end of India to the other. The people I encountered along the way were gracious and inspiring, with a wealth of knowledge and experience. So many shared my everyday beliefs about spirituality and Indian philosophy. What's more, they were living their dreams. It confirmed to me that I was on the right track.

I was most impressed by the photographer I worked with on an advertising campaign for Mahindra Homestays in India. From Tamil Nadu, his name was Prasana. He broke the ice by immediately noticing my toe rings. It took me by surprise.

'You're married?' he asked me. I was pleased that he didn't think they might just be fashion accessories, like many foreigners wore. I soon realised he was a perfectionist like me. Work days were long, as we pursued the best light and angles, giving us plenty of opportunity to talk. 'I completed my MBA and spent six months as a client servicing executive in an advertising agency. I hated it,' he confessed to me.

'So how did you end up as a photographer?' I was curious.

'It started off as a hobby and I taught myself. Then I quit my job and moved to Chennai to begin freelancing. I spent a lot of time struggling to prove myself in the industry. Finally got my big break.'

I recognised how bold and tenacious he'd been, particularly in

India where creative career choices aren't often encouraged or looked upon favourably.

'What did your family think?'

'Actually, my father's a doctor and my family's all academically inclined. They were really worried and upset, and initially opposed what I was doing. However, they've accepted it over time now that they can see it's my passion,' he explained.

I admired him. And, I was also quite astonished that I was in a position to relate to him. I thought back to the New Year's Eve party I went to in Kolkata, and to the filmmaker and musician I'd met there. At the time, I'd been so envious of how they'd left accounting and succeeded in their passions. I'd wondered if I could possibly follow in their footsteps but had no idea of where to begin or what direction to go in. Yet, a few years down the track, here I was. Miraculously, I'd done it!

It felt surreal to live the life of a travel writer, even more so to realise that it was *my* life. Lest you think it's all glamour, let me dissuade you. It can be an exhausting, mad life!

In June, as yet another southwest monsoon commenced making its way up the coast, I was staying in a cottage on a 90-acre coffee and spice estate in the Wayanad district of Kerala, in southern India. The road leading through the estate was thick with vegetation, including coconut palms, jackfruit trees and stunning red hibiscus flowers. The sun was about to rise. Soon, the whole valley came alive, illuminated in the sun's warm glow. I sat on my balcony, amid the swirling mist and intermittent bird calls, letting the fresh filtered coffee from the estate awaken me.

In July, I'd left the monsoon behind and travelled to the other end of India, 12,500 feet above sea level in the remote, high-altitude Spiti Valley of northern Himachal Pradesh. The stark alpine landscape was arid and barren, scattered with small villages and monasteries, and enclosed by soaring peaks crowned with snow. It was a world within a world.

I traipsed through the countryside on the back of a yak to the highest village in Asia. Village life was fascinating; tradition required families to donate their second eldest son to the local Buddhist monastery, to train to become a *lama*. Not all the children appeared to deal well with their fate; one little boy so disliked being told to study that I saw him belligerently throwing rocks at people. Farming was the principal source of income. It was a simple and uncomplicated way of life, but challenging. Winters were harsh. Heavy snowfall and below freezing temperatures forced residents to be housebound for months at a time, when they passed the time making handicrafts.

The trip wasn't an easy one for me. I was plagued by altitude sickness and became very weak. Headache, dizziness, vomiting, upset stomach – a different symptom each night. It felt like it would never end, and I felt so alone and helpless without anyone familiar there to help me.

I had only a few days to rest before my next journey. This time, it was to Chennai, to take part in an auto-rickshaw rampage, billed as an event for the 'clinically insane'. I was about to spend thirteen days in a rickshaw, driving it over 1900 kilometres and through four states, from Chennai to Mumbai. Fortunately, Aryan saw the funny side and agreed to join me.

We were given a lesson in how to drive an auto rickshaw. I struggled to come to terms with the fact that the accelerator was located on the rickshaw's handlebar. Every time I gripped the handlebar in fear, the rickshaw dangerously surged forward. India's roads are often narrow and filled with potholes, but it's the traffic that's the biggest hazard, consisting as it does of everything from trucks to bullock carts. Obstacles such as the holy cows required dodging as well.

The journey to Mumbai was arduous but enthralling. Life on the road developed into an exhausting routine of 6 a.m. starts, and all-day driving, but it was worth the pain.

Shortly after, I headed to Udaipur, in the desert state of Rajasthan. It was a long time since a city had so entranced me with its splendour, often called the most romantic city in India. I had a whirlwind 72 hours there as a guest of the Mewar royal family who have done a remarkable job of converting their palaces into hotels. My room overlooked the famed Lake Pichola and the Lake Palace Hotel. Stationery with my name embossed on it sat on my writing table, and an invitation to drinks with the head of the Mewar royal family lay alongside it. It really felt like I was caught up in a royal fairytale. Or perhaps an extra in the James Bond movie *Octopussy*, which was partly filmed on the premises.

When I arrived back in Mumbai, it was September and time for my favourite festival of the year, Ganesh Chaturthi. This eleven-day festival honours the birth of Lord Ganesh. Pot-bellied and elephant-headed, he's a strange-looking but widely adored Hindu god with the revered ability to remove obstacles. Eager chants of '*Ganpati Bappa, Morya!*' (Lord Ganesh, Hail!) filled the air, radiating excitement and anticipation.

Months before, tens of thousands of highly skilled artisans had been working to craft intricate sculptures of Lord Ganesh for the festival. These masterful creations were installed in carefully decorated *pandals* (canopied tents) all over the city, accompanied by a great deal of fanfare. I slipped off my shoes outside one of the tents, parted the curtains and stepped inside, into another world. Flickering fairy lights covered the ceiling, water trickled from a small fountain, and a dense cloud of incense swirled around. And there he was, lounging in all his glory on a throne on the podium, a towering Lord Ganesh, resplendent in his colourful robes. Gold jewellery dripped from his body and a gold crown graced his head. A hefty garland of gold and yellow marigolds was secured around his waist. At his feet were piles of coconuts, apples, bananas, pomegranates and platters of his favourite *modak* (a sweet made from rice flour, jaggery and coconut). They'd been provided by his devotees to ensure a trouble-free and prosperous year ahead.

'*Bahut sundar hai* (very beautiful),' I whispered to Aryan.

Many others had joined us in putting their busy lifestyles on hold to gather together and spend time with the beloved elephant-headed god. They prayed and sung, like others had for thousands of years, and would continue to do so for thousands more to come.

When the final day of Ganesh Chaturthi rolled around, everyone gathered to bid farewell to their favourite god and send him off in a huge street party. Maliha had a statue of Lord Ganesh at the end of her street, so I decide to join her. I got there in the evening at around seven o'clock, just as the statue of Lord Ganesh was carried out from his *pandal* and lifted onto the back of a large truck. Dozens of helpers, clad in saffron shirts and white hats, helped. I was handed a saffron-coloured ribbon bearing the familiar '*Ganpati Bappa, Morya!*' chant written in Hindi to tie around my head. Even babies wore one. Crackers exploded and fireworks decorated the sky.

Then the music started. So, too, did the dancing. The fabled red powder was thrown everywhere, and white foam sprayed for added fun. Later that night, I found myself pulled into a huge circle. We linked hands and danced, round and round. The monsoon season was still with us, and like many other evenings, it began to rain. Then it poured. We all kept dancing.

As midnight approached, it was time for the statue to be carted away to the ocean for immersion. I took a lingering look at Lord Ganesh, knowing that he would soon be destroyed.

It's natural to wonder why these painstakingly crafted and

beloved statues are discarded into the water, where they're left to crumble and be washed away. As with most things in India, the message behind the action is important and also poignant. Immersion symbolises the return of Lord Ganesh from the earth, after satisfying his devotees' wishes. Moreover, it serves as a reminder of the impermanence of everything in life, and the constantly changing state of the universe. Form eventually gives way to formlessness. Only the energy remains.

Although I'd adapted to life in Mumbai, at times I still missed the cleanliness, space and order of Australia. The photos that my friends sent me showed living conditions so pristine compared to mine in India. Did such a step up in the standard of living guarantee an equally large step up in happiness?

A house party at an immaculately decorated and roomy apartment in Bandra put it in perspective for me.

'You're going to a kitty party?' Aryan was dismayed when I told him of my plans to have dinner and drinks at a girlfriend's house. I'd met a group of foreign women also married to Indian guys, and we caught up from time to time. Like me, they found it difficult to relate to most of the expats in Mumbai. But together, we'd formed our own little niche.

I was just as dismayed. 'What's a kitty party?'

It was, I soon learned, a popular form of entertainment for housewives in India. They gather in large groups at someone's home, bring food, salaciously gossip and play games. At a *firangi* (foreigner) kitty party, however, the games were replaced by wine and we talked about life in general.

A Bollywood actress was at the party. She had a business relationship with my friend's husband.

'I'll be going to the US for two months but am not sure about where to live. I want a big place, but I'm concerned about getting good staff. It's important because I don't know how to operate a washing machine or a dishwasher, and I don't want to learn,' she explained.

It was almost 4 a.m. by the time the last guests left. It didn't concern me that I'd have to find my way home alone. I'd become adept at getting around Mumbai, and it felt safe to me. The actress took pity on me.

'Kandivali? Where's that? I've never even heard of it. Come with me, you can take my car and driver after he's dropped me home.'

We started chatting in the car.

'So, what do you like about Indian men?' she asked me, obviously curious about why I'd married one.

'Their values and sense of commitment,' I replied, thinking of Aryan. 'Indian men tend to be quite stable and caring as well, which is what's often missing in the west.'

'Really?' She seemed surprised by my response.

'And you? What are your views on Indian men?' I asked her, knowing that she'd recently broken up with her long-term boyfriend. 'They're too possessive and controlling. And they only see me as an actress, not who I really am.'

I remembered when I met Aryan, he'd expressed similar concerns about people not bothering to get to know who he really was.

'Hmmm, I guess I got lucky,' I said to her.

When I woke up in the morning, back in our small one-bedroom flat, the previous night seemed like a fantasy.

Living a simpler life had taught me to find joy in what I had. Even though our apartment was small, I had so much more freedom and flexibility than most people I knew. My days were mine to do what I wanted, when I wanted. There was a beach, a park and a huge shopping centre nearby. I worked when I wanted to work. I was writing and being creative. This new life had purpose and passion. My old life meant obligation, routine and entrapment into acquiring more and more unnecessary possessions. And it was bland compared to the unpredictability of India – unpredictability that had forced me to detach myself and let go.

I started feeling less like a foreigner in India and more like a white Indian. Mumbai had tested me but had failed to make me leave. I'd stayed on in the city against the odds, and proven how much I wanted my new life.

But Aryan wasn't satisfied working in the family business. While I'd finally found a fulfilling career, he'd sacrificed one. He wanted to keep his family and me happy, and prove to everyone that he was responsible and dedicated. Nevertheless, he had no passion for the job. He continued to devote all his spare time to music, spending long hours with friends producing music and dreaming of having his own studio. At work he'd taken to chanting *mantras* (spiritual verses) to keep his mind numbly blank and focused.

I also dreamed of a change. I spent long hours envisaging living in a cosmopolitan yet quiet area, with a 24-hour water supply, surrounded by a peaceful garden. In Mumbai? I didn't think it was possible. So, I contented myself with visiting public gardens and toyed with the idea of painting the walls of our apartment bright red and yellow.

Then Aryan arrived home one night with some unfathomable news.

'Lloyd called me. He asked me if I wanted to join him in working at a new lounge bar that will be opening up in Hiranandani Gardens. We'll be playing music there as well as producing music for the venue. The owner wants to release four albums of world fusion music a year.'

Hiranandani Gardens, a planned township in the central Mumbai suburb of Powai, is home to expats and well-to-do Indians.

The developer has built parks, hospitals and schools. There are world-class hotels, shops, supermarkets and restaurants. With its neoclassical architecture, the area looks more like Europe than India. But the real barometer of its cosmopolitan nature is that Indian women can be seen wearing shorts and miniskirts there. As Hiranandani Gardens was located almost an hour from where we lived, Aryan and I agreed that we'd have to relocate.

I felt a sense of accomplishment over being able to settle into a typical middle-class Indian lifestyle, eschewing that of an expat, even though it had taken its toll. I'd learned a lot about Indian society in the process and experienced things that most other foreigners wouldn't have. But what I really craved was to regain some anonymity. I had no intention of acquiring a bevy of servants or possessions, or even mixing in expat circles. I simply wanted to live serenely, without being such a subject of interest all the time.

I dreaded having to trudge though dozens of substandard apartments in the hunt for somewhere suitable to live. I wasn't even sure what was available within our budget. Yet, before I'd even finished compiling a list of requirements, Aryan called to tell me he'd found the ideal place for us.

It was a one-bedroom row house, located just opposite to where Lloyd would be living and where the music studio would be set up. It had three levels, including our own private rooftop and downstairs garden with a swing. We looked inside. To my delight, the walls were painted cheery shades of yellow, orange and red. The rent exactly fit our budget. We even had our own water tank! One of the last remaining row houses in a complex that existed before the area was developed, it was around ten years old and by no means luxurious like the surrounding apartment towers (in fact, I'd have to revert to cooking with a gas bottle as there was no gas pipeline). And, of course, there was an unappealing wet bathroom. Nevertheless, it was a house with a rare creative feel that was perfect for us. The owners, a kind-hearted elderly couple from Kerala, agreed to rent it to us.

Once again, what the universe had produced was better than anything I could have envisaged. I was humbled, grateful and in awe. My broken heart had led me into the unknown, and now my life had been transformed. I was doing what I was born to do. If my life hadn't been so torn apart, I never would be where I was. I wouldn't have had the courage or motivation to make changes to myself and my life.

I'd gone from self-awareness, to awareness of others, to awareness of the greater whole. I'd developed faith, and had been infused by the infinite sense of possibility in India. Old notions of who I was, defined by the roles that I'd played, had fallen away.

After years of searching and wandering, I'd completed the hardest and most rewarding journey of my life, and was at last living my dream.

Now, another new chapter could begin.

# Ackowledgements

WRITING this book was something I'd often thought about since my life started heading in this unusual direction. I'm not sure that I ever expected it to come to fruition. Therefore, I'm indebted to Helen Littleton for discovering my story and going out of her way to help bring it to life.

I'd also like to thank my husband for telling me to write it, for soothing me through the insanity of the writing process, and for bringing me food. There's a saying that being loved deeply by someone gives you strength while loving someone deeply gives you courage, and it's certainly the case for me.

I was heartened to gain both an agent and a publisher who'd also been to India, and could relate to my experiences. In addition, I'm very grateful to the talented people who edited this book and made it as marvellous as possible.

I've poured my heart and soul into the book, and it's fair to say that revealing so much of my life, warts and all, to the world has been daunting. Hence, I'd like to thank Angela Rojas, a wonderful intuitive healer, who helped turn my fear into enthusiasm. And last but not least, I'd like to thank everyone – friends, family and readers of my blog – for their support and interest in my book. It's really helped boost my confidence and keep me motivated.

# MORE TITLES FROM PAN MACMILLAN

Jane Stork
**Breaking the Spell**

*Breaking the Spell* is Jane Stork's extraordinary life story. Equally moving and disturbing, it chronicles the rise and fall of the religion Rajneeshism and the Rolls Royce guru, and Jane's part in the events that led to its collapse.

Growing up in post-war Western Australia, Jane Stork had a conventional Catholic upbringing, and married her university sweetheart at age 21. Embarking on the familiar path of marriage and raising children, Jane's semblance of a normal life began to unravel as she entered her thirties. She sought answers at a meditation centre, and quickly became devoted to the Indian guru Bhagwan Shree Rajneesh, changing her name, adopting the orange robes of a *sannyasin*, and uprooting her family to live first in an ashram in India and then in the Bhagwan-created city of Rajneeshpuram in Oregon, USA. For Jane, what started out as a journey seeking spiritual enlightenment began to descend into darkness as she sacrificed her marriage and children, and eventually – through a monstrous act of attempted murder – her freedom.

After serving time in the US, Jane started a new life in Germany, but soon realised she could never truly be free until she had faced up to the past. With an international arrest warrant hanging over her head, and a son who is gravely ill, Jane finally does so with devastating clarity.

Gregory David Roberts
**Shantaram**

He was Australia's most wanted man. Now he's written Australia's most wanted novel.

*Shantaram* is a novel based on the life of the author, Gregory David Roberts. In 1978 Roberts was sentenced to nineteen years' imprisonment as punishment for a series of robberies of building-society branches, credit unions, and shops he had committed while addicted to heroin. In July 1980 he escaped from Victoria's maximum-security prison in broad daylight, thereby becoming one of Australia's most wanted men for what turned out to be the next ten years.

For most of this period he lived in Bombay. He set up a free health clinic in the slums, acted in Bollywood movies, worked for the Bombay mafia as a forger, counterfeiter, and smuggler and, as a gun-runner, resupplied a unit of mujaheddin guerrilla fighters in Afghanistan. This is the setting of *Shantaram*.

Apart from having this highly unusual personal background, Greg Roberts is a very gifted writer. His book is a blend of vivid dialogue, unforgettable characters, amazing adventures, and superb evocations of Indian life. It can be read as a vast, extended thriller, as well as a superbly written meditation on the nature of good and evil. It is a compelling tale of a hunted man who had lost everything – his home, his family, and his soul – and came to find his humanity while living at the wildest edge of experience.

Hannah Tunnicliffe
**The Colour of Tea**

Lost among the gaudy, busy streets of Macau, Grace's life is
slowly unravelling. Her marriage to Pete, her Australian husband,
is fraying and her dreams of having a family seem hopeless.

With the heralding of a new year she resolves to do something
bold. Something her impetuous Mama might do. In this pocket of
China, filled with casinos and yum cha restaurants, she opens her
own small cafe called Lillian's. This sanctuary of macarons and
tea becomes a place where the women of Macau come together,
bridging cultural divides, to share in each other's triumphs and
pain. But Grace's immersion in the cafe is taking its toll on her
marriage, and when things start to crumble in the cafe, Lillian's
suddenly feels like a burden rather than an escape. The recipe for
disaster is complete when Pete does the unthinkable . . .

Infused with the heady aromas of Macau and peppered with
inspirational characters, *The Colour of Tea* takes you on a mouth-
watering journey of the senses as Grace rediscovers what it is to
love, to live with hope and embrace real happiness.

Peter Baines
**Hands Across the Water**

Peter Baines started out as a police officer in the mean streets of Cabramatta in the early nineties. Becoming a specialist in crime scene forensic investigations he was called upon to bring his skills to the Bali bombings in 2002.

But it was the 2004 Boxing Day tsunami that forever changed the direction of his life. Helping the people of Thailand identify their dead, he met the countless children who had been left behind, orphaned, with nowhere to go. With a colleague he decided to make a difference, and set about creating the charity Hands Across the Water, building an orphanage and raising funds to raise and educate the children.

Today, Hands Across the Water has grown to support an ever increasing number of children in need, and Peter has become a well-known corporate speaker in demand around the world.

This is Peter's story about how one knockabout Aussie bloke can change the lives of thousands by offering a hand.

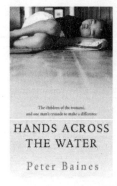

The children of the tsunami,
and one man's crusade to make a difference

HANDS ACROSS
THE WATER

Peter Baines

Christine Stinson
**It Takes a Village**

Growing up in conservative, postwar Australia isn't easy. For eight-year-old Sophie, who has just been told that she's a *bastard*, it seems that she lives in a world of secrets, unanswered questions and whispers.

Who is her father and why did her mother never tell anyone who he was?

With only her reclusive grandfather to raise her, and more than one neighbour expecting her to go off the rails like her mother – after all, apples rarely fall far from the tree – Sophie struggles to find her place in the world.

In a time when experiences are shared around the kitchen table, over the back fence or up at the corner shop, Sophie learns that life is rarely simple, love is always complicated and sometimes it takes more than blood ties to make a family.